Nordic Dialogues on Children and Families

This book brings together key authors from the Nordic countries (Sweden, Finland, Norway, Denmark and Iceland) to discuss theoretical and empirical research on families and children. Sharing the Nordic perspective from each of the five countries, the book highlights key ideas within and across the countries. The chapters provide an understanding of the history of the Nordic perspectives of family and children, present current innovative research on solutions to complex issues, and explore contemporary issues. Nordic countries continually attain high scores in lifestyle measures, quality of life and children's outcomes. Much of this has to do with the specific culture and policy of the Nordic countries. Written by academics within the region who are well regarded for contributing to academic and public debate, this book will appeal to an international audience interested in the Nordic perspective and social policy around family and children.

Susanne Garvis is Professor of Child and Youth Studies at the Department of Education, Communication and Learning, University of Gothenburg, Sweden.

Elin Eriksen Ødegaard is Professor of Early Childhood Education at the Center of Educational Research, Western Norway University of Applied Sciences, Norway, and Visiting Professor at UiT – The Arctic University of Norway.

Evolving Families

Series Editor: Sivanes Phillipson

This series focuses on issues, challenges and empirical best practices surrounding evolving families that impact upon their survival, development and outcomes. The aim of this series is twofold: (1) to showcase the diversity of evolving families and the multiple factors that make up the function of families and their evolution across time, systems and cultures; (2) to build on preventative, interventionist, engagement and recovery methods for the promotion of healthy and successful evolving families across generations, social and political contexts and cultures.

1. **Early Childhood Intervention**
   Working with Families of Young Children with Special Needs
   Edited by Hanan Sukkar, Carl J. Dunst and Jane Kirkby

2. **Nordic Dialogues on Children and Families**
   Edited by Susanne Garvis and Elin Eriksen Ødegaard

Nordic Dialogues on Children and Families

Edited by Susanne Garvis
and Elin Eriksen Ødegaard

Routledge
Taylor & Francis Group
LONDON AND NEW YORK

First published 2018 by Routledge

2 Park Square, Milton Park, Abingdon, Oxfordshire OX14 4RN
52 Vanderbilt Avenue, New York, NY 10017

Routledge is an imprint of the Taylor & Francis Group, an informa business

First issued in paperback 2019

British Library Cataloguing-in-Publication Data
A catalogue record for this book is available from the British Library

Library of Congress Cataloging-in-Publication Data
A catalogue record for this book has been requested

ISBN: 978-1-138-67339-7 (hbk)
ISBN: 978-0-367-27195-4 (pbk)

Typeset in Galliard
by Apex CoVantage, LLC

Contents

List of Contributors vii

1 **Introduction** 1
SUSANNE GARVIS AND ELIN ERIKSEN ØDEGAARD

2 **The collectivity of family conduct of life and parental self-understanding** 13
CHARLOTTE HØJHOLT, PERNILLE JUHL AND DORTE KOUSHOLT

3 **Family life in Nordic countries** 28
LENA BÄCKSTRÖM

4 **Constituting cultures of compassion in early childhood educational settings** 39
LASSE LIPPONEN

5 **Pedagogical leadership and families in Swedish preschool** 51
SONJA SHERIDAN AND PIA WILLIAMS

6 **Early childhood education, gender relations and equality among parents and families in Sweden** 63
INGEGERD TALLBERG BROMAN AND INGRID PRAMLING SAMUELSSON

7 **Divorce, families and children** 79
PER ARNE RØD

8 "We have this family 'under the microscope' so to speak": schools, child abuse and family support 94
YLVA ODENBRING, THOMAS JOHANSSON AND JOHANNES LUNNEBLAD

9 Economic, social and cultural status (ESCS) and mathematics performance of immigrant students in the Finnish metropolitan area in PISA 2012 108
HEIDI HARJU-LUUKKAINEN, MIRJA TARNANEN, KARI NISSINEN AND JOUNI VETTENRANTA

10 Coming and staying or coming and going? Immigrant families in Denmark: challenges and opportunities for integration 126
ANNETTE HILTON

11 Parental engagement in Icelandic preschools 143
JOHANNA EINARSDOTTIR AND ARNA H. JONSDOTTIR

12 The importance of aesthetic activities in Norwegian kindergartens 157
TONA GULPINAR AND LEIF HERNES

Index 173

Contributors

Lena Bäckström has a PhD and is senior lecturer in educational psychology at the University of Kristianstad, Sweden. She teaches in preschool and primary school education. She is also a clinically active psychologist and psychotherapist at Family Health Care Centres and supervisor of personnel in health care. Her research interests include: childcare, family, parenthood, educare and discourses of quality in preschools and primary schools.

Ingegerd Tallberg Broman is a senior professor in education and researcher at the Department of Children Learning and Society at Malmö University, Sweden. Her main research field is early childhood education and care in a gender and historical perspective and the development of a profession for education and care related to the youngest children in an international perspective regarding the relations between the state, the family and the preschool teacher. She has been responsible for research programs like Multi-contextual Childhood and The Teacher and the Cultural Grammar (together with professor Lena Rubinstein Reich) and for research schools for preschool teachers focusing on childhood and learning. Her ongoing research concerns the professional assignment in preschool in transition.

Johanna Einarsdottir is a professor of early childhood education and the dean of the School of Education, University of Iceland. She has extensive experience in the field of early childhood education and early childhood teacher education. Professor Einarsdottir has been involved in several international research projects as a researcher and a consultant in her areas of expertise and published together with international colleagues. She is an editor of several books published in Icelandic and English. She has presented numerous papers and research results on early childhood education and educational transitions to professional and community groups nationally as well as internationally. Recently she has mainly been conducting research on children's views on their preschool education and research on transition to primary school from the perspectives of children, parents and educators.

Susanne Garvis is a professor of child and youth studies at the University of Gothenburg, Sweden. She worked in Australia before moving to Sweden.

Professor Garvis has expertise in narrative research with children, families and teachers. She is particularly interested in the lived experience of understanding phenomenon and often implements a narrative constellation approach.

Tona Gulpinar works as a lecturer in the kindergarten teacher education program at Oslo and Akershus University College (HiOA), Norway. She is part of the research project Searching for Qualities (2012–2017), where her research focus is aesthetic learning. She is also a visual artist and musician and has produced art productions specifically for children, such as *Be Cubed on Hennie Onstad*, a collaboration between Thomas Wiederberg and Vigdid Storsveen, and *Be Extended* at Galleri RAM, supported by the Norwegian Arts Council, a collaborative project with Anneke von der Fehr. She has several album releases and has performed both nationally and internationally.

Heidi Harju-Luukkainen, PhD (education), holds a qualification in management and a special education teacher qualification from Finland. She also holds a title of docent in student assessment from the University of Jyväskylä, Finland. At the moment Dr. Harju-Luukkainen is a visiting scholar at the University of Southern California (UCLA), CRESST. Her research interests are in international student assessments and justice in education. Dr. Harju-Luukkainen has worked in several universities in the Nordic countries, and she has conducted international research around Europe and Saudi Arabia in some 20 different research and developmental projects. Dr. Harju-Luukkainen has published more than 80 articles, reports and books on her specialties.

Leif Hernes is a choreographer and has produced many dance works for stage, film and television nationally and internationally. He is a professor of drama at Oslo and Akershus University College (HiOA), Norway, and has taught for many years at the Arts Academy in Oslo, Ballet Academy. He is the author of numerous publications of theatre and dance. At HiOA he has been involved in the EU-supported art project Glitterbird – Art for the Very Young about art mediation for children. He manages one of the largest research projects in Norway that focuses on the youngest children in kindergarten, Searching for Qualities (2012–2017); his focus is aesthetic learning.

Annette Hilton is an associate professor in research leadership at the University of Technology Sydney, Australia. Prior to this, she lived in Copenhagen for two and a half years, where she held the position of associate professor in science education at the Danish School of Education, Aarhus University. She has previously worked as a lecturer in science and mathematics education and general pedagogies at the University of Queensland and the Australian Catholic University and as a secondary school science and mathematics teacher. Her research interests are in conceptual development in science and mathematics as well as teachers' professional growth.

Charlotte Højholt is a professor of psychology in the Department of People and Technology at Roskilde University, Denmark. Her research interests centre on children's everyday lives across contexts as families, schools, kindergartens, institutions for children's leisure time and special help arrangements – as well as cooperation among involved adults. She has published widely in the areas of development, learning, family life, professionalism, interdisciplinary work and methodology, including the co-edited volumes *Children, Childhood and Everyday Life* and *Psychology and the Conduct of Everyday Life*. She is head of the PhD program Social Psychology of Everyday Life at Roskilde University.

Thomas Johansson has a PhD in sociology and is a professor of education in the Department of Education, Communication and Learning at the University of Gothenburg, Sweden. His main research interests are in the field of gender studies, the sociology of the family and youth research.

Arna H. Jonsdottir is an assistant professor in early childhood education and educational leadership and a department chair in early childhood education in the School of Education, University of Iceland. Her research has been mainly in the field of professionalism, professional identity and leadership of preschool teachers and head teachers. She has led a research project on professionalism within the Centre for Research in Early Childhood Education and has also worked on a research project within the Centre for Research in Educational Leadership, Innovation and Educational Evaluation on the effects of the financial crisis in Iceland on all school levels.

Pernille Juhl is an assistant professor at the Department of People and Technology, Roskilde University, Denmark. Her research interest is families' everyday lives and parenthood, children's everyday lives across contexts as families, school, and day care, and social interventions focused on marginalized children and parents. Her PhD project resulted in the thesis *På sporet af det gode børneliv: Voksnes bekymring og børns perspektiver på problemer i hverdagslivet [Searching for the Good Life for Children: Adults' Concerns and Children's' Perspectives on Problems in Everyday Life]* and the international article: "Toddlers Collaboratively Explore Possibilities for Actions across Contexts: Developing the Concept Conduct of Everyday Life in Relation to Young Children."

Dorte Kousholt is an associate professor at the Department of Education, Aarhus University, Denmark. Her research interest is children's and families' everyday lives, children's communities in and across different institutional contexts and parenthood. She has done ethnographic research in and across various contexts of children's lives. She has published on children's everyday lives across contexts, parental cooperation, family work and collaborative methodology, including "Collaborative Research with Children: Exploring Contradictory Conditions of Conduct of Everyday Life" (2016) and "Family Problems: Exploring Dilemmas and Complexities of Organising Everyday Family Life" (2012).

Lasse Lipponen is a professor of education, with special reference to early childhood education, at the Department of Teacher Education, University of Helsinki, Finland. His research work is directed to cultures of compassion, children's agency and teacher education. During the past years his development and research work has been funded by the European Union (EU), Singapore Ministry of Education, Academy of Finland, the Finnish Funding Agency for Innovation, and Finnish Ministry of Education and Culture. Lipponen has authored more than 100 research articles on teaching and learning.

Johannes Lunneblad has a PhD in education and is an associate professor of education in the Department of Education, Communication and Learning at the University of Gothenburg, Sweden. His main research interests are in the fields of urban education and multicultural education.

Kari Nissinen, PhD (statistics), is a university researcher in the Finnish Institute for Educational Research, University of Jyväskylä, Finland. His main responsibilities are management and statistical analyses of large-scale assessment (PISA, TIMSS, PIRLS and PIAAC) data sets. He has much experience in statistical data analysis, and his expertise areas are linear and generalized linear models, multilevel and mixed models, multivariate statistics and survey methodology.

Elin Eriksen Ødegaard is a professor in early childhood education at the Centre of Educational Research, Western Norway University of Applied Sciences, Norway, and a visiting professor at UiT – the Arctic University of Norway. Her areas of expertise are narrative research about children and teachers, kindergarten as an arena for cultural formation, child culture, pedagogy and professionalism.

Ylva Odenbring has a PhD in education and is an associate professor of education in the Department of Education, Communication and Learning at the University of Gothenburg, Sweden. Her main research interests are in the fields of gender studies and social justice in education.

Per Arne Rød is a clinical social worker, PhD, and associate professor at the Department of Social Science and Social Education, Bergen University College, Norway. Rød has practical experience in child protection services, child psychiatry and family therapy. As a researcher, he has conducted studies on the analyses and decisions of the child protection services and on children's experiences of conflict-ridden relationship breakups.

Ingrid Pramling Samuelsson is a professor of early childhood education at the Department of Education, Communication and Learning at the University of Gothenburg, Sweden. Her main research fields are young children's learning and curriculum questions of early years education. Her many research studies of children's learning and play in the preschool context have led to the development of a didactics approach, labelled developmental pedagogy. One of her most popular books is *The Playing-Learning Child* (originally in Swedish but also translated to German), which is based on the ideas that children are playing-learning individuals and that preschool didactics need to integrate play and learning. Her latest research concerns children's possibilities to learn in relation to group size and about immigrant families. She has an UNESCO Chair in Early Childhood Education and Sustainable Development and is the former world president of Organisation Mondiale pour l´Èducation Présolaire (OMEP).

Sonja Sheridan is a professor in education at the Department of Education, Communication and Learning, University of Gothenburg, Sweden. She specializes in research on quality issues related to the preschool quality, the preschool profession and children's learning and development in preschool. She was the vice head of the department with responsibility for research between 2010–2015 and has been the leader of several research projects, with many international publications.

Mirja Tarnanen is a professor of language education in the Department of Teacher Education at the University of Jyväskylä, Finland. Her research interests lie in the areas of language teaching and learning in the different settings, teacher education and curriculum reform. Her recent publications deal with literacy and assessment practices across curriculum; migrants in professional communities; learning in multilingual settings; and language awareness and beliefs of pre-service teachers and connections between curriculum reform, school culture and practice.

Jouni Vettenranta, ScD (forestry), is a senior researcher at the Finnish Institute for Educational Research, University of Jyväskylä, Finland. His main responsibilities are conducting the Finnish TIMSS-study and working as a science expert in the PISA study. His research interests lie in the areas of regional variation of learning results and social and cultural conditions. By connecting geographical information and international assessment data, he figures out how possible local characteristics affect learning.

Pia Williams is a professor in child and youth studies at the Department of Education, Communication and Learning, University of Gothenburg, Sweden. She has much experience in working as a lecturer in higher education. Her research is directed towards early childhood education with special interest in conditions for children's learning and development in preschool in relation to preschool teachers' competence. Another research interest focuses on children's peer collaboration, communication and interaction in preschool.

1 Introduction

Susanne Garvis and Elin Eriksen Ødegaard

Introduction

This book explores the concept of Nordic perspectives of family and children. In addition to families, institutions are spaces where social mobility, change and life-long learning take place. Needless to say, numerous mechanisms will synthetically form ways that families and children live their lives. Political, cultural-historical and geographical conditions are crucial mechanisms, but as we will learn throughout this book, the Nordic perspective will visualize and document the importance of the children's agency, their activities and experience within families and institutions. Understanding children and family is of crucial importance for a wide scope of professionals within education, social work, care and health. New ways of living and a change of the status of children challenge established views and practices.

Social and educational institutions in the Nordic countries will often claim to work within a 'Nordic model', even if programs, methods and philosophy are imported from other parts of the world. We therefore need to address the concept of the 'Nordic model' to get to the Nordic perspectives on family and children. Because globalization, exchange of ideas and transnational agreements and common grounds exist across geographical borders and boundaries, it is reasonable to critically ask if there is a Nordic perspective and, if yes, why it is of interest.

Our answer to that question is yes; we can talk about a Nordic dialogue. Even if the 'Nordic' can seem blurred, and it is not difficult to come up with examples of common ground across other geographical axes, there are compelling reasons for paying attention to a Nordic perspective on family and children. In an era of globalization, Nordic dialogues must consequently be seen in a prism. What we claim to be Nordic perspectives are closely linked to national and global economies as well as transnational cultural ideas and ideals on families and children.

The universal idea and continuous challenge of how to shape better lives for children motivate the cooperating authors. In this book we see children as participants in families and society, and a premise is the fact that a body of scientific evidence shows that economic growth and conditions are not only mechanisms that ensure and provide a good life for children. It is, however, of interest that economic equal distribution, often referred to as the Nordic welfare system (the 'Nordic model') can seem a reasonable factor for a high level of trust, openness and tolerance, factors often referred to as common features in Nordic countries. Openness generates trust in other people, in legal systems and in politicians, something that is said to be unique in a global context (Høybråten, 2015). For this reason, we will elaborate on how the Nordic welfare system deals with conditions for families in the introduction.

The concept of family is broadly understood and elaborated to embrace both nuclear and extended families. Also historical and new ways of living and understanding children, childhood and generations are relevant when understanding family. What constitutes a family could mean a family or group in which the decision-making processes over and with children and members of the family are taking place over time. The members of a family will not necessarily live in the same household but be emotionally attached, detached or related by kin. When it comes to the laws and regulations in welfare states, however, definitions about living in the same household might be a condition for benefits.

Contemporary knowledge sees family and children, on the one hand, as resources, partners who can be more involved in activities, development and creation of curriculum and change. On the other hand children and families are also seen as at risk, underprivileged, underdeveloped, hard to involve and difficult to change (Rogoff, 2003; Hedegaard, Aronsen, Højholt & Ulvik, 2012). In practice these two opposite perspectives are often blended. Involvement, development and change in institutions have traditionally been reserved for professionals, but ecological, cultural and systemic bases of knowledge take into account that children are parts of family systems and relations that affect the development and well-being of children.

Furthermore, the aim of the book is to share the Nordic perspective from each of the five countries in the Nordic region: Island, Finland, Sweden, Denmark and Norway.[1] The research chapters highlight key ideas within and across countries. Key academics from across the Nordic region share an understanding about the history of the Nordic perspectives of family and children as well as providing current innovative research about problems and solutions to complex issues related to family and children.

Each of the chapters shares examples of empirical research as well as theoretical perspectives in arguing the Nordic perspective. The common contribution is this interdisciplinary body of articles that renews the understanding of family and children from among the Nordic authors. The book brings new knowledge and insights into the cultural understanding of the Nordic region of interest beyond the Nordic region.

The Nordic model

What is then the 'the Nordic model'? It refers to the combination of a market-based economy with a significant tax-financed welfare policy and an emphasis on social transfer and equality goals across gender and class. There is a high labour force participation rate for both men and women. Wages and income have been kept equal for many years, sustained by labour unions. The open economy also includes a tendency for an openness towards new technologies. There is participative democracy and traditions for local authorities and local influence, including neighbour-organized communities

The first key consideration is the innovative design of policy and practice to deal with contemporary issues within society. The second is that Nordic countries are grappling with problems that other countries will have to deal with in due course, such as how to organize society when almost all women work and how to listen to children's voices when parents divorce. Nordic perspectives appear to reject tired, orthodox approaches and provide innovative solutions. In addition, the system has paradoxical consequences, and claims of the perfect realization are often exaggerated.

The Nordic countries have a collective population of only 26 million. This is not a substantial population compared to other regions, yet the Nordic region is considered a powerhouse in many policies and practices within societies. This is evident in Nordic countries scoring highly in lifestyle measures, quality of life and most livable places to work and live. The Nordic countries are able to dominate league tables in indices of country competitiveness as well as well-being, democracy and peace. The countries have for 200 years kept peace among each other and have substantial cooperation across national borders.

The objective is therefore not to convey the Nordic perspective as a homogeneous perspective, nor to give an impression that all Nordic citizens, families and children, institutions and policy makers think and behave in the same way. The 'Nordic model' is still a work in progress, and there are contemporary efforts that the Nordic countries are using to update their model to retain and make it distinctive (Høybråten, 2015). This book provides some understanding about 'the work in progress'.

A brief Nordic comparison

To help provide an overview of Nordic countries, we have decided to include tables to show the implementation of policy around childhood, parental provision and welfare support for children. The tables show key dates and provision for support for families. The tables also show the differences across the countries of Sweden, Norway, Finland, Denmark and Iceland. This suggests that whereas there might be a general model around the 'Nordic dialogue', different perspectives also dominate across countries in regard to rights, provision and support.

The first table (Table 1.1) highlights the different country's perspectives in regard to policies around childhood. Although all countries have similar ways in regard to corporal punishment laws, universal access to kindergarten, starting age of school, provision for schooling and curriculum frameworks, there are differences in when policies were implemented and the actual provision given. For example, school starting age varies across the Nordic region, as does universal access. The actual cost of kindergarten and formal schooling also varies across the countries. What the countries do share, however, is a commitment to universal access for children, higher ages for starting school compared to Anglo-Saxon

Table 1.1 Nordic policy around childhood

	Sweden	*Norway*	*Finland*	*Denmark*	*Iceland*
Ratification of UN Rights of the Child Convention	1990	1991	1991	1991	1992
Corporal punishment law	1979 (UN) 1958 (forbidden to hit children in schools)	1987(UN) 1936 (in schools)	1983(UN) 1890 (in Schools)	1997(UN) 1967 (In schools)	2003(UN)
Universal access to kindergarten	3–6 years are free for 15 hours a week since 2003 Children can start from 1 year of age since 1995 6-year-old right to free preschool class since 1975	Every child, age 1–6, has a legal right to a place in kindergarten since 2009	8 months to five years since 1990 6-year-old kindergarten class since 1996	Children should be offered a place in day care facilities (dagtilbud) if their parents want it. Some local authorities guarantee a place since 1997. Since 2000–2003 there has been a financial agreement between the central government and local authorities of offering all parents day care places.	Day care obligatory for bilingual children from 3 years Children can start from 1 year of age
School starting age and years of compulsory schooling	7 9	6 10	7 9	6 10	6 10

Profile of frameworks for early childhood	Play and learning Democracy Systematic documentation Qualification socialization and subjectification	Play and learning Democracy Continuous observation of whole child development and happiness Socialization, qualification and subjectification	Play and learning Individual plans Democracy socialization, qualification and subjectification	Play and learning Democracy Language Screening of 3-year-olds Socialization, qualification	Play Learning Democracy Equality Assessment of every child's development Socialization, qualification and subjectification
Provisions provided in education	Basic right to free education, including necessary equipment, textbooks, school transport and meals	6–18 basic rights to free education, including necessary equipment, textbooks and school transport	Basic right to free education, including necessary equipment, textbooks, school transport and meals	Maximum cost is 2.551 (Copenhagen) Low family income; free or low fee	Parents pay 30% of actual cost in public institution and up to 50% in private institutions

countries and heavily subsidized early childhood and schooling. The countries also have a universal understanding to ban corporal punishment and ratify the Rights of the Child. Another similarity is in the early childhood curriculum frameworks, which have a strong focus on play, learning and democracy.

The second table (Table 1.2) provides a comparison of parental policy in the region. This includes the amount of maternity and paternal leave provided, father's rights and access to prenatal care. All countries appear to offer maternity and parental leave at between 70 to 90 per cent of income. Whereas the actual time and amounts vary, all of the countries have split policies for both the mother and the father. Fathers are also entitled to leave to look after their newborn children and have rights to initially take time off when the child is born. Free prenatal care is also available to all expecting mothers. Once children are born, they are entitled to free health care.

The final table (Table 1.3) shows comparisons across policies for welfare support for children. All countries have free medical care for children until the age of 18, with Sweden offering free health care until the child is 20. In some countries dental care is also covered under this health provision. Some of the countries have also made allowances for parents to look after sick children and still receive between 80 to 100 per cent of their salary. This may be a unique feature of the Nordic perspective in supporting working parents to also have entitlements to care for sick children. Each country also has provision for child benefits, with some countries making the payment dependent on income and other countries paying all families. Whereas support is given for children who attend kindergarten, some countries also have support for children who do not attend kindergarten as part of the thinking around equality. Again although the exact details of time and amounts differ across the region, there is a general trend of providing free health care, supporting families to care for sick children and providing access to kindergartens as well as providing funded alternatives. Overall the policies show strong support for children and their families to ensure adequate standards of living.

Other countries often admire the 'Nordic model' for families and children and quote their successes in achieving good outcomes. This book is intended to dig deeper into these policies to see what they look like within each of the contexts for families, children and professionals. How do such policies and provisions work in contemporary times? What is the relationship among families, children and professionals? The purpose of the book is to explore such questions and look at the Nordic dialogue across the different countries in regard to families, children and professionals.

Overview of the book

The Nordic dialogue brings together a number of different authors from across the region. The first chapter provides an introduction to the book and summarizes. In Nordic society, family members' lives are historically structured and distributed in the sense that children and parents share a common, everyday life together. In the

Table 1.2 Policy for parents in Nordic countries

	Sweden	*Norway*	*Finland*	*Denmark*	*Iceland*
Amount of maternity and parental leave	Both parents are entitled to up to 8 months of paid leave per child, which makes it possible for a total time of 16 months per child Of this amount, 13 months are paid at 80% of the most recent income up to a ceiling of approximately 443,000 SEK (€51,100) per year in 2016	Mother can take 35 weeks at full pay or 45 weeks at 80% pay Fathers can take up to 10 weeks on the mother's income. Together the parents can receive an additional 56 weeks of full pay or 56 weeks of 80% pay	Maternity leave is for 18 weeks Parental leave is for 26 weeks Paternity leave is for 9 weeks and covers the first year of a child's life Benefits during maternity, paternity and parental leave are between 70 to 90% of previous annual earnings	18 weeks of maternity leave Fathers get 14 days Parents can then split an additional 32 weeks	Parents can split 9 months of post childbirth leave Mothers get 3 months and then fathers get 3 months Both parents receive 80% of their salaries
Father's rights	A new father or the other parent also has the right to 10 days with compensation when a child is born	Fathers (other parents) can get 10 weeks on the mother's salary, and they split the rest	Fathers can take 18 weeks of paternity leave while the mother is on maternity leave	14 days paid leave at birth, then until 32 weeks paid parental leave Can extend the leave on reduced pay	Fathers are given 3 months and the possibility to an additional 3 months to share with the mother
Provision	Free prenatal care	Free prenatal care	Free prenatal care Maternity package	Free prenatal care	Free prenatal care

Table 1.3 Welfare support for children

	Sweden	*Norway*	*Finland*	*Denmark*	*Iceland*
Health care provision	Children below 20 are entitled to free health care (including dental care)	Children below the age of 18 receive all of their medical care free (including dental care)	Children below the age of 18 receive all of their medical care free.	Every legal resident gets a free health care Free dental care for children until 18)	Children below the age of 18 receive all of their medical care free Pay for medicine
Entitlement to care for sick children	120 days per child per year for children under 12 years Salary is at 80%	20 days per child per year for children under 12 years Salary is 100%	Parent has the right to stay home to look after sick children.		12 days per child under 13 years per year For chronically ill children 80% salary for 9 months
Child benefit	Child allowance amounting to SEK 1,050 (about €122) per month and per child with supplements for large families	Child allowance amounting to NKR 970 (€107) per month and per child under 18, with supplements for large families	Working parents are entitled to work shorter hours from the end of the parental leave period until the end of the child's second year of school A flexible care allowance encourages parents of children under the age of 3 to combine part-time work with part-time care An amount of €244.18 per month is paid to parents working a maximum of 22.5 hours per week or 60%, of their normal full-time hours, and €162.78 to those working a maximum of 30 hours per week, or 80% of their normal full-time hours	Families (mothers) with children 0–2: DK 17 772 (€ 2390) per child per year 2–6: 14,076 per child per year 7–17: 11,076 per child per year	Child allowance is provided for low-income families depending on income, number of children and their ages

Cost and access for kindergarten	Preschool is free for children 3–5 years for 15 hours a week Parental fees are directly proportional to parents' income and inversely proportional to the number of children in a family The fee can be up to 3 per cent of the family's monthly income but no more than 1,260 SEK (about €146) per month	Maximum price is NOK 2.480 (€264) Low-income families get reduced or free cost	The monthly fee per child varies between €0 and €283 in 2015 depending on family size and income Education for 6-year-old children (pre-primary) is free	Maximum price is DK 2.551 (€ 343) with lunch included	Prices vary between municipalities Meals are included For those who cannot get a place in lekskola, can get subsidies for private day care
Support for children who do not access kindergarten	A flat rate allowance of untaxed 3,000 SEK (€312) per month	Families who do not use kindergarten service at all get NOK 6,000 (€639) per child per month If the child uses kindergarten service less than 20 hours a week, the family gets NOK 3,000 per child per month	Parents are also entitled to paid childcare leave with an allowance after the end of parental leave if they do not use day care This enables parents to look after a child under the age of 3 without giving up their jobs In 2015 this basic childcare allowance was €342.53 per month per one child	Children from families in need for language support can get access to a language stimulation program 15 or 30 hours a week	No support

second chapter, Charlotte Højholt, Pernille Juhl and Dorte Kousholt draw upon research projects exploring children's everyday lives across a variation of contexts through participatory observations and interviews. They focus on the parents' perspectives on their lives across family, day care, family relief and children's lives in relation to settling into school. The chapter takes a point of reference in the collectivity of everyday life and self-understanding as a family.

The third chapter by Lena Bäckström presents family life in Nordic countries from the children's perspectives. She reports on data collected from 11-year-old children about their family life and upbringing as a starting point. The findings suggest that the children talked about the concept of a 'good family' that includes many different types of family structures. Given the high rates of divorce and separation in Nordic countries, the chapter provides an important contribution about family life in general as well as the support structures available.

In his chapter on compassion (Chapter 4), Lasse Lipponen discusses the emotional worlds of early childhood settings in a Swedish context. He focuses on the formation of compassion related to the rules that govern how it is and should be expressed in early childhood settings. He then relates this to the emotional worlds of families. He concludes that each family has its own emotional world and that almost every day, especially when parents leave and pick up their children, the two worlds (family and kindergarten) negotiate boundaries on emotions.

The chapter by Sonja Sheridan and Pia Williams from Sweden (Chapter 5) explores pedagogical leadership and families within a Swedish preschool context. The chapter discusses pedagogical leadership from the perspective of management and monitoring and as a fundamental aspect of preschool teacher competence. Their chapter also illustrates the problems leaders deal with when demands from society are in conflict with parents' and teachers' wishes to make decisions that are necessary for preschool.

The next chapter, Chapter 6 by Ingegerd Tallberg-Broman and Ingrid Pramling Samuelsson explores early childhood education, gender relations and equality between parents and families in Sweden. In the chapter, they discuss the historical conditions and examine the basis of current studies on contemporary relationships between preschools and families. They also discuss the challenges facing Sweden in regard to global and local events that directly influence children and their families.

In Chapter 7, Per Arne Rød presents statistics that show that Nordic families are typically patriarchal and discuss what that means when children live in divorced families in conflict. He shows how dysfunctional relationship breakups are characterized by unclear boundaries and cause psychological damage to one or more members of the family. He discusses the fact that parents' rights as adults in conflict take precedence over the parents' duties as parents and that children cannot protect themselves against their parents' conflicts, even though the court has taken formal responsibility regarding decisions on child custody. The chapter gives substantial insight into children's experience and perspectives when living in families with serious conflicts.

Sweden was the first country to ban child abuse in 1979; however, research suggests that children still do experience abuse. In Chapter 8, Ylva Odenbring, Thomas Johansson and Johannes Lunneblad explore the shaping of domestic abuse and child neglect within a discourse on parents and their 'problematic' behaviour. They authors note that when Swedish parents abuse their children, it is often understood and explained in terms of social or psychological problems. Alternatively, with immigrant parents the behaviour is described in terms of culture. The chapter provides important knowledge on the processes and challenges involved in the collaborative work accomplished among school officials and other professionals.

In Finland, the number of students from immigrant backgrounds has increased over the last decades and especially with the influx of aslum seekers in 2015. In Chapter 9, Heidi Harju-Luukkainen, Mirja Tarnanen, Kari Nissinen and Jouni Vettenranta present information about the economic, social and cultural status and mathematics performance of immigrant students in the Finnish PISA results. Their chapter aims to understand how students' family-related factors affect educational attainment and how they are distributed from a geostatistical perspective. Findings provide important insights about educational equality and equity in Finland and raise questions about geographical accumulations that may go undetected.

In the chapter on immigrant families (Chapter 10), Anette Hilton provides an exploration about family integration and opportunity. Her chapter sheds light into the challenges associated with families moving to Denmark. In a series of case studies, she shares personal experiences of immigrants deciding if they should stay or leave. Her findings explore challenges of language barriers, employment as well as perceptions about newcomers, social norms and feelings of 'outsiderness'. She also explores concepts of 'double identity' and 'otherness'.

Johanna Einarsdottir and Arna H. Jonsdottir, in Chapter 11, share insights from Icelandic parents about working with preschool, with a focus on power and influence. Guidelines in Iceland suggest that educators, parents and children should be active participants and be involved in decisions that influence the preschool. Einarsdottir and Jonsdottir conducted focus groups with parents to explore the relationship. Their findings show many challenges and implications in relation to practice. Two dimensions of the parent-professional relationship were also found.

Chapter 12 by Tona Gulpinar and Leift Hernes explores the perceptions of families in relation to aesthetic subjects in Norwegian preschools. The study is part of a larger scale exploring the quality of early childhood. The chapter presents information about the Norwegian law system in regard to children's arts and culture before sharing findings from two surveys on parent expectations. Norwegian parents appear to have strong expectations of the kindergarten as a mediator for culture.

At the end of each chapter, a short summary is made across the main themes and ideas for Nordic countries. These are also discussed in terms of contemporary times, especially given the changing landscape in the Nordic region.

Conclusion

This book is intended to provide readers with an up-to-date perspective of families and children in the Nordic countries. The chapters share information about history and policy in Nordic countries as well as share a contemporary understanding of the current cultural context and how families navigate different educational institutions. As part of the contemporary understanding, several of the chapters also discuss immigration and cultural minority groups. It is hoped that as readers unpack the Nordic perspective, they will begin to discover the unique features of policy and practice in this part of the world as well as the challenges and barriers within the perspective. This book has drawn together academics from across the different countries to provide a snapshot understanding to report current research and ideas as well as raise questions for the future. Perhaps as a reader you will find similarities or differences to your own country. Perhaps you will find the historical perspectives refreshing or challenging. It is hoped, however, that as you ponder the Nordic dialogue, you also engage in deep reflection about possible futures and begin conversations with others about possibilities and challenges.

Note

1 Also Åland, the Faeroe Island and Greenland are part of the Nordic region.

References

Hedegaard, M., Aronsen, K., Højholt, C., & Ulvik, A. S. (2012). *Children, Childhood and Everyday Life – Children's Perspectives.* Charlotte, NC, USA: Information Age Publishing.

Høybråten, D. (2015). *The Nordic Perspective – Strategy for International Branding of the Nordic Region 2015–2018.* Retrieved from www.norden.org

Rogoff, B. (2003). *The Cultural Nature of Human Development.* Oxford: Oxford University Press.

2 The collectivity of family conduct of life and parental self-understanding

Charlotte Højholt, Pernille Juhl and Dorte Kousholt

Introduction

How do families develop their shared everyday life? How do parents develop their self-understanding as 'a family' who takes care of children – in relation to the variety of challenges, for instance, related to children's continually changing lives as toddlers and as schoolchildren?

This chapter takes a point of reference in the collectivity of developing everyday life and self-understanding as a family. In Nordic societies, family members' lives are historically structured and distributed in the sense that children and their parents share a common everyday life together and, at the same time, they live their lives across several different contexts more or less separately. However, separately is not an adequate term because modern families in many respects gather around supporting these different trajectories across contexts, and this implies getting involved in the life contexts of each other.

Children's lives in a variety of institutions represent new tasks and social situations for their parents, who seem to reflect their personal way of arranging life in relation to these multifaceted tasks together with other parents. This forms a background for new kinds of conflictuality in relation to family life.

In family research as well as in professional practice, there appears to be a tendency to problematize how parents execute their family tasks and to regard the family as a quite isolated unit. This goes together with a tendency to regard societal demands as quite abstract and as unambiguous government of families as something each individual must live up to. Such problems connect to theoretical challenges in relation to conceptualizing how family life at one and the same time is quite a personal matter involving great differences in regard to life forms, care practices and perspectives on the development of children *and* a common matter related to the welfare society's general responsibility for children. In this way, the care for children is also a conflictual matter related to the institutions in a society and the historical conditions for developing as parents of growing children. How can we understand such interrelatedness and conceptualize everyday living as something subjects actively do, arrange and coordinate? How can we focus on *the personal conduct* of family life and care for children? Trying to deal with such challenges, we will involve theoretical conceptualizations about how persons conduct their compound, intertwined and cross-contextual lives together (Holzkamp, 2013; Dreier, 2008). Furthermore, the article builds on empirical material from fieldwork consisting of interviews with children, parents and professionals and participatory observations of everyday life across family life, family interventions, day care and school (Højholt & Kousholt, 2014).

Central themes in family research

Historically, the Western modern nuclear family can be seen as formed through structural and economic changes during the late 18th and 19th centuries, causing the family to 'turn inwards' as an arena for emotional fulfilment and 'shut off' the influence of the outside community (Shorter, 1979). From the 1950s, taking a point of departure in Parsons's structural-functionalistic approach, the family came to be regarded as a decisive unit of socialization and hence a foundation for social integration (Parsons & Bales, 1956). This structural-functionalistic approach has been widely criticized by, among others, feminist family researchers arguing against the idea of the nuclear family as universal and natural (Leira, 1993; Hartmann, 1981). Analysis of connections between the 'internal' structure of the family and the structure of the patriarchal society became a central part of Western feminist family research (Finch, 1993). What we want to draw attention to is that historically family research has placed the responsibility for the 'correct development' of the child on the parents in a quite private and individualized family. Even though this perspective has been criticized, it remains a central issue. Therefore, it is a central challenge for family research to analyze the practices of family life as fundamentally social and in connection with changing societal conditions.

In recent decades, there has been an increasing focus on discourses of involvement and time investment (e.g., Forsberg, 2009) and increased 'responsibilization of parents' in relation to the educational needs of children (Knudsen & Andersen 2014). Based on statistic demographic data, similar arguments are put forward by Schneider (201). He emphasizes that in large parts of Europe, parenthood has developed towards professionalization and the parents' duty to secure the 'best interest of their child' – where 'best interest' is increasingly associated with educational possibilities. In general, the research deals with increasingly specific developmental and educational 'needs' that parents are supposed to fulfil. The argument of increased professionalization and responsibilization of parents has a strong presence in the debate about family life and parental cooperation with various public institutions (cf. Højholt & Kousholt, forthcoming). The growing number of preventive programs aimed at increasing parental knowledge and competences, as well as early interventions, can be seen in this light – and seem to problematize the modern parents as insecure and self-doubting, confronting vast demands and pressures related to upbringing. These research perspectives raise critical awareness of increasing demands on and ideals for modern parenthood. However, we see a tendency that in such a research interest, the parents appear as individuals who must each live up to standards and ideals imposed on parents in a quite abstract way. This calls for conceptualizations about how parents are actively dealing with and also transforming their everyday practices.

In regard to these research challenges, it appears fruitful that David Morgan (1996) introduced the concept of 'family practices' to deal with problems relating to the concept of 'the family' that often come to signify a rather static unit permeated with normative standards. Morgan (2013) argues for the concept of family practice to capture the active, *doing* family, the everyday character of daily life – imbued with regularity, change and fluidity at the same time. With his approach to family practices, Morgan contributes with analysis of family life as an everyday common activity and the unity of regularity and change. Furthermore, recent developments in Nordic family research have emphasized the way parenting is formed by the everyday lives of children across different institutional settings and how that entails the parental work of dealing with the coordination and connections of the 'chains of care' in cooperation with various professionals (e.g., Andenæs, 2011; Andenæs & Haavind, 2016; Højholt & Kousholt, 2016; Juhl, 2014). Concepts about shared care (Singer, 1993) or chains of care direct attention to the fact that the everyday lives of children take place across different contexts and highlight that care for children involves several caregivers and coordination among them. This challenges conceptions that isolate parenting within the family and addresses the attachment between parent and child as the primary topic in relation to understanding family relations and problems (cf. Kousholt, 2012).

Taking these research challenges as a point of departure, we will argue for conceptualizations capable of grasping family life as both part of a personal life across different contexts and as collective practice that must be continuously rearranged in relation to the development of the children and shifting possibilities in and demands from different contexts.

Analytical challenges

Searching for research insight into family life leaves us with the impression that we are in need of conceptualizations that may guide exploration of the conduct of everyday life of families in a *concrete* way, connecting historical and socio-structural conditions for everyday life to the subjective meanings and experiences of action possibilities. To overcome an apparent tendency to reproduce a political concern about uncertain and problematic parents more or less caught in the demands of a modern society, we need the analytical possibility to explore (and intervene into) the social possibilities for family life and explore the personal ways of experiencing and dealing with these.

Theoretically, we confront the challenge of conceptualizing different but entangled lives and subjective 'arranging' of everyday life conditions in a certain historical time with certain demands as well as possibilities for taking part and obtaining access to, for example, educational trajectories. Dealing with such possibilities and demands implies continual development of personal preferences, priorities and plans in relation to selecting, coordinating and adjusting to conditions – it implies the development of a personal 'conduct of life'.

Employing the concept of conduct of life, we want to analyze the active, creative, exploring, coordinating and anticipating processes involved in leading a complex everyday life (Holzkamp, 2013). In continuation of this, our theoretical aim is to expand how we in family research understand the collective processes of developing conduct of everyday life and 'self-understanding'. Family members conduct their lives *together* and in *relation* to each other, and the focus on family conduct of life turns our attention to the work of arranging a complex practice where different lives, interests and perspectives must be integrated and coordinated. Ole Dreier (2008, 2011) has developed this approach with a focus on the cross-contextual aspects of everyday life, and researchers from different fields have further expanded conceptualizations about the personal and social aspects of the conduct of everyday life (see, e.g., Chimirri, 2013; Højholt & Kousholt, 2016; Juhl, 2015; Røn Larsen & Stanek, 2015; Schraube & Højholt, 2016).

These endeavours can also be seen as related to a methodological point about anchoring everyday living in people's participation in social practice and as inspired by sociocultural theory (Hedegaard & Fleer, 2013; Rogoff, 2003; Chaiklin, Hedegaard & Jensen, 1999) and social practice theory (Lave, 2011; Axel, 2011).

Thus, the analytical challenge is to link how the very mutuality 'inside' the family develops through changing distribution of contributions, responsibility and influence among the family members *and* through the exchange with a plurality of other persons, participation, demands and possibilities of other places. The aim is to be able to conceptualize how subjects develop their common practices and come to cooperate in new ways. This contrasts with the perception of development as a linear movement from independence and government to autonomy and freedom. The conduct of everyday life is neither an adjustment to order and control, nor an individualistic display of inner needs, but rather an intersubjective collectivity.

Empirically, the chapter draws on different research projects exploring children's everyday lives across a variation of contexts (among others: family, day care, kindergarten, school, special help arrangements and institutions for children's leisure time). We will focus on research investigating toddlers' lives across family, day care and respite family; their parents' perspectives in relation to that; and children's lives in relation to settling into school and their parents' perspectives in relation to this situation. By presenting examples from two research projects, we want to illustrate variations and avoid a homogenous picture of Nordic family life. Our fieldwork involves participatory observations in different life contexts and the children's transitions between them as well as interviews with parents, professionals, children and experts. The researchers have participated in these trajectories for several years and cooperated with the professionals in relation to the development of family work and parental cooperation.

The following examples are meant to illustrate general points about the collectivity of family conduct of life. From two different empirical trajectories, we address three interwoven analytical themes; firstly, how parenthood is developed collectively and how being a parent involves contradictory and changing tasks, which are negotiated and adjusted in cooperation with other parents, professionals and children; secondly, how parents develop their self-understanding in relation to their everyday lives and how this involves processes of participating in shared conflictual practices; and thirdly, how the processes of developing care practices entail complex and contradictory processes and how this brings about explorative and situated investigation of the children's daily interplay and situations. This goes for the help and support one as a parent provides for one's children as well as for the help provided by professional institutions to parents and children in difficulties.

Continuously changing conditions and mutuality in family life

As a part of children's trajectories across different institutions, they continuously change their demands, interplay and conflicts with their parents. The *mutuality* between child and parents changes in specific ways. Hanne Haavind (1987) has, with a vantage point in cultural psychology, formulated this as a process of "extending mutuality", where the child becomes involved in new tasks and relationships, tackles expanded responsibilities and develops new kinds of contributions and increased motivation. From this inspiration, as well as a point of departure in the concept of participation, we have conceptualized such processes as a change – and exchange – in the ways children and their caregivers take part in their common arrangements and how they divide possibilities of contributions and influence. Parents and children constitute the conditions for the development of each other; and for that reason, the distribution of influence and responsibility between them is a continual challenge and involves dilemmas (Højholt, 2006, 2011; Kousholt, 2011, 2012; Juhl, 2014).

However, the conditions for such relational processes are also set in other places and are related to historical and structural distributions of the responsibility for children as well as related to societal demands for specific competences, contributions and participation.

The following example illustrates how the arrangements of everyday life and changes in the mutuality among family members are brought about through the children's movement from one societal institution to another, with quite different expectations to the children as well as to their parents.

In interviews with parents investigating their perspectives on how children settle into school, a recurring theme is that the change of institutional contexts means new conditions for being a parent. The interviews contain many stories of children behaving unexpectedly and changing moods and parents being 'puzzled'. Parents reflect upon the question: how are we to understand this new behaviour?

In an interview with the parents of twins in first grade, Naja and Peter, the father says:

> We had an expectation that it would be difficult for Peter . . . It took us by surprise that it is actually Naja . . . it has been tough on her . . . the social part.

The mother reflects upon how the transition to school led to Naja experiencing a change in her social position: from being the "oldest, secure, well-liked and very competent" in relation to the practices of day care, to struggling with "how to find one's place among all the other children and how to assert herself". Within the first years of school, Naja was frequently 'called home' because of stomach pain. Her mother says:

> [W]e [the parents] talked about it again the other day, when she was called home – it has been really surprising for us to have a child always in a good mood, 'on top of things' and competent and suddenly to have a child who is very vulnerable. It's like . . . almost a change in personality . . . she is in a bad mood, she cries in the morning – not for any particular reason, she is just like . . . not able to get dressed.

The children's transition to school not only means new routines in relation to arranging family life (getting the whole family ready and having the child brought to school at 8:00, preparing lunchboxes and school bags – which are some of the more practical differences of having a child in day care institution vs. in school in Denmark). The parents also experience changes in relation to how they perceive their child, what the child is able to do and his or her strengths and weaknesses. New challenges in the life of the child mean that the child changes his or her participation in family life (parallel to Hedegaard, 2016). The parents continuously deal with intertwined processes of 'trying to catch up' with the changes in their child's way of taking part in the everyday life of the family and how they need to adjust their support for and demands on their child. Such processes involve talking to each other and reflecting in dialogue with other parents and teachers.

In this example, it becomes a matter for the parents of adjusting their everyday lives so that the mother can pick up Naja early from school. They experience her as 'exhausted' and therefore pay more attention to her and adjust their demands and expectation of her accordingly. They need to support her more during the mornings (getting dressed and ready to leave), and they allow her more 'quiet time' at home (e.g., playing games on the iPad). Naja's parents try to explore, in conversations with Naja and with each other, what the stomach pain is about. Then they get an insight into stories about conflicts between some of the other girls and Naja not being able to play with a particular girl who she wants to play with. This means that the parents engage in dialogue with the teacher about the girls' ways of arranging play and excluding each other, and at the same time, they try to support Naja's relations with the other girls by making 'play dates' outside school. The parents continuously explore the relations between contribution (how the child takes part) and responsibility (what the child can manage and what kind of support is needed), and in this manner the mutuality is continuously changing.

The detailed description of the changing practices in the family illustrate that children's development is not a linear movement towards more and more independence and responsibility. Taking on new challenges (i.e., investigating new conditions and possibilities for taking part in the children's communities in school) can entail becoming less 'competent' for a while (cf. Hviid, 2008). Parents experience new challenges and must consider whether to adjust their perceptions or understanding of their child – and consequently how to behave as parents to support the well-being and development of their child. This often entails that interplays, positions and practices within the family are transformed (as in the case where the parents' concerns shift from Peter (is he mature enough and able to handle the demands of school) to Naja.

During the interview, the parents elaborate further on other aspects of what came as a "surprise": In a meeting with the professionals from the after-school centre, they talk about Peter in a way that the parents "cannot recognise at all", and this is in contrast to the impression they get from the school. According to the parents, the professionals in the after-school centre talk about Peter as very "disruptive" and socially challenged and hint at an "autism disorder". His mother explains:

> [W]e were glad that we had just been to the other [meeting with the teachers] because otherwise we would have thought that we didn't have any sense of things . . . okay . . . we damn well know our own children, right, it was really such a surprise.

Through reflecting with each other and talking with the other parents about their impressions of the after-school centre, the parents calm down and reassure each other that they are not totally wrong in their own understanding of their boy. Together with some of the other parents (who are also very unsatisfied with the after-school centre), they arrange a meeting with the professionals.

The parents are 'searching' and questioning – what do these conditions and situations mean for my child? It is characteristic that these investigations are closely entangled with collaborations with the teacher in school and with other professionals and the information parents receive from other parents. How the teachers understand and respond to the challenges of the child is crucial in relation to how the parents experience their agency in relation to dealing with these challenges.

It is not just the children and their parents who constitute conditions for each other's development – other parents, other places, other children (i.e., in the school) and professionals who organize learning communities and parental collaboration also make up conditions for personal self-understanding with regard to developing as a parent. The examples illustrate that it is significant how parents can use each other to reflect and support their continuous 'search for understanding' and coordinate actions in relation to, for example, the professionals with whom they have a dispute. In this case, the parents have each other, and they have good relations to other parents in the class. They are not isolated with their doubts, pressures and conflicts with the professionals when their parental abilities are questioned. This example therefore illustrates how parents may reorganize their everyday lives in a collective coordination with other parties. However, not all parents have the opportunities to involve networks and social resources in this way, and the conditions for redistribution of tasks, responsibility and care among the family members are quite different.

When conducting everyday life becomes overwhelming

Organizing family life is about prioritizing and coordinating contradictory needs and considerations, and this involves relating to acute conflicts in situated ways as well as developing concrete adjustments, strategies and understandings of oneself and the social situation of family life. Such conflicts are common and are part of conducting an everyday life (Kousholt, 2011). At the same time, such common conflicts become a matter for professional support when one is a parent to children defined as children at risk.

We have also conducted fieldwork in the everyday lives of families where the municipal authorities have initiated preventive interventions aimed at helping the often very young and isolated mothers to develop their ways of caring for their children (Juhl, 2014). The health visitor has the task to evaluate the mother's competencies as a parent, and in relation to this, he or she evaluates issues of concern in the family and provides instructions and advice about child care. Diana, a young mother living alone with her two children (11 months and 36 months), elaborates on how, for the moment, she has found a way of dealing with the very contradictory demands at night, when her youngest child needs peace and quiet and her eldest child fights about bedtime:

> When Matt freaks out and does not want to go to bed, I give Daniel his bottle, and then he just lies down. In that way, I only have to struggle with Matt . . . (this) makes it possible for (Daniel) to lie on his own when eating. That is how I make the evenings work just fairly well.

The bedtime situation requires accommodation to the needs of both children when a single parent is trying to organize tranquillity and peace after lots of practical, relational and emotional demands and conflicts related to picking up the boys from their two different institutions, making food, eating together, playing, comforting, cheering up the boys and dealing with their conflicting wishes. The example is therefore fruitful for analyzing how the specific organization of the situation provides an insight into the mother's conditions and her perspective on the concrete possibilities and constraints in everyday family life. Her specific dilemmas are connected to the general challenge that in their complex everyday lives, persons pursue many concerns more or less simultaneously (Dreier, 2011, p. 12).

However, the health visitor problematizes the bedtime procedure of leaving Daniel to himself with the bottle. The problematizing seems embedded in quite isolated principles about children's needs (Woodhead, 1991) and overlooks how the reasons for the arrangement are grounded in certain contradictory and overwhelming demands. In a paradoxical way, the help in this situation becomes experienced quite unambiguously as social control, and in this situation the help appears to contribute to the mother feeling inadequate as a mother and confronted with contradictory concerns that cannot be reconciled. In their care for the children, the professionals often focus on specific feeding practices, eye contact, health promotion and situations of bodily contact and concentration, whereas the young parents talk about how to pursue a plurality of matters at the same time – such as caring for several children, the housekeeping, education or employment, the conflicts between the parents and friends or partners and so on.

The parents' development of self-understanding is related to their participation in social practice and entails an investigation of one's own way of dealing with concrete dilemmas in continuity – or rupture – with the way one as a person arranges everyday life. Self-understanding refers to an understanding of oneself as a person with certain commitments who leads life a certain way, seizing certain opportunities, responding to situations, challenges and setbacks, preferring certain activities, rhythms and relations and so forth (Dreier, 2011, p. 14). Self-understanding is linked to participation in social practice together with other subjects, and it arises from and also guides the realization of the conduct of everyday life (Højholt & Schraube, 2016, p. 23).

The development of self-understanding as a collective affair

By becoming involved in these many-sided personal processes, the preventive help sometimes adds to the very problems and marginalization it is meant to remedy. In other situations, the help opens up for parents becoming aware of new action possibilities. This is partially the case for another mother, Linda, who is also a single mother of a 2-year-old girl. The family lives in a small apartment and has a respite family who helps and supports the mother. Linda has asked for help because of her own background in a violent family. She experienced how she often feels powerless in situations where her daughter is being cross, and she asked for help in the hope of learning alternative ways to handle conflicts and frustrations. The mother explains how cooperation with the respite family and the possibility to learn from others' ways of being parents, contribute to her development of self-understanding from a potentially violent parent to a parent with alternative action possibilities in difficult situations:

> How to handle Ditte when she is cross and screams? I learned what to do and say, and that works very well, I think. I have become more self-confident, and I trust myself to be able to handle situations without becoming violent.

The self-understanding and changing practice as a parent emerges from being part of the respite family practice and experiencing other ways of handling frustrations. At the same time, the cooperation with the respite family leads to new conflicts in the family between the mother and her daughter. The mother explains how there are big differences between the material goods at home and in the respite family and also between the routines and perspectives on childrearing – the respite family parents are much more indulgent towards the daughter; they do not demand that she eats vegetables or that she tidies up her toys and so on. At home the family space is limited in comparison to the respite family home, and the mother therefore wants her child to tidy up, which creates conflicts between the mother and her child.

Such conflicts among children and parents are common in relation to Nordic family life and can be seen in the light of the changing distribution of contributions to the family community among family members – as discussed in the previous section. In general, parents coordinate and negotiate together with other parties about how to deal with childrearing, which rules should be applied where, who has the responsibility for what and how to distribute influence. But the young mothers in this project lack a network to exchange and investigate such conflictual changes. Furthermore, they are met as mothers with incompetence, and they confront unnegotiable demands from the municipality.

Listening to Linda illustrates how parents understand their own way of conducting family everyday life in relation to insights into other parents' (or parent figures') ways of conducting life. As we have seen, the community with the respite family opens up new action possibilities for the mother in relation to handling conflicts with her child, but the community and being part of the respite family life is contradictory:

> I sort of become insecure . . . about myself because these people have high educations and so on, and they also get paid by the municipality so . . . well, they kind of know a lot about children . . . they are hired by the municipality to help me so . . . I just feel that their opinion is worth more than mine . . . even though it is my child.

At the same time as developing her self-understanding as a mother who can handle conflicts without being violent towards her daughter, the mother also experiences that her perspective on issues related to her child is marginalized in relation to the respite family parents because they are positioned by the municipality and the authorities as helpers and the mother as the one needing the help. The possibilities for exchanging dilemmas with other parents and sharing challenges regarding family life appear significant. This is parallel to the analyses of parents to children settling into schools, but the mothers in this project seem to share restricted conditions for belonging in parents' communities and thereby for investigating possibilities for new strategies and ways of going beyond 'giving up' on matters important to them and their children.

In a mothers' group for marginalized and young mothers organized by the municipality, two professionals (a health visitor and a family counsellor closely supervised by a psychologist) meet with the mothers and their children once a week during the children's first three years. The professionals' purpose is helping the mothers better understand and interpret their children's signals.

The mothers concurrently explain that the best aspect of attending the group is that the group offers a possibility for the mothers to listen when another mother asks a question and receives an answer. Also, the mothers appreciate the possibility of the mutual exchanges of problems in relation to childcare and daily routines, as well as in relation to being young and mothers at the same time, and how to deal with boyfriends, education, relationships and so on. In the mothers' group, they are engaged in conflictual and mutual negotiations about common dilemmas related to conducting a family life with their specific conditions.

One mother explains how she was very surprised at first when she experienced how the other mothers struggled with some of the same issues she did. However, the discussions about dilemmas and complexity in relation to organizing everyday life mainly take place outside the central activities in the mothers' group. Hence, the discussions and also the conflicts between the mothers take place during breaks, when all the mothers go outside on a terrace to smoke. The professionals stay inside waiting for the mothers to return. This appears paradoxical because it is exactly in the mother's group that the mothers have the (only) opportunity to access more experienced adults' perspectives on different issues, so this is also an opportunity to get help in finding new action possibilities. In the mothers' group, the majority of the questions brought forward by the mothers are rejected by the professionals as irrelevant to the themes of the mothers' group (e.g., children's need for sleep, childrearing, healthy nurturing and emotional contact). When outside smoking, the mothers discuss issues such as how to deal with sharing custody with the children's fathers, how to cook quick meals, how to deal with the employment service, how to cooperate with day care and so on. When asking the mothers about what is the best part of attending the mothers' group, several of the mothers answered like one mother, Lene: "the smoking breaks!"

Discussion across analytical themes

The analyses have confronted the challenge of conceptualizing family life as a concrete and collective practice, in a way attempting to move beyond an account of isolated families, abstract demands and government. In continuation of this it has been discussed how family life is about arranging everyday life conditions in a certain historical time with certain demands and possibilities for taking part and obtaining access to and influence on different life contexts. The examples illustrated how the mutuality of the family is undergoing change and how these changes are interwoven with the family members' participation in other places. So, the development of family conduct of life is a practical challenge in continuous change and also a reflexive matter parents share with other parents learning from the parallels, the differences and the conflicts they meet and investigate, negotiate and deal with together.

Based on such analytical points, we argue that parenthood is about continuously exploring children's engagements and difficulties across places, together with other children and adults. Parents have to continually investigate the personal meanings of their children's social lives in other places as well as in the interplay of the family. As we have seen, the parents anticipate, for instance, what kinds of meanings school life will have for their different children, but they become surprised and have to re-evaluate the situations of the children to investigate the basis for the mutual interplay they have with their children. This raises questions about how to support the children's new social lives outside the family and how to develop the distribution of influence and responsibility among themselves and their growing children.

The Nordic welfare countries imply quite pressing and contradictory demands, for instance, in relation to adequate parental care for toddlers with the appropriate balance between flexibility and predictable conditions. Regarding school life, the discussions are often about the priorities in relation to demands for academic competences and discipline contra cooperation about the interplay and conflicts among the children in schools. In both contexts, such aspects are *connected* and coexist in the everyday lives of the children, but when worries and difficulties dominate, these aspects become separated into more unambiguous principles and demands on parents (Kousholt, 2011). Instead of the situated investigation of the concrete and sometimes conflictual aspects of everyday life, the problems then seem to be investigated based on more abstract categorizations (Røn Larsen, 2012).

At the same time, these connected aspects of everyday life with children represent dilemmas that parents speculate about, investigate and exchange experiences about with others. The conditions for dealing with these dilemmas together with others appear quite different – the young mothers and their children are met differently, and their possibilities for taking part and coordinating their lives across contexts can be conceptualized as 'situated inequality' in relation to general complexities of conducting family life (Højholt, 2016).

As we have tried to illustrate, the contradictions of concerns in everyday life are sometimes overwhelming, and parents may experience themselves as exposed to contradictory tasks, dilemmas and conflicts. Such situations call for concrete investigation and cooperation about rearrangements of everyday life, but exactly such cooperation can become restricted by the individual categorization of parents as being 'the problem'. Rather than a more or less unambiguous point of reference in 'weak social background' or intergenerational transmission, we will argue for investigation of specific dilemmas and of collective processes where those involved – professionals, parents and children – experience restricted influence and give up on each other (Højholt & Kousholt, 2016).

Parents seem to develop their self-understanding as parents on the basis of their perspectives on and possibilities for influence on common and matters related to children's learning and development. Is it possible to feel 'belonging' in parental communities and to recognize problems and perspectives here? Is it possible to influence the conditions their children encounter, for instance, in school and peer groups? The analyses point to the *common* development of conduct of everyday life as well as the social basis for personal self-understanding. In other words, how personal 'identity' of being a parent and a family is based and developed through participation in the social world.

The psychological concepts about parental ability and attachment appear all too isolated and abstracted from social conditions and interplay, and this may complicate interventions aimed to strengthen the care of parents. The analysis points to a more comprehensive and democratic exploration of the social situations of families in trouble and in this way to a continual development of flexible interventions connected to the challenges that the parents experience in relation to their conduct of family life.

References

Andenæs, A. (2011). Chains of care: Organising the everyday life of young children attending day-care. *Nordic Psychology, 63*(2), 49–67.

Andenæs, A., & Haavind, H. (2016). Sharing early care: Learning from practitioners. In M. Fleer & B. van Oers (Eds.), *International Handbook on Early Childhood Education*. The Netherlands: Springer.

Axel, E. (2011). Conflictual cooperation. *Nordic Psychology, 20*(4), 56–78.

Chaiklin, S., Hedegaard, M., & Jensen, U. J. (1999). *Activity Theory and Social Practice*. Aarhus: Aarhus University Press.

Chimirri, N. (2013). Expanding the conduct of everyday life concept for psychological media research with children. In A. Marvakis, J. Motzkau, D. Painter, R. Ruto-Korir, G. Sullivan, S. Triliva, & M. Wieser (Eds.), *Doing Psychology Under New Conditions*. Toronto: Captus Press, 355–364.

Dreier, O. (2008). *Psychotherapy in Everyday Life*. Cambridge: Cambridge University Press.

Dreier, O. (2011). Personality and the conduct of everyday life. *Nordic Psychology, 63*(2), 4–23.

Finch, J. (1993). Problems and issues in studying the family. International perspectives. In A. Leira (Ed.), *Family Sociology – Developing the Field. Conference Proceedings*. Oslo: Institute for Social Research, 16–33.

Forsberg, L. (2009). *Involved Parenthood: Everyday Lives of Swedish Middle-Class Families*. Linköping: Linköping University.

Haavind, H. (1987). *Liten og stor. Mødres omsorg og barns utviklingsmuligheter.* [*Small and Big. Mothers' Care and Children's Possibilities for Development*]. Oslo: Universitetsforlaget.

Hartmann, H. (1981). The family as the locus of gender, class, and political struggle: The example of housework. *Signs, 6*, 366–394.

Hedegaard, M. (2016). Children's cultural learning in everyday family life exemplified at the dinner setting. In M. Fleer & B. van Oers (Eds.), *International Handbook on Early Childhood Education*. The Netherlands: Springer.

Hedegaard, M., Chaiklin, S., & Jensen, U. J. (1999). Activity theory and social practice: An introduction. In M. Hedegaard, S. Chaiklin, & U. J. Jensen (Eds.), *Activity Theory and Social Practice*. Aarhus: Aarhus University Press, 12–30.

Hedegaard, M., & Fleer, M. (2013). *Play, Learning and Children's Development: Everyday Life in Families and Transition to School*. Cambridge: Cambridge University Press.

Holzkamp, K. (2013). Psychology: Social self-understanding on the reasons for action in the conduct of everyday Life. In E. Schraube & U. Osterkamp (Eds.), *Psychology From the Standpoint of the Subject: Selected Writings of Klaus Holzkamp*. Basingstoke, UK: Palgrave Macmillan, 233–341.

Højholt, C. (2006). Knowledge and professionalism – From the perspectives of children? *Journal of Critical Psychology*, 18, 81–106.

Højholt, C. (2011). Cooperation between professionals in educational psychology – Children's specific problems are connected to general dilemmas in relation to taking part. In H. Daniels & M. Hedegaard (Eds.), *Vygotsky and Special Needs Education – Rethinking Support for Children and Schools*. London: Continuum, 67–85.

Højholt, C. (2016). Situated inequality and the conflictuality of children's conduct of life. In E. Schraube & C. Højholt (Eds.), *Psychology and the Conduct of Everyday Life*. London and New York: Routledge, 145–163.

Højholt, C., & Kousholt, D. (2014). Participant observation of children's communities: Exploring subjective aspects of social practice. *Qualitative Research in Psychology, 11*, 1–19. doi:10.1080/14780887.2014.908989

Højholt, C., & Kousholt, D. (2016). Children participating and developing agency in and across various social practices. In M. Fleer & B. van Oers (Eds.), *International Handbook on Early Childhood Education*. The Netherlands: Springer.

Højholt, C., & Kousholt, D. (forthcoming). Parental collaboration in relation to children's school life: Advanced self-regulation or naive solidarity? Submitted to *Subjectivity*.

Højholt, C., & Schraube, E. (2016). Toward a psychology of everyday living. In E. Schraube & C. Højholt (Eds.), *Psychology and the Conduct of Everyday Life*. London and New York: Routledge, 1–14.

Holzkamp, K. (2013). Psychology: Social self-understanding on the reasons for action in the conduct of everyday Life. In E. Schraube & U. Osterkamp (Eds.), *Psychology From the Standpoint of the Subject: Selected Writings of Klaus Holzkamp*. Basingstoke, UK: Palgrave Macmillan, 233–341.

Hviid, K. P. (2008). "Next year we are small, right?": Different times in children's development. *European Journal of Psychology of Education, 23*(2), 183–198.

Juhl, P. (2014). *På sporet af det gode børneliv: Voksnes bekymring og børns perspektiver på problemer i hverdagslivet.* [*Searching for the Good Life for Children: Adults' Concerns and Children's' Perspectives on Problems in Everyday Life*]. PhD thesis, Roskilde University, Department of Psychology and Education.

Juhl, P. (2015). Toddlers collaboratively explore possibilities for actions across contexts: Developing the concept conduct of everyday life in relation to young children. In G. B. Sullivan, J. Cresswell, A. Larraín, A. Haye, & M. Morgan (Eds.), *Dialogue and Debate in the Making of Theoretical Psychology*. Toronto: Captus Press Inc, 202–210.

Knudsen, H., & Andersen, N. Å. (2014). Playful hyper responsibility: Toward a dislocation of parents' responsibility? *Journal of Education Policy, 29*(1), 105–121. doi: 10.1080/02680939.2013.791929

Kousholt, D. (2011). Researching family through the everyday lives of children *across* home and day-care in Denmark. *ETHOS, 39*(1), 98–114.

Kousholt, D. (2012). Family problems: Exploring dilemmas and complexities of organising everyday family life. In M. Hedegaard, K. Aronsson, C. Højholt, & O. S. Ulvik (Eds.), *Children, Childhood, and Everyday Life: Children's Perspectives*. Charlotte, NC: Information Age Publishing, Inc, 125–139.

Lave, J. (2011). *Apprenticeship in Critical Ethnographic Practice*. Chicago: The University of Chicago Press.

Leira, A. (1993). *Family Sociology – Developing the Field*. Olso: Institute for Social Research.

Morgan, D. H. J. (1996). *Family Connections: An Introduction to Family Studies*. Cambridge: Polity.

Morgan, D. H. J. (2013). *Rethinking Family Practices*. London: Palgrave Macmillan.

Parsons, T., & Bales, R. F. (1956). *Family: Socialization and Interaction Process*. London: Routledge & Kegan Paul Ltd.

Rogoff, B. (2003). Development as transformation of participation in cultural activities. In B. Rogoff (Ed.), *The Cultural Nature of Human Development*. New York: Oxford University Press.

Røn Larsen, M. (2012). A paradox of inclusion: Administrative procedures and children's perspectives on difficulties in school. In M. Hedegaard, C. Højholt, O. S. Ulvik, & K. Aronsson (Eds.), *Children, Childhood and Everyday Life: Children's Perspectives.* Charlotte, NC: Information Age Publishing, Inc, 143–160.

Røn Larsen, M., & Stanek, A. H. (2015). Young children and their conduct of everyday life. *Nordic Psychology* (Online), *67*(3), 195–209. doi:10.1080/19012276.2015.1062256

Schneider, N. F. (2011). Family and parenthood in contemporary Europe: Sociological considerations and their political implications. *Family Science*, *1*(3), 135–143. doi:10.1080/19424620.2010.570009

Schraube, E., & Højholt, C. (Eds.). (2016). *Psychology and the Conduct of Everyday Life.* New York: Routledge.

Shorter, E. (1979). *The Making of the Modern Family.* United Kingdom: Fontana Books.

Singer, E. (1993): Shared care for children. *Theory & Psychology*, *3*(4), 429–449.

Woodhead, M. (1991). Psychology and the cultural construction of 'children's needs. In R. Carr, P. Light, & M. Woodhead (Eds.), *Growing Up in a Changing Society: Child Development in Social Context.* London: Routledge.

3 Family life in Nordic countries

Lena Bäckström

Introduction

When children's development, upbringing and socialization are observed in relation to their families and family life, two different perspectives often emerge. The cohabiting nuclear family is described either as an indispensable, necessary and sometimes closed space around the children or as something that no longer exists and is not really needed at all for the development, upbringing and socialization of children. The two notions from Dahlström (1989) – *the indispensability theory* and *the withering away theory* – describe these two perspectives.

Representatives of the first perspective, the indispensability theory, argue that family life today, when compared to past times, shows variability, differences and instability, whereas families' daily lives are rather characterized by permanence and stability (Bäck-Wiklund, 2012).

Representatives of the second perspective, the withering away theory, argue about families that are in crisis, weakened, dissolved or broken or families as eliminated and languishing (Castells, 1997). They interpret the trends that exist in society as destructive in relation to family and parenthood in past times. The importance of social networks for children and adults, the increasing numbers of single-parent families (e.g., single-parent families headed by mothers) will be neglected. The fact that adults choose to live in different serial families during their lifespans is seen as a threat to the former traditional nuclear family life and children's development and education: "the crisis of the patriarchal family" (Castells, 1997).

The history of family

In a historical perspective, the family formed out of necessity to ensure human survival (Kristjánsson, 2001). Results from historical family research in Nordic countries and the Western world show that the nuclear family has been the dominant family form in the past. The nuclear family, with close contact and dependence on relatives and neighbours, is obvious – but not all relatives lived together in the same place. Instead, these family relationships were mediators between family and work and among different social institutions.

The man was the sole guardian and custodian of the family at the turn of the 20th century in Nordic countries. The universal right to vote for every adult changed these circumstances. Although the relationship between mother and child was defined by biology, fatherhood was defined through the father's social relationships with the mother and their children.

The progress of Nordic welfare states, and that of the Western world, towards a democratic equal society where equality of every individual is sought, has been emphasized, especially by conservative family researchers, as a factor that weakened the family. It is thought that the family as an institution is losing its function in the welfare state, when tasks and duties which in the past could be performed within the families and by the parents themselves are now performed by other adults and by institutions that parents are referred to (Dahlström, 1989, 1992). Castells (1997) assumes that the family as a heterosexual institution has to move towards a sharing of responsibilities for the children and that parenting will imply a "renegotiated heterosexual family contract" consisting of a "completely mutual parenting responsibility" for domestic work and economy as well as of equality between parents. Women and men working away from home, global feminism and homosexual liberation are presumed to fundamentally threaten the values of the existing patriarchal society (Castells, 1997). The progress of Nordic and Western family life can be viewed as proof of Castells's (1997) thesis about the crisis of the patriarchal family. But the increase in the number of divorces and separations in our time may be because adults choose each other on the basis of love and adults choose their partners based on romantic love. Parenting in the postmodern family is based on a love relationship that is more active and open but conditional and therefore more fragile (Roman, 2003).

Family today

Family researchers today agree on three areas: (1) the family as *a cohesive social framework* around adult(s) with children; (2) the family as *a shared life project* that is negotiated among family members; (3) the *need to study families' daily lives* to obtain knowledge. The family is held together by emotional ties – over time but not always in the same room. Parents are adults who have chosen each other. Most children who are born in Nordic countries are wanted by their parents (Dencik, 1993), and more women are giving birth today than ever before in history; we have "more mothers per child" (Dencik, 1993). More women than men choose to have children as single parents. But paternity research reveals that we have even "more fathers per child" as the fathers also choose single parenthood to a higher degree today than before (Haas & Hwang, 2000; Wissö & Plantin, 2015). Kristjánsson (2001) highlights three important functions that families have for their members: a psychosocial, a recreational and a consumptive function. The psychosocial function is associated with trust, hope and meaning. Family members have the opportunity for recognition and acknowledgment. The recreational function within families is all about recreating and fostering mental and physical strength and health for children and parents. The consumptive function is linked to the families' survival, primarily in physical respects, ensuring that the children and parents have food, warmth and shelter.

For many women and men, parenting and family life comprise just one of many life projects (Bäck-Wiklund & Bergsten, 1997). Becoming a mother or a father is an individual project, whereas parenthood and family life are a common, collective project. The family exercises fellowship, loyalty and solidarity in relation to values and disclosures. Good parenting and family life are characterized by reciprocity and respect for each other (Beck & Beck-Gernsheim, 2002). Parenting is a durable and lasting relationship in family life – extended over time (Allat, 1996).

Maccoby (1999) describes a cooperating team of two parents as the optimal environment for raising children. Through increased autonomy, communication and negotiation, family members' insights on both equality and inequality – within and outside the family life – and their own relationship are seen and discussed (Beck & Beck-Gernsheim, 2002). Research on children's family life often focuses on the idea that there is an interaction between children and parents which is both context- and situation-bound (James, 1999; Kuczynski & Grusec 1997; Maccoby, 2000; Morrow, 1998; Sorbring, Deater-Deckard & Palmérus, 2006). Children themselves tell us about what they view as 'a good family' and how they develop strategies to influence their parents' behaviour, particularly in conflict situations (Bäckström, 2006; Sorbring, 2005). Listening to what children need and what a good family life requires in the form of care, sacrifice, cooperation and solidarity, versus upsetting children and partners, seems to be the ultimate guarantor of good development and socialization of children as well as adults. 'Family' and 'parenthood' can have different meanings and purposes for different family members. For children, this may mean that having access to many parents (e.g., more than one family) may be an opportunity to recognize their varying needs and interests: biological, social and legal (Bäckström, 2006, Sorbring, 2005).).

Welfare states based on democratic values regard the family as a base for children's development, education and socialization. At the same time, research shows that parenting and family functions, at least in terms of care and responsibility for children and the division of work within and outside the family, are carried out traditionally, as they have been for generations. Family life inside the families is traditional in relation to gender and what women and men are supposed to do as parents: mothers and fathers. Nordic research reports argue that it is most often fathers who see their children only occasionally (not as full-time parents) after divorce or separation. There seems to be a voluntary type of parenthood, mainly used only by fathers. One can see this as 'conditional parenting' in which men can either choose or deselect fatherhood. Mothers' choices in this respect are more limited (Bekkengen, 2002). According to current legislation, both parents are expected to share custody of the children, whether the children want to spend time with both of them or not. Most children of divorced and separated parents have some form of contact with the parent with whom they do not live on a regular basis. The most common arrangement in Nordic countries is parents having joint custody of the children. But arrangements to care for the children can vary between parents.

Relations between the child and the biological parents, as well as step-parents in extended families, are characterized by both unity and distinction. Negotiation relations marked by loyalty and justice must be developed and perceived as important by all family members (Sjöberg Larsson, 2012).

Nordic and international studies show that the structural conditions and institutional as well as cultural conditions in different countries are important for how family life and parenthood are arranged in everyday life (Bäck-Wiklund, 2012; Emmenegger, Hausermann, Palier & Seeleib-Kaiser, 2012). But the research results also show that women today combine unpaid domestic work with paid employment to a greater extent than men. In retrospect, the Nordic welfare model on family life and parenthood appears to be a social attempt to enable (especially women) to combine responsibility and care for the children and family with paid professional work. But the men were never involved – or integrated – in this social attempt. Hochschild and Machung (1989) call this "the second shift" in family life. They can see "faster-changing-women" and "slower-changing-men" in the society in their studies. The researchers believe that the society must make it easier for families and parents by offering municipal services and social arrangements similar to those designed in the Nordic welfare states (Hochschild & Machung, 1989).

Lifelong family lives: issues about cohesion and departure

Most children in Nordic countries and the rest of the Western world (75 per cent) live with their parents (both biological and/or adoptive parents are included) (Barnombudsmannen, 2010, p. 1; Emmenegger et al., 2012). Almost all Swedes and Scandinavians (90 per cent) become parents (Dencik, 2001). During the past two decades, divorces and separations between parents declined, mainly parents with young children. In Nordic counties it is mothers who take most of the parental leave. They spend twice as much time as fathers with the children and take responsibility for childcare. Women and mothers also take care of most of the housework. Their work outside the home is more likely than men's to be part time, most of it in the health-care sector (SCB, 2015, p. 154).

Parallel to this, 25 per cent of Nordic children live in family arrangements other than the traditional nuclear family. Most of these are families headed by single mothers, but other forms include families headed by single fathers, families with step-parents/step-children; families with same-sex parents, adoptive parents and foster families. Working-class children are more likely to experience divorces and separations between the parents, and they more often grow up in single-parent families. Divorces and separations are most common in families where the children have a Nordic mother and a father with a foreign ethnicity (SCB, 2015, p. 154). Children may reside full time with one parent, or they may live alternately with each parent. One-third of children (33 per cent) living with single mothers have no contact with their fathers (Barnombudsmannen, 2010, p. 01). Adopted or foster children often seek out their biological parents, usually the mother (Irhammar, 1997; Juusela, 2015). Children of single parents, who are usually the mothers, often have fantasies and beliefs about the absent parent, usually the fathers (Mariotti, 1997).

Golombok (2000), in a research study, examined the factors in family life that are likely to be important for children who have grown up in different family forms: divorced and separated biological parents, single parents and adoptive, step- and same-sex parents. Her conclusion was that the composition of the family is less important than children's experiences of everyday family life – the presence of a qualitative dimension: "Family structure, in itself, makes little difference to children's psychological development. Instead, what really matters is the quality of family life" (Golombok, 2000, p. 99). Socio-economic conditions and the family environment are stronger predictors of, or against, (good) development and socialization than children's and parents' experiences of divorce and separation, emphasizes Golombok (2000). Pryor and Rodgers (2001) formulate some cautious conclusions about their research review and believe that children's experiences and the experiences of their parents' divorce undoubtedly constitute a risk factor in children's lives, but it is hardly the main risk factor in that respect. Hetherington (1999) points out that it is rather the conflicts between parents, whether they choose to live together or apart, which may have consequences for a child's development, education and socialization. Hetherington (1989) described the children either as survivors, losers or winners six years after their parents' divorce. The interpersonal relations were highlighted as critical, but other factors such as the children's age, sex and socio-economic status were significant (Hetherington, 1989).

Moxnes (1999) shows in a comparative research survey between divorced parents in Norway and the United States that there are moves that the children are forced to make and adverse changes in family finances in connection with the divorce that coincide as risk factors in the two countries. Most children of divorce do well in the continuation of life (Moxnes, 1999). Single parents who were interviewed about the advantages and disadvantages of being single parents responded that the greatest benefits for the children and themselves were that they no longer had to cope with conflicting requirements from family members. Here, women showed a positive mental improvement, whereas the men's situations after divorce was more vulnerable (Clarke-Stewart & Brentano, 2006). Being alone with worries about the children and the poor economy of single-parent families were problematic for both women and men.

Lifespan and the generative aspects: complementary family life and parenting

Demographics in Nordic countries are shifting so that there are more and more elderly people compared to young people. Within a 25-year period, the elderly population in the Nordic region has increased by 8.6 per cent. Life expectancy is increasing in all Nordic countries, and people can now expect to live to 80 years old. This is because people are healthy and in relatively good health longer, and people are having fewer children than before. However, Nordic countries have a higher birth rate compared to almost all other European countries.

Social networks around families are more extensive than ever before in history (Bäck-Wiklund & Johansson, 2012; Pryor & Rodgers, 2001). Part-time work is often combined with unpaid care work for family members. This is most common in women's life cycles.

Nine out of 10 adults become parents sometime in our part of the world. Never before in history have children grown up with so many adults who have personal experiences of following children's development and fostering and socializing them from infants to young adults. Every second Nordic child born in this century will experience its 100th birthday. These children will grow up with four or sometimes five generations in a close network: siblings, parents, grandparents and great-grandparents.

Around 22 per cent of all families in the Nordic countries have children. Of these families, most – around 77 per cent – are married or cohabiting couples (Haagensen, 2014).

A Norwegian study of the life course, ageing and generation (Slagsvold et al., 2012) revealed that today's grandparents are a very important resource for families with young children. Approximately 50 per cent of the families who participated in the study had access to their own parents as a deputy parental resource for their children. The grandchildren said in interviews that they felt valued by their grandparents and that there was a mutual exchange of knowledge between generations: children received homework assistance and care, and the grandparents received help with digital technology from their grandchildren (Fergusson, Maughan & Golding, 2007).

International studies have found that Nordic countries have more governmental institutions that support families with children than do other European countries. According to Kristjánsson (2001), the Nordic countries' ambitious public investment in family support might have its ideological origins in the fact that the nuclear family was the most common form of the family in the past, and nuclear families require more help and support than extended generational families typically do.

Discussion and conclusion

The welfare of children and families is at the hub of the welfare state. The concepts of child and family have been redefined in the Nordic countries, and in the Western world more generally, in compliance with the Convention on the Rights of the Child. Anyone under the age of 18 is considered a child. The family is the basic unit in society. Children have the right to be protected and supported in an atmosphere of happiness, love and understanding in their families (UNICEF, 1989).

The *bourgeois family* can be seen as a model for family life and parenting in Nordic countries as well as in the whole Western world. It can be described as a closed and more organized nuclear family, where the conditions are mainly about the economy and education of the children. As a result of the increasing urbanization and industrialization in the Western world, other factors within the family have gained greater prominence and updated explanations and meanings. Today, the emotional and moral relations among family members are highlighted (Jørgensen, 1999). The notion of the *nuclear family* was introduced by Murdock (1949) to mean two adults living together in a shared household with a shared economy and emotional and (hetero-)sexual intimacy. The nuclear family is in contrast to the extended family, which for practical reasons often forced relatives to live together in large family groups comprising several generations and with a broader family crowd – which has been uncommon in the Nordic countries.

Family research is seeking and collecting broader concepts of the various forms of everyday family life. In Nordic family research, the following concepts have been used: *family generational* and *communities and blended families* (Liljeström & Kollind, 1990), *linked families/family systems* (Sjöberg Larsson, 2012), *network families* (Bäck-Wiklund & Johansson, 2012), *rainbow families* (Malmquist, Hydén & Zetterqvist Nelson, 2012) and *star families* (Engarås, 2008). Star families include all types of family constellations: one parent, two parents, adoptive, rainbow, step, foster families or family donation families. Even childless families can be included in the concept. Using a star as a metaphor shows the diversity of star rays that surround us. The Convention on the Rights of the Child uses the concept of *extending family* (UNICEF, 1989).

All these family concepts together describe the fact that families have both been transformed and are continuously changing over time as the children grow up. The nuclear family is a narrow and short-sighted family notion, and a broader family notion must be used. Today, children can be given four or five parents: an egg donor, a sperm donor, a surrogate mother and one or two parents. Then we must take into account that families' lives both change and last over time – and families exist over time as well.

These new family concepts also show the need for a generative aspect in which parents are always parents. The children that grow up in Nordic countries today will probably meet their parents, grandparents and great-grandparents during their lifetime. This is a new situation for the 21st century as life expectancy will be longer than before. That gives the generative aspect importance even in the future. It is also important to have in mind that 'family life' in a historical perspective has probably been 'families' lives' for a very long time: change and variableness have been the signatures of everyday life for children and parents who live together in families. First of all the need for food, warmth, trust and meaning as well as the need for recreation are fundamental for human survival. Everyday life in families involves social frameworks and shared ideas of a state of belonging in the present time for children and adults. The fact that parenthood and family life are voluntary choices for human adults might, in Nordic countries, be a guarantee for a good family life in terms of love and understanding between the parents – at least in the beginning of family life and childrearing. The diversity adults create in their lives when living with children in other arrangements than nuclear families in the past can be seen as providing more comprehensive and rich lives for children as they are growing up.

The implementation of child care centres, day care institutions, preschools and after-school centres in Nordic countries shows how the statement 'It takes a village to raise a child' can work in practice. In the welfare society there is a need for 'deputy parents', 'vicarious parents' and 'acting adults' who can complement the roles of parents and stand in when they are absent. The research of Heckman, Stixrud and Urzua (2006) highlights the importance of the families in nurturing and fostering children during their upbringing. Parents' understanding of the relevance of education to children is paramount in relation to the development of cognitive and non-cognitive abilities – as well as sociability. The possibility for this is the generally organized welfare system that provides supporting systems of primary health and care for children and their families (Emmenegger et al., 2012). The fact that childcare, schools and health services as institutions for families and children would not exist without the existence of families is seldom called into question in the field of childhood and family research. Such a proposal shows that children and their families as institutions, with good reason, can be assumed to function as services for society as well (Oldman, 1994).

References

Allat, Pat. (1996). Conceptualizing parenting from the standpoint of children: Relationship and transition in the life course. In Julia Brannen & Margret O'Brien (Eds.), *Children in Families: Research and Policy.* London and Washington, DC: Falmer Press.

Bäckström, Lena. (2006). *Barn i Bon. En intervjustudie med 11-åringar om familj, fostran och dagligt liv.* [*Children in Nests*]. Lund University, Sweden: Pedagogiska institutionen.

Bäck-Wiklund, Margareta. (2012). *Familj och modernitet.* [*Family and Modernity*]. In Margareta Bäck-Wiklund & Thomas Johansson (Eds.), *Networkfamily.* Stockholm: Natur och Kultur, 17–47.

Bäck-Wiklund, Margareta, & Bergsten, Birgitta. (1997). *Det moderna föräldraskapet: en studie av familj och kön i förändring.* [*The Modern Parenthood: A Study of Family and Gender in Change*]. Stockholm: Natur och Kultur.

Bäck-Wiklund, Margareta, & Johansson, Thomas (Eds.). (2012). *Nätverksfamiljen.* [*The Network Family*]. Stockholm: Natur och Kultur.

Barnombudsmannen rapporterar 2010:01 [The Barnombudsman reports]. Örebro: Statistiska Centralbyrån.

Beck, Ulrich, & Beck-Gernsheim, Elisabeth. (2002). *Individualization: Institutionalized Individualism and Its Social and Political Consequences.* London: SAGE.

Bekkengen, Lisbeth. (2002). *Man får välja.* [*Men Get to Choose*]. Malmö: Liber.

Castells, Manuel. (1997). *The Information Age: Economy, Society and Culture. Volume II: The Power of Identity.* Malden, Mass, UK: Blackwell Publishers Ltd.

Clarke-Stewart, Alison, & Brentano, Cornelia. (2006). *Divorce Causes and Consequences.* New Haven, CT: Yale University Press.

Convention on the Rights of the Child. Retrieved from www.unicef.org/crc/

Dahlström, Edmund. (1989). Theories and ideologies of family functions, gender relations, and human reproduction. In Katja Boh, Maren Bak, Cristine Clason, Maja Pankratova, Jens Qvortrup, Giovanni, B. Sgritta, & Kari Wærness (Eds.), *Changing Patterns of European Family Life: A Comparative Analysis of 14 European Countries.* London: Routledge.

Dahlström, Edmund. (1992). Debatten om kön och familj under svensk efterkrigstid. [The debate about sex and family during the Swedish post-war]. In Joan Acker, Annika Baude, Ulla Björnberg, Edmund Dahlström, G. Forsberg, Lena Gonäs, Harriet Holter, & Arne Nilsson (Eds.), *Kvinnors och mäns liv och arbete.* [*Women's and Mens' Life and Work*]. Stockholm: Studieförbundet Näringsliv och Samhälle.

Dencik, Lars. (1993). Barnens färd mot välfärd. [The children's journey toward welfare.] *Moderna Tider* [*Modern Times*], *32/33*(Årgång 4), 31–36.

Dencik, Lars. (2001). Föreläsning vid Ph.d. kursus "Barndoms-og Familieforskning". Lesson at PhD studies, Centre for Childhood & Family Research, Department of Psychology, Roskilde University, Januari 2001.

Emmenegger, Patrick, Hausermann, Silja, Palier, Bruno, & Seeleib-Kaiser, Martin. (2012). *The Age of Dualization: The Changing Face of Inequality in Deindustrializing Societies.* New York: Oxford University Press.

Engarås, Ingrid. (2008). Retrieved on 1 August 2016, from https://sv.wikipedia.org/wiki/Stj%C3%A4rnfamilj

Fergusson, Emma, Maughan, Barbara, & Golding, Jean. (2007). Which children receive grandparental care and what effect does it have? *Journal of Child Psychology and Psychiatry*, *49*(2), 161–169(8).

Golombok, Susan. (2000). *Parenting: What Really Counts?* London: Routledge.

Haagensen, Klaus Munch. (2014). *Nordisk statistisk årsbok 2014.* [*Nordic Statistical Year Book 2014*]. Nord 2014:001. Volume 52. http://dx.doi.org/10.6027/Nord2014-001

Haas, Linda, & Hwang, Philip. (2000). Programs and policies. Promoting women's economic equality and men's sharing of child care in Sweden. In Linda Haas, Philip Hwang, & Graeme Russell (Eds.), *Organizational Change & Gender Equity. International Perspectives on Fathers and Mothers at the Workplace.* Thousand Oaks, London and New Delhi: Sage Publications Inc.

Hareven, Tamara. (1985). Historical changes in the family and the life course: Implications for child development. In Alice Boardman Smuts, & John W. Hagen (Eds.), History and Research in Child Development. *Monographs of the Society for Research in Child Development, Serial Number*, *50*(4–5), 8–23(15).

Heckman, James, Stixrud, Jora, & Urzua, Sergio. (2006). The effects of cognitive and non-cognitive abilities on labour market outcomes and social behavior. National Bureau of Economic Research, Cambridge. *Journal of Labor Economics*, *24*(3), 411–482.

Hetherington, Mavis E. (1989). Coping with family transitions: Winners, losers, and survivors. *Child Development*, *60*(1), 1–14(14).

Hetherington, Mavis E. (Eds.). (1999). *Coping With Divorce, Single Parenting, and Remarriage. A Risk and Resiliency Perspective.* Mahwah, NJ and London: Lawrence Erlbaum Associates, Publishers.

Hochschild, Arlie, & Machung, Anne. (1989). *The Second Shift: Working Parents and the Revolution at Home.* New York: Avon Books.

Irhammar, Malin. (1997). *Att utforska sitt ursprung.* [*To Explore Its Origin*]. Lunds universitet: Psykologiska institutionen, Avdelningen för barn-och ungdomspsykiatri.

James, Allison. (1999). Parents: A children's perspective. In Andrew Bainham, Shelly Day Sclater, & Martin Richards (Eds.), *What Is a Parent? A Socio-Legal Analysis.* Oxford: Hart Publishing.

Jørgensen Schultz Per. (1999). Familieliv – i børnefamilien. [Family life – in family with children]. In Lars Dencik & Per Schultz Jørgensen (Eds.), *Børn og familie i det postmoderne samfund* [*Children and Families in the Postmodern Society*]. København: Hans Reitzels Forlag A/S.

Juusela, Mary. (2015). *Adoption: The Great Homeland Journey.* Stockholm: Miller & Books.

Kristjánsson, Baldur. (2001). *Barndomen och den sociala moderniseringen. Om att växa upp i Norden på tröskeln till ett nytt millennium* [*Childhood and Social Modernization. About Growing up in the Nordic Countries on the Threshold of a New Millennium*]. Stockholm: HLS Förlag.

Kuczynski, Leon, & Grusec, Joan E. (1997). Future directions for theory of parental socialization. In Joan E. Grusec & Leon Kuczynski (Eds.), *Parenting and Children's Internalization of Values: A Handbook of Contemporary Theory.* New York: John Wiley & Sons.

Liljeström, Rita, & Kollind, Anna-Karin. (1990). *Kärleksliv och föräldraskap* [*Love, Life and Parenthood*]. Malmö: Carlssons.

Maccoby, Eleanor E. (1999). The custody of children of divorcing families. Weighing the alternatives. In Ross A. Thompson, & Paul R. Amato (Eds.), *The Postdivorce Family: Children, Parenting and Society.* Thousand Oaks, London and New Delhi: Sage Publications Inc, 50–70.

Maccoby, Eleanor E. (2000). Parenting and its effects on children: On reading and misreading behaviour genetics. *Annual Review Psychology, 51*, 1–27(27).

Malmquist, Anna, Hydén, Margareta, & Zetterqvist Nelson, Karin. (2012). Familjeliv hos samkönade par och andra regnbågsfamiljer. [Family life between same sex parents and other rainbow families]. In Margareta Bäck-Wiklund & Thomas Johansson (Eds.), *Nätverksfamiljen* [*The Network Family*]. Stockholm: Natur och Kultur.

Mariotti, Paola. (1997). Creativity and fertility. The one-parent phantasy. In Joan Raphael-Leff & Rosine Jozef Perelberg (Eds.), *Female Experience: Three Generations of British Women: Psychoanalysts on Work With Women.* London: Routledge.

Morrow, Virginia. (1998). *Understanding Families: Children's Perspectives.* London: National Children's Bureau.

Moxnes, Kari. (1999). Børn og skilsmisse. [Children and divorce]. In Lars Dencik & Per Schultz Jørgensen (Eds.), *Børn og familie i det postmoderne samfund.* [*Children and Family in Post-Modern Societies*]. København: Hans Reitzels Forlag A/S.

Murdock, George Peter. (1949). *Social Structure.* New York: The Free Press.

Oldman, David. (1994). Childhood as a mode of production. In Berry Mayall (Ed.), *Children's Childhoods: Observed and Experienced.* London and Washington, DC: The Falmer Press.

Pryor, Jan, & Rodgers, Bryan. (2001). *Children in Changing Families. Life After Parental Separation.* Malden, MA: Blackwell Publishers.

Roman, Christine. (2003). Sociologiska perspektiv på "familjen". Från "komplementära könsroller" till "den rena relationen". [Sociological Perspectives on the "family". From "complementary gender roles" to "pure relationship"]. In Margareta Bäck-Wiklund & Thomas Johansson (Eds.), *Nätverksfamiljen.* [*The Network Family*]. Stockholm: Natur och Kultur.

Sjöberg Larsson, Kristina. (2012). Mamma, pappa, styvpappa – barn. Föräldraskap i länkade familjesystem. [Mother, father, step-father – children. Parenthood in linked families]. In Margareta Bäck-Wiklund & Thomas Johansson (Eds.), *Nätverksfamiljen*. [*The Network Family*]. Stockholm: Natur och Kultur.

Slagsvold, Britt, Veenstra, Marijke, Daatland, Svein Olav, Hagestad, Gunhild, Hansen, Thomas, Herlofson, Katharina, Koløen, Kristine, & Solem, Per Erik. (2012). Life-course, ageing and generations in Norway: The NorLAG study. *Norsk Epidemiologi*, *22*(2), 95–102(7).

Sorbring, Emma. (2005). *Girls' and Boys' Views of Conflicts With Parents*. Göteborg University, Sweden: Department of Psychology.

Sorbring, Emma, Deater-Deckard, Kirby, & Palmérus, Kerstin. (2006). Girls' and boys' perceptions of mothers' intention in using physical punishment and reasoning as discipline methods. *The European Journal of Developmental Psychology*, *3*(2), 142–162(20).

Statistiska Centralbyrån 2015: 154. Barn och familjestatistik [Sweden Statistics: Children and families]. http://www.scb.se/

UNICEF. (1989). *Convention on the Rights of the Child*. Retrieved from www.unicef.org/crc/

Wissö, Therese, & Plantin, Lars. (2015). Fathers and parental support in everyday family life: Informal support in Sweden beyond the welfare state. *Families, Relationships and Societies*, *4*(2), 267–280(14).

4 Constituting cultures of compassion in early childhood educational settings

Lasse Lipponen

Introduction

There is a long tradition of studies focusing on children's emotional development from various theoretical perspectives as well as in different contexts. As Fleer and Hammer (2013) state, the emphasis in most research on emotions in early childhood is on their individual construction and generally in family contexts. On the other hand, recent studies on children and emotions tend to focus on the development of curricula and programs to teach young children socio-emotional skills and self-regulation strategies for expressing their emotions (Madrid, Fernie & Kantor, 2015). These studies demonstrate the importance of understanding the role emotions play in children's learning, development and well-being. Despite these insights, however, less research attention has been given to how emotions are constructed, enacted and negotiated in naturalistic social interactions in everyday life in homes and kindergartens or to the rules and norms that regulate their expression. Studying emotions in naturalistic interaction is likely to yield new information on how they emerge and manifest themselves in daily life and how they are organized as aspects of a particular culture.

My aim in this paper is to investigate the emotional worlds (Madrid et al., 2015) of early childhood education in a Finnish setting, focusing on acts of compassion and their constitutive practices. I conceptualize and analyze compassion as a collective activity comprising the acts of helping, including, comforting, and sharing in the everyday life of a kindergarten. These acts of compassion are dynamic, being negotiated, constituted and produced in interaction. I focus especially on the formation of compassion related to rules that govern how it is and should be expressed in early childhood settings.

Constituents of compassion

Most previous empirical studies on compassion have been conducted in experimental or health-care settings. Experimental studies (for an extensive review, see Goetz, Keltner & Simon-Thomas, 2010) focusing on other than real, everyday interaction, conceptualize compassion as an individual skill or trait and as an emotion that one feels when others are in need or suffer and that motivates the desire to help and understand them. According to Goetz et al. (2010), compassion is a distinct emotion and should not be confused with distress, sadness or love or with empathy, which is perhaps the closest in meaning. Whereas empathy means the capacity to understand what another person is experiencing, however, compassion goes further in leading to actions such as helping, including, caring, comforting and sharing. Experimental studies (see Goetz et al., 2010) have demonstrated that it is more difficult to feel compassion when there are differences among people in status, culture, religion, language, skin colour, gender or age, for example. These studies have also revealed that deservingness is essential to the appraisal processes that give rise to compassion and that feeling compassion is sensitive to the possible costs involved in helping someone else (see Goetz et al., 2010).

Studies in health-care settings have relevance to early childhood education given that caring is one of the leading forms of activity in both fields. Some researchers (Taggart, 2016) even argue that care foregrounds the ethical dimension of early childhood work and that compassionate pedagogy is at the core in the ethics of care. Studies conducted in the health-care sector (see Fotaki, 2015; Lown, 2015; Mannion, 2014; Shea, 2015) have shown that high-quality care and compassion are closely related. It has been demonstrated, for example, that being cared for by compassionate practitioners speeds up recovery (Gilbert, 2009) and that clinicians who feel that they are compassionately treated by their organization and each other tend to be more creative and more open (Cole-King & Gilbert, 2011). However, most studies on compassion in the health-care sector treat it as an individual attribute enabling health professionals to provide high-quality, responsive care (Fotaki, 2015). As Fotaki (2015) points out, compassion should be understood as a social phenomenon that "shapes and is shaped by conditions of inequality and coercion extending to the notions of social justice and solidarity" (p. 200).

Research on children and compassion in early childhood settings is very rare, although there is a long tradition focusing on the development of pro-social behaviour in childhood (see, e.g., Eisenberg, 2013). Research within this tradition describes such behaviour as a set of skills that an individual possesses but does not deal with compassion per se or with its interactional nature. We demonstrated in our earlier work (Paananen & Lipponen, 2016) that supporting compassion is not a top priority in the development of early childhood education or in the practices of kindergartens. On the contrary, these aims are systematically dislodged when they are conflicting, which happens especially when the decision-making is engulfed in the discourse of individualistic rights and a variety of governance measures narrows down the teacher's decision-making scope (Paananen, 2018).

Family is a basic and, in most cases, the first emotional world of children. (Family is a complex concept, but I do not discuss the different conceptualizations in this paper.) It offers children an environment in which to learn a whole range of emotions as well as how they should be understood, expressed and enacted in different situations (Frost, 2014; Madrid et al., 2015). For example, children learn that if somebody hurts himself or herself, they are expected somehow show to empathy, or even compassion, and do something to comfort the sufferer or to help the one in need. Furthermore, every kindergarten and every family is unique, each with its own emotional world. These emotional worlds of the two activity systems interact every day in a variety of ways. Everyday encounters take place when parents pick up their children from a kindergarten or leave them there. Other encounters are dramatic and unique in peoples' lives. As Park, Leekeenan and Given (2015) demonstrate, a traumatic family event such as a conflagration may turn into a shared process of emotional learning and into acts of compassion. Such acts of compassion come not only from the teacher but also from the whole community, the aim being to help the family to survive and to recover. Collaboration between the kindergarten's and the family's emotional worlds is not always smooth. Bialostok (2015) describes his emotional journey and his emotional work on the borderline between kindergarten and home when he was trying to find a kindergarten for his son, who suffered from Asperger's syndrome. People with Asperger's do not have a sophisticated understanding of the emotional worlds of other children or adults and tend not to show empathy or compassion. Moreover, as Bialostok (2015) notes, the teachers also found it very difficult to understand the emotional worlds of this boy and to express empathy with and compassion for him. Research has also shown that people feel more compassion for those who matter the most to their well-being, such as offspring and family members (Goetz et al., 2010). However, as Nussbaum (2014) points out, this can lead to the division of the world between 'us' and 'them', and compassion for one's own children can so easily slip over into a desire to promote their well-being at the expense of that of other people's children. All in all, there is a lack of studies that treats compassion as a culturally and materially constructed phenomenon, especially in early childhood settings.

Cultural-historical activity theory as a framework for studying acts of compassion

There are various theories concerning the classification and conceptualization of rules (see, e.g., Bernstein, 1996; Ferraris, 2013; Searle, 1969; Thornberg, 2009). With regard to school rules, for example, Thornberg (2009) found that they mediated the relation between subject and community in two main ways: they regulate pupils' everyday behaviour and socialize them into the moral life of school. Searle (1969) proposed a distinction between regulative and constitutive rules: the former regulate an activity (such as traffic), whereas constitutive create a possibility for rules in activities (i.e., playing a card game). I turn to cultural-historical activity theory (CHAT) in this paper to elaborate on the notion of rules as part of the constitution of compassion as a collective and interactional everyday practice of a kindergarten and as mediators between subject and community.

The origin of CHAT is in Russian psychology aimed at bridging the traditional divide between individual and society (e.g., Leont'ev, 1978). The theory was further developed and formulated by Engeström (1987) in particular. The focus is on the complex, situated and distributed nature of ongoing activity in an activity system. Activity systems are systems in which people engage in solving problems or making or designing something (Greeno & Engeström, 2014). They are "dynamic, open, semiotic system(s) of meaningful actions and meaning-making processes" (Lemke, 1990, p. 191). An activity system may be as small as an individual working with a computer or as large as an organization with hundreds of employees. It is inherently historical; in other words it is under continuous change and transformation. As an analytical tool, CHAT allows the tracking of multiple relations among institutions and individuals and the division of labour, artefacts and rules that mediate the relations.

The basic elements of an activity system include the subject, the instruments, the division of labour, the community, rules, the object of the activity and the outcome. The present kindergarten case serves to concretize the model, the activity system being the kindergarten. The subject is a teacher or another member of staff whose agency is the chosen perspective in the analysis (e.g., it could be a child or a cleaner). The selection of the subject depends on the perspective from which the activity is examined. Let us consider the work activity of a kindergarten teacher. The object of her or his work is the child and the child's learning and development, and the outcome is the child's well-being. The instruments the teacher applies include the curriculum, the children's individual ECE (early childhood education) plans and their learning portfolios. The community consists of the whole staff of the kindergarten: the principal, teachers, nurses and other employees. The division of labour determines the tasks and decision-making powers of the staff members. The relation between the subject(s) and the community is mediated by rules, referring to the explicit and implicit regulations, norms and conventions that, in varying degrees, liberate or constrain practices, interactions and social relations within the activity system (Engeström, 1987). Rules dictate what it is to be a member of a particular community, such as a kindergarten: individuals cannot have rules of activity that are theirs alone. To some extent, rules are shared and collective. Some of them may be very explicitly expressed and enacted, but every activity system has implicit rules that are not put into words and are only reified in practices.

Study design: constituting cultures of compassion

This study is a case analysis and a pilot study drawn from a broader research project, 'Constituting Cultures of Compassion in Early Childhood Education (CoCuCo)', the objective of which is to investigate acts of compassion and their constitutive practices in early childhood settings. My focus in this article is on the following questions. What institutional rules and regulations contribute to the constitution of a culture of compassion? How is compassion enacted and expressed in the everyday life of a kindergarten and in family interaction?

The study was conducted in the Children's House kindergarten (fictive name), located in the city of Helsinki. Children's House caters to about 60 children divided in three groups: two groups of 1- to 4-year-olds and one group of 4- to 6-year-olds. My research group and I worked with the group of 4- to 6-year-olds.

The children represented the lower and middle classes of Finnish society in terms of socio-economic background.

We gathered the data on site in October and November 2015. The data consisted of the Children's House curriculum and observational notes. Every kindergarten in Finland is expected to design its own curriculum based on the National Guidelines on Early Childhood and Care in Finland (Heikkilä, Ihalainen & Välimäki, 2005). Thus, the Children's House curriculum is an interpretation and implementation of these guidelines. The national guidelines are not normative, meaning that it is not mandatory to follow them. Analysis of the curriculum sheds light on how the rules of compassion are formed and articulated as a part of the Children's House activity system.

The observation data were collected during five ethnographic visits to Children's House. Each visit lasted between 2 and 4 hours, and the total number of hours of observation was 16. During the visits the researcher took part in the everyday life of the kindergarten community and observed the daily interactions, focusing especially on the acts of helping, including, comforting and sharing. Whenever such acts were observed, the researcher made notes about the situation, the people who were present, what was talked about and the tools that were used and how the episodes began and ended. All these notes facilitated interpretation of the rules related to the constitution of compassion. Thus, my interest in this paper is not in how an individual child behaves or how compassionate she or he is but in how acts of compassion are produced as part of the everyday life of a kindergarten.

Analysis

The aim in the analysis, which follows ethnographic logic (Castanheira, Crawford, Dixon & Green, 2001), was to demonstrate the extent to which the constitution of compassion relates to rules that govern how it is and should be expressed in early childhood settings. The data analysis proceeded in a series of cycles during which questions were posed and data was represented, in this case in the form of curriculum documents and observations. An essential aspect of the analysis is the multiphase process. Firstly, I read the curriculum documents carefully and marked all the occasions on which a rule concerning the constitution of compassion emerged. Secondly, I investigated the observation data. Keeping the research questions in mind, I explored the data several times in an attempt to identify regularities and patterns (Mitchell, 1984; Roth, 2005). The final step was to translate the Finnish transcripts of the significant episodes into English.

Ethical considerations

I asked for written authorization from the city of Helsinki and the children's parents. All the parents allowed their children to participate in the study. Every attempt was made during every phase of the study to protect the children's anonymity and privacy and to treat them, their parents and teachers with dignity.

Findings: compassion as a part of everyday life in kindergarten

Next I report on the constitution of compassion as an interactional activity and as part of everyday kindergarten life. I illustrate my theoretical discussion with illustrative vignettes from the data. In addition to substantiating my theoretical claims, the examples demonstrate the importance and relevance of the theoretical conceptualizations with respect to research on compassion.

Rules mediate the subjects' activities in an activity system such as a kindergarten. Rules regulate the subjects' practices, social relations and interaction within the system either explicitly or implicitly (Engeström, 1987). Thus, in the present case, there is a connection between the rules the community uses to make sense of their social world in which compassion is experienced and expressed. Rules inform the community about what is correct or expected behaviour in particular situations, for example, and what is not. Whatever the staff members and children do on a daily basis at the kindergarten, their activities are mediated by rules, either implicitly or explicitly.

The activity system, the curriculum and the rules of compassion

The analyses of the Children's House curriculum revealed seven rules that were explicitly related to acts of helping, including, caring, comforting and sharing. These rules of compassion are not based on any law or formal regulations but appear to have developed as part of the general working culture of this particular kindergarten. The following rules were identified (with the action they represent in parentheses):

- Interfere instantly in cases of bullying (including)
- Be a friend to all the children (including)
- Apologize, help and care (helping and caring)
- Encourage the children to say if they experience injustice (including)
- Acknowledge the reality from other peoples' perspectives (helping, including, caring, comforting and sharing)
- Help children to make new friends (helping and including)
- Comfort children who pine for their parents (caring and comforting)

These rules or conventions, needless to say, regulate and mediate how to behave in relation to other people in this particular activity system and how to live with them (Engeström, 1987; Nussbaum, 2014; Thornberg, 2009). Most of the rules conveyed in the curriculum refer to acts of including. This could be interpreted as an attempt to make the kindergarten into an inclusive space in which dignity and safety are norms, diversity is recognized and accepted and everyone feels encouraged, supported and included. In a way, these rules represent policies for fairness in early childhood settings. The Children's House curriculum is a public document and thus is easily accessible to families: one could assume that because

> and says that she wants to go to home. Child B listens and joins the discussion, saying that she also wants to go home. The teacher reaches out, and Child B comes and hugs her and sits down next to her. The teacher gently asks what the matter is. Child A says in response that her mother and father always go to work. The teacher comforts her, saying that she understands that she is feeling gloomy and simultaneously puts a hand on her own chest. The teacher goes on to say that the best medicine to combat gloom is play. The teacher and the children start to negotiate about what games to play or what activities to do. They decide to start a pirate game. All three children enthusiastically engage in playing.

It is commonly believed that compassion is something that somebody gives and somebody else receives. As this vignette shows, it can also be requested. Child A, who was missing her parents, is a potential recipient. On her own initiative she approaches the teacher, sits on her lap, and only then verbally indicates a desire for compassion by saying that she misses her parents. Interestingly, emotion and desire for compassion appear to be transmitted from one child to another – in this episode from Child A to Child B. To alleviate the children's gloomy feelings, the teacher directs their attention away from 'missing the parent' to a new activity, negotiating about what to play. This 'shifting away from suffering' appeared to be common practice in Children's House. According to the curriculum, caring and comforting is a rule, but how it is enacted in everyday situations varies: people not only carry out rules; they also reformulate and expand them and produce new ones (Engeström, 1987). Albeit not inscribed in the curriculum, many episodes of caring and comforting also contained an element of physical comfort, such as touching.

Discussion

Despite the acknowledged importance of emotions in children's lives, little attention has been given to how they are constructed, enacted and negotiated in naturalistic social interactions in everyday life at home and in the kindergarten. This paper contributes to enhancing understanding of children's emotional worlds (Madrid et al., 2015), focusing on the formation of compassion related to rules that govern how it is and should be expressed in an early childhood setting. In elaborating on the notion of rules as constitutive of compassion, I applied ideas from cultural-historical activity theory (CHAT) (Engeström, 1987).

The analysis demonstrates that rules for compassion are clearly inscribed in the curriculum and appear to be important elements in the existence of the emotional world of Children's House. Such rules mediate and regulate social life and at the same time teach moral behaviour to the whole community (Thornberg, 2009). They have significance, even if the teachers and children do not explicitly refer to them, and do not thereby justify their situational acts. Registering the curriculum rules and making them accessible to many give them social significance, which is necessary for any activity system, and without which emotional worlds would not exist in the same way.

The most common rule, inscribed in the curriculum was 'including', which probably implies that the Children's House kindergarten aims to be an inclusive space in which everybody is accepted and everyone' needs are recognized. In everyday interactions, however, most of the concrete acts of compassion were acts of comforting and caring. This is perhaps not surprising, given that the need for comfort and care is very visible in everyday life. The needs of a crying child missing his or her parents, or a child who has hurt him- or herself, are easy to recognize. Albeit not mentioned in the Children's House curriculum, comforting was frequently accompanied and augmented with touching. Holding in the arms and taking onto the lap were so common as to appear almost the rule, formulated in everyday interaction as a situated practice and based on an evaluation of whether or not the 'suffering' one deserved to be comforted and touched (see Goetz et al., 2010). Every activity system has its explicitly expressed and enacted rules, but there are also implicit rules that are not put into words but are only reified in practices.

Interestingly, most of the acts of compassion were directed by teachers towards children and, as previously mentioned, were mainly acts of comfort. My interpretation is that both adults and children follow the implicit rule that it is the 'adult's job to comfort children'. On the basis of this study, I suggest that children should be guided to express empathy more actively and to evoke acts of compassion towards other children. The large number of acts of caring and comforting may well reflect the idea that early childhood education is still very much about caring. As Fotaki (2015) points out, studies done in the health-care sector demonstrate that high quality is related to responsive care and compassion. Further, the number of genuine acts of compassion was smaller than expected. It could be that daily life in a kindergarten runs so smoothly that there is neither the need nor the opportunity to recognize, offer and receive compassion.

Conclusions

Emotional worlds, and acts of compassion at home and in the kindergarten, are not separate entities, and it is more than likely that they differ to some extent. Each family (and kindergarten) has its own emotional world and its rules on how compassion should be expressed and when it is deserved, for example (Frost, 2014). Almost every day, and especially when parents leave and pick up their children, the two activity systems, home and the kindergarten, negotiate on the boundary of two emotional worlds. The cooperation between the mother and the kindergarten teacher was smooth in my example (Vignette 2), but it could have been otherwise. Tensions and disruptions are very common on the boundaries of two activity systems, in which the rules have a double function: simultaneously, they constrain and licence what people are allowed and not allowed to do. Given their nature and institutional value, rules are powerful tools: they have control and influence over people and events and have serious consequences for the construction of social reality in early childhood settings. Arriving at a deeper understanding of why teachers, children and parents act in the way they do in the context of Children's House requires an analysis of the history of this activity system. As Engeström (1987) points out, the challenges and potential of rules can only be understood against their own history and as a local history of an activity system, such as a specific kindergarten or a home.

CHAT generally very seldom focuses on emotions, which nevertheless play integral roles in Leont'ev's (1978) work on activity. CHAT researchers should pursue activity-theoretical studies on emotions in further investigations and focus especially on the dialectical role of motives and emotions in activity.

The identification of episodes of interaction in which acts of compassion and compassion-related rules are constituted is valuable not only for academic research on early childhood education: it also has pedagogical potential for the development of emotional worlds in kindergartens and families. Every teacher should be alerted to the possibility of harnessing compassion in their learning communities and should be able to collaborate with families on this issue.

Acknowledgements

I thank my master's students majoring in early childhood education at the Department of Teacher Education, University of Helsinki, for their engagement in the data collection: Reetta Kaasalainen, Pilvi Kattainen, Helena Korte and Tytti Lagercrantz.

The research reported in this article was funded by the Academy of Finland.

References

Bernstein, B. (1996). *Pedagogy, Symbolic Control, and Identity*. Boston: Rowman & Littlefield Publishers, Inc.

Bialostok, S. (2015). Guinea pigs, Asperger's syndrome, and my son. In S. Madrid, D. Fernie, & R. Kator (Eds.), *Reframing the Emotional Worlds of the Early Childhood Classroom*. New York: Routledge, 39–53.

Castanheira, M. L., Crawford, T., Dixon, C., & Green, J. (2001). Interactional ethnography: An approach to studying the social construction of literate practices. *Linguistics and Education, 11*, 353–400.

Cole-King, A., & Gilbert, P. (2011). Compassionate care: The theory and the reality. *Journal of Holistic Health Care, 8*, 29–37.

Eisenberg, N. (2013). *The Development of Prosocial Behavior*. New York: Academic Press.

Engeström, Y. (1987). *Learning by Expanding*. Helsinki: Orienta-Konsultit.

Ferraris, M. (2013). *Documentality: Why it is necessary to leave traces*. New York: Fordham University Press.

Fleer, M., & Hammer, M. (2013). Emotions in imaginative situations: The valued place of fairytales for supporting emotion regulation, mind, culture, and activity, *20*, 240–259.

Fotaki, M. (2015). Why and how is compassion necessary to provide good quality healthcare? *International Journal of Health Policy Management, 4*, 199–201.

Frost, M. (2014). Compassion in international relations. In M. Ure & M. Frost (Eds.), *The Politics of Compassion*. New York: Routledge, 97–106.

Gilbert, P. (2009). *The Compassionate Mind: A New Approach to Life's Challenges.* London: Constable.

Goetz, L., Keltner, D., & Simon-Thomas, E. (2010). Compassion: An evolutionary analysis and empirical review. *Psychological Bulletin, 36,* 351–374.

Greeno, J. G., & Engeström, Y. (2014). Learning in activity. In R. K. Sawyer (Ed.), *The Cambridge Handbook of the Learning Sciences* (2nd ed.). Cambridge: Cambridge University Press, 128–147.

Heikkilä, M., ihalainen, S-L., & Välimäki, A-L. (2005). *National Guidelines on Early Childhood and Care in Finland.*

Retrieved from https://www.julkari.fi/bitstream/handle/10024/75535/267671cb-0ec0-4039-b97b-7ac6ce6b9c10.pdf?sequence=1.

Lemke, J. L. (1990). *Talking Science.* Norwood, NJ: Ablex.

Leont'ev, A. N. (1978). *Activity, Consciousness, and Personality.* Englewood Cliffs: Prentice-Hall.

Lown, B. A. (2015). Compassion is a necessity and an individual and collective responsibility. *International Journal of Health Policy Management, 2,* 613–614.

Madrid, S., Fernie, D. E., & Kantor, R. (2015). Introduction to reframing emotions. In S. Madrid, D. Fernie, & R. Kator (Eds.), *Reframing the Emotional Worlds of the Early Childhood Classroom.* New York: Routledge, 1–15.

Mannion, R. (2014). Enabling compassionate health care: Perils, prospects and perspectives. *International Journal of Health Policy Management, 2,* 115–117.

Mitchell, C. J. (1984). Typicality and the case study. In R. F. Ellens (Ed.), *Ethnographic Research: A Guide to General Conduct.* New York: Academic Press.

Nussbaum, M. C. (2014). Compassion and terror. In M. Ure & M. Frost (Eds.), *The Politics of Compassion.* New York: Routledge, 89–207.

Paananen, M. (2018). The imaginaries that survived: Societal roles of early childhood education in an era of intensification. *Global Studies of Childhood, 8.*

Paananen, M., & Lipponen, L. (2016). Pedagogical documentation as a lens for examining quality in early childhood education. *Early Child Development and Care, 186,* 1–11.

Park, C., LeeKeenan, D., & Given, H. (2015). A family, a fire, and a framework: Emotions in an anti-bias school community. In S. Madrid, D. Fernie, & R. Kator (Eds.), *Reframing the Emotional Worlds of the Early Childhood Classroom.* New York: Routledge, 19–35.

Roth, W.-M. (2005). *Doing Qualitative Research: Praxis of Method.* Rotterdam: Sense.

Searle, J. (1969). *Speech Acts.* Cambridge. Cambridge University Press.

Shea, S. (2015). Is it possible to develop a compassionate organization? *International Journal of Health Policy Management, 4,* 769–770.

Taggart, G. (2016). Compassionate pedagogy: The ethics of care in early childhood professionalism. *European Early Childhood Education Research Journal, 24,* 173–185.

Thornberg, R. (2009). The moral construction of the good pupil embedded in school rules. *Education, Citizenship and Social Justice, 4,* 245–226.

5 Pedagogical leadership and families in Swedish preschool

Sonja Sheridan and Pia Williams

Introduction

Pedagogical leadership in preschool is a complex issue being managed by professionals in different positions, contexts and objectives. Its complexity is reflected in its diverse focus: children, families, colleagues, politicians and so on. Various factors such as objectives, authorization, competence, group size, staff-child ratio and facilities related to the preschool context affect leadership and preschool collaboration with families. Consequently, pedagogical leadership in preschool has different meanings in specific, cultural and organizational contexts as well as the receiver and varies during different times. Historically, leadership in Swedish preschool was not in focus either for research or debate. Nevertheless, leadership has always required specific expertise in both the head of the preschool and the preschool teachers. Today, pedagogical leadership is regulated and formulated, both in the Swedish Education Act (2010: 800) and in the revised preschool curriculum (Ministry of Education and Science, 1998/2011), where the guidelines for preschool teachers' responsibilities are clearly prescribed. The preschool quality is likewise to be continuously monitored, evaluated and developed.

The aim of this chapter is to discuss pedagogical leadership from a perspective of management and monitoring and as a fundamental aspect of preschool teacher competence. The chapter builds on a literature review and research on preschool teacher competence, preschool quality and leadership in preschool. Guiding this article are the following questions: what required competencies are associated with pedagogical leadership in Swedish preschool in relation to the intentions of policy documents and curricula and changes in society, the views of children and families and conceptions of children's learning? What competencies are needed to advance pedagogical leadership as an aspect of the preschool profession?

Pedagogical leadership in preschool

Leadership in preschool is characterized by extensive tasks, such as raising and educating children, administration and economics as well as provision of support for families and children. Siraj-Blatchford and Hallet (2014) claim that leadership in preschool is both ethical and caring, characterized by taking decisions and contributing to involve others. That requires multidisciplinary knowledge and competencies, depending among other things on the development of society, preschool's position in the educational system, conditions and expectations of preschool, intentions in current policy documents and curricula and the society's approach to children and children's learning. How leadership is communicated in practice depends thus on several interacting factors. These include the changes that have occurred over time and constantly happen at a macro level but also the effect of increased demands and expectations of preschool on how pedagogical leadership can be practiced in reality (Sheridan, Sandberg & Williams, 2015). In the following case we will give an example of how the multifaceted task of leadership can be expressed in a preschool context.

> The 'City Preschool' is divided into four departments with a total of 70 children age 1 to 5 years. Currently, the working team consists of Kim, the head of the preschool, six educated preschool teachers, 10 day care attendants and one preschool student teacher, supervised by the preschool teacher Lisa. One of the preschool teachers has a long-term illness, and therefore one untrained substitute teacher is included in the team. It is a popular preschool, and many parents wish to get a place for their child there. Every week, Kim gets telephone calls and emails from parents, even though they know that there is a formal way to apply for a place. Continuously, Kim also gets calls from the municipality head director, who is responsible for all preschools in the municipality, wondering if 'City Preschool' can receive some more children in the groups. Kim works hard to maintain the current group size but understands that it might be impossible when many children are waiting to get a place and the preschool budget is strained.
>
> One typical day, two in the working team are ill. Kim solves the problem by rescheduling the working time for some of the employees to avoid recruiting a replacement staff member. The working team is not satisfied with Kim's decision as they miss out their time for planning. They also know by experience that it will be difficult to get a break during the day when they are short of staff. Lisa has to work a longer day than scheduled to cover for her absent colleagues, with the effect that there will be no time for supervising the students as planned. Suddenly two children in the toddlers' group get sick. Lisa has to make an instant decision. She leaves the activity she was engaged in with five of the older children. Lisa calls the parents and asks them to interrupt their jobs and fetch their sick children. It gets loud and noisy in the group the short moment Lisa disappears. One child starts to cry. Lisa hurries back, comforting the child, and tries to bring order back to the group. Later that day, a parent takes contact with Kim and wants to talk about her worries about her child. She believes that there are too many children in the group, the rooms are too small in relation to the amount of children, and she is afraid that her child is not getting the attention, supervision and opportunities for learning that the child has a

> right to, according to the curriculum. The day ends with a staff meeting where Kim informs the staff that they probably need to increase the group size to keep the budget. The team gets upset. Kim hesitates about how to inform the parents about this issue.

Researchers such as Harris (2005), Rodd (2006), Siraj-Blatchford and Manni (2007) and Spillane (2006) point out various factors related to the context affecting pedagogical leadership in preschool. These may include historical, demographic, social, political and cultural characteristics and requirements that the leader of an organization and community relate to. In her research Hujala (2004) uses a contextual leadership model based on Bronfenbrenner's (1979, 1986) ecological system theory. She argues that leadership in preschool consists of the interaction between the process and leadership context and can be characterized by extensive tasks, such as raising and educating children together with their families, administration and economics as well as providing support for families and children. Leadership in preschool is a socially constructed, situational and interpreted phenomena, which means that it is not only the leaders' ideas about leadership which define leadership but also the views of all actors involved in the preschool, including families and financiers. The results show that parents had a stronger focus on the interaction when they defined leadership than what other groups had. Rönnerman and Olin (2013) emphasize that dialogue, participation, confidence and knowledge are important for accountability and leadership. Swedish preschools appear to shape society in a way that the preschool provides parents (legal guardians) opportunities for professional work and study and contributes to greater democratization and equality between women and men as well as parents' and children's rights to participation and influence (Tallberg-Broman, Rubinstein-Reich & Hägerström, 2002). Most Swedish parents today choose preschool for childcare, and they are satisfied with it. The National Agency parent survey (Swedish National Agency for Education, 2013), in which the parents of 124,000 children participated, revealed that 90% felt that the staff did a good job, that children were safe and that preschool pedagogy was good. Research suggests that high-quality preschools with well-educated teachers have the potential to improve equity and equality for children from diverse backgrounds (Sylva, Melhuish, Sammons, Siraj-Blatchford & Taggart, 2010). To invest in the youngest children in a society has been found socio-economically profitable (Heckman, 2006). Most effective for the individual, family and society are investments aimed at children between 1 and 3 years (Britto & Ulkuer, 2012).

Even if Swedish parents are satisfied with preschool, its international status has decreased as well as children's overall situation in Sweden. From being a top-ranked country, Sweden is now in 11th place when it comes to children's well-being, safety, health, education, and so on (UNICEF, 2013). Pedagogical leadership will thus become increasingly important to create conditions for children to access a good and equal start in life, regardless children's living conditions and background.

The Swedish preschool context and leadership

Preschool is an important part of society in that 85% of all children between the ages of 1 to 5 are enrolled in a preschool (Swedish National Agency for Education, 2013). To meet and support families' needs for care, preschool is usually open from 6.30 a.m. to 6.00 p.m. The average time spent at preschool per child is 30 hours a week. Often the children are organized into toddler groups (1–3 years old), sibling groups (1–5 years old) and older groups (3–5 years old). The sizes of these groups can vary (Williams, Sheridan & Pramling Samuelsson, 2016). Whilst an average toddler group often has around 12 to 16 children and three teachers, sibling groups can have up to 26 children or more with a staff/child ratio of approximately 5.3. Most of the teachers are qualified, with about 43per cent% of them having a 3.5-year-long university degree, the other group of teachers having a nursery nurse certificate gained after 2 years at an upper-secondary/ senior high school.

In recent decades the importance of preschool has been strengthened by different economic, structural and educational reforms, making preschool part of the Swedish educational system. In 1996, the responsibility for preschool was brought under the control of the Ministry of Education. In 1998 the first national curriculum for preschools was established and revised in 2010 (Sweden Ministry of Education and Science, 1998/2011). Organizationally Swedish preschool has an open and flexible structure. The curriculum encompasses a number of goals to aim for, but guidelines about how preschool practice and education should be organized as a means of attaining the envisaged outcomes are lacking.

The curriculum for preschool embraces the fundamental values, tasks, goals and guidelines for preschool activities. Democracy forms the foundation of the work done in preschools, and all activities are carried out in accordance with the fundamental democratic values of helping children acquire the values on which Swedish society is based. Care, nurturing, and learning together form a coherent whole. The goals are formulated as something the preschool should strive to ensure that each child develops. The goals specify the orientation of the work of the preschool and thus the desired quality targets in the preschool. Through the revision a stronger focus was directed on children's learning and development of various content areas like early mathematics, literacy, natural science and technology. This means that preschool should be more pedagogical and learning oriented but not in an academic way (Bennett, 2010). Following the preschool tradition, different goals and content areas are to be integrated with one another in different themes, for example, themes of spring, circus and so on using preschool didactics (Pramling & Pramling Samuelsson, 2011). For by the thematic work approach, learning is also to be integrated with play and care and build on children's interests and previous experience.

The curriculum does not only regulate preschool objectivities and activities. It also regulates the cooperation with home and parents. Together with the Education Act (2010: 800) the curriculum describes how this cooperation is to be conducted. It is the head of preschool together with the preschool teachers who are responsible for taking initiative to and uphold the contact with the children's homes and parents.

Policy documents regulating leadership and cooperation between home and preschool

The Education Act (2010: 800) stipulates that education in preschool aims at children acquiring and developing knowledge and values. It should promote all children's development and learning and a lifelong desire to learn. An important task of the preschool is to impart and establish respect for human rights and the fundamental democratic values on which Swedish society is based. Each and every person working in the preschool should promote respect for the intrinsic value of each person as well as respect for our shared environment.

Children's development into responsible persons and members of society should be promoted in partnership with the home. The preschool should help families by supporting them in their roles of bringing up and helping their children grow and develop. The task of the preschool means working in cooperation with parents so that each child receives the opportunity of developing in accordance with their potential.

In the preschool curriculum the goals specify the orientation of the work of the preschool. The guidelines for the staff in the preschool specify not only the responsibility of preschool teachers to ensure that work is carried out in accordance with the goals in the curriculum but also in cooperation with the home concerning the child's upbringing, along with discussion with parents about the rules and attitudes in the preschool. The preschool's work with children should thus take place in close and confidential cooperation with the home. Parents should have the opportunity within the framework of the national goals to be involved and influence activities in the preschool. A prerequisite for children and parents to have the opportunity of exercising influence is that the preschool is clear about its goals and what its work involves. The guidelines state that preschool teachers are responsible for each child, together with their parents, receiving a good introduction to the preschool; for ensuring that parents receive opportunities to participate and exercise influence over how goals can be made concrete in pedagogical planning; for the content of the development dialogue, its structure and how it is carried out; and for involving guardians in assessing the work of the preschool.

Pedagogical leadership – two functions and perspectives

The curriculum also regulates the leadership in preschool, which in Swedish preschools has two functions and perspectives. Pedagogical leadership in preschool is to be carried out both by the head of preschool and by the preschool teachers in their work with the children, parents and colleagues. In some situations, the meaning and task of pedagogical leadership will differ from these two functions and perspectives; in others they will coincide. We will now discuss how they differ and coincide.

Pedagogical leadership – the head of the preschool

The head of the preschool is the pedagogical leader for the preschool. She or he is the head of the staff and has the overall responsibility for activities to be carried out in agreement with the goals in the Swedish revised preschool curriculum and the assignment as a whole as well as the preschool quality. The head of preschool is also responsible for developing forms of cooperation between the preschool and the home and ensuring that parents receive information about the goals of the preschool and its methods of working. The task also means working in cooperation with parents so that each child receives the opportunity of developing in accordance with their potential (Sweden Ministry of Education and Science, 1998/2011).

In the restructuring of the Swedish educational system, the head of the preschool has received a crucial as well as supporting position to create conditions so that the activities in preschool comply with the curriculum goals and intentions. The assignment includes financial, educational and administrative responsibility. It involves child and parent contacts, safety issues, cooperation with other educational systems such as school and after-school activities, child health as well as personal dialogue and educational and didactical discussions with the teachers, planning of competence development and contacts with different administrations and managements. The head of the preschool is often included in different networks and development teams with other headmasters and administrative managers (Sweden Ministry of Education and Research, 2007).

Dahlgren and Åsén (1987) describe how the assignment has changed for the preschool leader. In the context of decentralization the pedagogical leaders have become an important link between society, management, preschool work and families. Many preschool leaders describe it as positive to have greater responsibility and opportunities to make decisions and take initiatives. But they also express that pedagogical issues often get sidelined due to administrative tasks. During the 1980s it was common to just be responsible for one preschool. Today there are major differences in how leadership is organized. It is common to be responsible for several preschools with large staffs, not working in the child group, being the administrator and the educational leader and being the official connection between preschool and home.

A report, based on a survey sent in the early 1990s to 925 headmasters in preschool about their job situations, shows that it is a female-dominated profession where most have worked in preschool for six years or more. They seemed to enjoy their work, even if personnel issues were expressed to be a pressure. They felt that they lacked competencies related to administration, economics and organization and asked for better organizational conditions and clear goals to develop their pedagogical leadership and preschool as a whole. Much has happened in preschool since this study was conducted, but it is of interest to study how changes in the educational system have affected leadership in preschool and the positions and competences the head of the preschool is expected to possess (Frank, Lundmark & Söderström, 1990).

Pedagogical leadership – the preschool teacher

Cooperation between preschool and home has had different meanings over time. It has developed from a philanthropic view, where focus was on fostering the whole family morally and dutifully (Johansson, 1992; Westberg, 2008) to an approach of collaboration between home and preschool (Ministry of Education and Science, 1998/2011) in which parents are seen as the most vital for the child. Today a preschool teacher's responsibility and pedagogical leadership are stated in the revised curriculum as ultimately responsible for children's learning, development and care in line with the intentions (Sweden Ministry of Education and Science, 1998/2011). In this way, the preschool teacher is also in a leading position to ensure that the work is done in accordance with the preschool assignment. It is up to the teachers themselves to interpret the goals and to decide how they should be concretized (Sheridan, Williams, Sandberg & Vuorinen, 2011).

Scrivens (2003) argued that there is not just one way to be a leader and that leadership varies from culture to culture and situation to situation. As a preschool teacher, the main task is to lead the daily work with the children and impel constructive changes in the work, which requires competencies to communicate ideas to colleagues and work together in a joint and targeted work. Research shows (Sheridan et al., 2015) that to lead is closely related to being social and engaged, building relationships and being a role model. Leadership in preschool is handled primarily through communicating intentions, creating dialogue and reflecting together with colleagues, children and parents. Important competences are related to communication and social skills, the skills to be able to relate to others and the skills to be a driving force and act professionally. More general competencies are also to be clear, to be interested, to pay attention to others, to compromise and to allow others to take leadership roles. However, leadership is also to influence and persuade others in the working team, which means that different opinions are coordinated and that the focus is directed towards common goals. This can especially be a compound task as there are different professionals within the working team. Thus, it demonstrates a complicated and dynamic guidance, based on communication, listening to another person, trying to understand each other's perspectives and at the same time striving towards important goals. On the other hand, it is a form of leadership where reciprocal agreements seem more important than providing a vision of the future.

Thus leadership in preschool is about having a relevant education as the preschool teacher competencies are prominent in leadership. It is about being committed, being able to interact with others and having a solid theoretical knowledge that can be applied in practice. One preschool teacher says, "I use myself as an instrument. My personal commitment and my competence to relate to others are expressed in my leadership. My formal training and theories that I have learned, I try to transform in practice".

The preschool teacher's responsibility as a pedagogical leader can be described as always being 'one step ahead' and to oscillate between past, present and future, which in turn requires authority and legitimacy. In a study (Sheridan,

Williams & Pramling Samuelsson, 2014) preschool teachers describe leadership as a pedagogy practiced in dialogue with others. It is about initiating and making well-considered choices and decisions and also about taking responsibility for decisions and actions taken by children, parents and colleagues. Important skills are to drive and stimulate the development of the work in preschool forward. A preschool teacher expresses that

> leadership is a strategy. A way to act that lets children follow you or colleagues, depending on what it is about. That is, they listen to what you have to say. Of course, you don't have to always agree, but if you have them with you it will be a discussion. And the same applies to parents.

Leadership can be either promoted or hindered depending on behaviour, style and methods. The preschool teacher makes this visible in the previous quotation. She has a strategy for leadership, to act so that people concerned are listening to the message. Leadership in preschool is practiced mainly in communication and interaction and means that you are a person who others are listening to. This applies to children, parents and colleagues. Making one's voice heard does not decide what others should do. It is rather to initiate discussions where intentions become visible, even if all agree completely (Sheridan et al., 2014).

To lead colleagues differs from leading individual children and a child group. When a preschool teacher becomes the leader of colleagues, it is about leading the team and practicing a democratic and horizontal leadership. This requires communication skills: being able to communicate intentions and reflect together with colleagues, creating debate and arguing for something specific as well as disseminating and sharing information, representing others and asserting their views to stakeholders. Some preschool teachers view themselves as authorities among colleagues and managers. Based on their knowledge and experience, they expect to gain support for what they consider is important in relation to the children. Their strategy is to be clear and convincing. To practice leadership in relation to colleagues is not entirely unproblematic. Often it is a question about being able to compromise as leadership is informal and equally distributed among the participants in the team.

Vital is preschool teachers' pedagogical leadership with individual children and children in a group. Teachers' professional skills become visible through their leadership with the children. Leadership with children involves both leading individual children and the group. Many preschool teachers express that they try to see both the individual child and all children in the group (Sheridan et al., 2014). They are sensitive to what children express and guide them in their development. In interaction and communication with the children, they use their knowledge in different content areas and try to be good role models for them. Their leadership aims to highlight the children's abilities by helping them develop different skills.

To lead a group of children and capture the interest of the group requires other competencies. Preschool teachers believe that leadership is more pronounced when working with the whole group of children. Then it is necessary to take a more formal leadership position, which they believe gives the children a sense of belonging and participation. Important for preschool teachers is to exercise democratic leadership with the children. It is about the balance of simultaneously listening to the children and leading them so that children can influence ongoing activities and make their voices heard and that their opinions are taken seriously. A preschool teacher says, "Children can affect and influence their daily life in preschool". To lead children is also a question about spontaneous and situated leadership in which teachers need to act in the situation, acting in the moment and acting on the basis of children's behaviour as well as seizing the opportunity.

Leadership with parents is a question of establishing and maintaining a good relationship between home and preschool and is emphasized in several studies (Aarnon & Reichel, 2007; Huntly, 2008; Vuorinen, Sandberg, Sheridan & Williams, 2013). Research shows that consistency across preschool and home and between preschool staff and parents promotes happiness and achievement for children (Siraj-Blatchford & Hallet, 2014; Sylva, Melhuish, Sammons, Siraj-Blatchford & Taggart, 2004). Despite this knowledge, the communication between preschool and home is more of a one-sided relationship. The direction of information about children usually moves from the preschool setting to the parents and seldom in the opposite direction (Siraj-Blatchford & Hallet, 2014). Although the authors point out that there is a growing need and expectation for the development of partnerships with parents and families and reciprocity in sharing of information. Parents and care holders should be encouraged to inform about their child as there is a clear positive impact on children's well-being when working effectively with parents.

A Swedish study (Vuorinen et al., 2013) showed that preschool teachers view the ability to establish dialogue with parents and gain their trust as particularly important for establishing and maintaining collaboration between preschool and home. Although the competencies preschool teachers emphasize in the encounter with parents and the competencies they perceive parents as requesting do not always coincide. The teachers put forward competencies concerning children's learning and the ability to interpret and visualize the tasks formulated in the preschool curriculum, whereas parents seem to seek personal qualities, focusing on social and communicative skills and experience rather than formal competence. Preschool teachers make a deliberate effort to draw attention to competencies of importance to their profession as well as to distinguish preschool teachers from day care attendants, and in this process the interpretation and implementation of the curriculum become central. Experience is highly valued by preschool teachers and is seen as a prerequisite to achieving successful collaboration between the home and preschool as the ability to individualize evolves through experience (Vuorinen et al., 2013).

One can conclude that preschool teachers' leadership is a complex task as it on a face-to-face level is directed towards several stakeholders as children, parents and colleagues.

Conclusion

To be a leader in today's and future preschools requires professional competencies to be able to interrelate theory and practice and apply knowledge in action. The aim with the exemplified case with the City Preschool, in the beginning of this chapter, was to show how both preschool teachers and the head of the preschool in their leadership face complex professional, ethical, educational, cultural and political demands. The case illustrates the problems leaders have to deal with when demands from society are in conflict with parents' and teachers' wishes to make decisions that are necessary for a preschool. Leadership in preschool is thus a question of solving overall decisions but also of focusing on conditions for children's learning, development and well-being. According to the preschool curriculum, leadership includes knowing how to interpret and specify the contents and subjects where children are seen, listened to, challenged and given equal opportunities to learn and be involved in the learning process. As the work is carried out within a team, it is of importance to develop an educational consensus, which means that activities are planned and implemented on the basis of a common understanding of the intentions of the curriculum. Rönnerman's and Olin's (2013) study about quality work in preschool is illustrated from three levels of management, namely administration (quality coordinator), preschool (preschool managers) and operations level (preschool teachers supervising colleagues). The study shows the need for dialogue, participation and trust for it to be possible to carry out responsibilities. Pedagogical leadership is about leading and managing activities that are oriented towards children, families and colleagues where form and content are emerging in a mutual communication. Important questions for preschool teachers to reflect on are, for example, what leadership means for preschool teachers. How do they perceive leadership? And how does the leadership influence professional competence?

Leadership is practiced continuously and in the best case in communication, interaction and dialogue with and among the team, with colleagues and with the head of preschool, parents and children. Being a leader in preschool today and simultaneously facing the challenges of the future are therefore complex tasks as they involve working not only with adults but with young children and their families and with various professional groups: preschool teachers and child minders with managers and other persons who may influence or be influenced by the preschool organization.

References

Aarnon, S., & Reichel, N. (2007). Who is ideal teacher? Am I? Similarities and differences in perception of students of education regarding the qualities of a good teacher and of their own qualities as teachers. *Teachers and Teaching: Theory and Practice*, *13*(5), 441–464.

Bennett, J. (2010). Pedagogy in early childhood services with special reference to Nordic approaches. *Psychological Science and Education*, *3*, 16–21.

Britto, P., & Ulkuer, U. (2012). Child development in developing countries: Child rights and policy implications. *Child Development*, *83*(1), 92–103.

Bronfenbrenner, U. (1979). *The Ecology of Human Development: Experiments by Nature and Design*. Cambridge, MA: Harvard University Press.

Bronfenbrenner, U. (1986). Ecology of the family as a context for human development: Research perspectives. *Developmental Psychology, 22*, 723–742.

Dahlgren, G., & Åsén, G. (1987). *Föreståndarna och förskolans ledning*. Rapport 7/1987. Institutionen för pedagogik. Stockholm: Högskolan för lärarutbildningen.

Frank, C., Lundmark, A., & Söderström, M. (1990). *1000 föreståndare om arbetssituation och arbetsmiljö. En empirisk studie av ledningsfrågor, arbetsmiljö och utvecklingsbehov för föreståndare inom barnomsorgen*. Uppsala universitet: IPD-rapport nr 10.

Harris, A. (2005). *Crossing Boundaries and Breaking Barriers: Distributing Leadership in Schools*. London: Specialist Schools Trust.

Heckman, J. (2006). Skill formation and the economics of investing in disadvantaged children. *Science, 312*(5782), 1900–1902.

Hujala, E. (2004). Dimensions of leadership in the childcare context. *Scandinavian Journal of Educational Research, 48*(1), 53–71.

Huntly, H. (2008). Teachers' work: Beginning teachers' conceptions of competence. *The Australian Educational Researcher, 35*(1), 125–145. doi:10.1007/BF03216878

Johansson, J.-E. (1992). *Metodikämnet i förskollärarutbildningen: bidrag till en traditionsbestämning*. Göteborg: ACTA Gothoburgensis universitatis.

Ministry of Education and Research. (2007). *Tydligare ledarskap i skolan och förskolan – förslag till en ny rektorsutbildning*. Departementsserien (2007:34). Stockholm: Utbildningsdepartementet.

Pramling, N., & Pramling Samuelsson, I. (Eds.). (2011). *Educational Encounters: Nordic Studies in Early Childhood Didactics*. Dortrecht, Holland: Springer.

Rodd, J. (2006). *Leadership in Early Childhood*. Maidenhead: Open University Press.

Rönnerman, K., & Olin, A. (2013). Kvalitetsarbete I förskolan belyst genom tre ledningsnivåer. *Pedagogisk forskning i Sverige, 18*(3–4), 175–196.

Scrivens, C. (2003). Educational leadership: What might we learn from research in schools? *Early Education, 31*, 29–35.

Sheridan, S., Sandberg, A., & Williams, P. (2015). *Förskollärarkompetens i förändring*. (Preschool teacher competence in change- in Sweden). Lund: Studentlitteratur.

Sheridan, S., Williams, P., & Pramling Samuelsson, I. (2014). Group size and organizational conditions for children's learning in preschool: A teacher perspective. *Educational Research, 56*(4), 379–397.

Sheridan, S., Williams, P., Sandberg, A., & Vuorinen, T. (2011). Preschool teaching in Sweden – A profession in change. *Educational Research, 53*(4), 415–437.

Siraj-Blatchford, I., & Hallet, E. (2014). *Effective and Caring Leadership in the Early Years*. London: Sage Publications Ltd.

Siraj-Blatchford, I., & Manni, L. (2007). *Effective Leadership in the Early Years Sektor. The ELEYS Study*. London: Institute of Education, University of London.

Spillane, J. P. (2006). *Distributed Leadership*. San Francisco: Jossey-Bass.

Sweden Ministry of Education and Science. (1998/2011). *Curriculum for Pre-school*. Lpfö 98. Revised in 2010. Stockholm/Skolverket: Fritzes.

Swedish Education Act (2010:800). (2010). Stockholm: Ministry of Education and Science.

Swedish National Agency for Education. (2013). *Beskrivande data 2013. Förskola, skola och vuxenutbildning* (Skolverkets rapport nr 399). Stockholm: Skolverket.

Sylva, K., Melhuish, E., Sammons, P., Siraj-Blatchford, I., & Taggart, B. (2004). *The Effective Provision of Preschool Education (EPPE) Project: Final Report.* London: DfEs/Institute of Education, University of London.

Sylva, K., Melhuish, E., Sammons, P., Siraj-Blatchford, I., & Taggart, B. (2010). *Early Childhood Matters: Evidence From the Effective Pre-School and Primary Education Project.* London: Routledge.

Tallberg-Broman, I., Rubinstein-Reich, L., & Hägerström, J. (2002). *Likvärdighet i en skola för alla. Historisk bakgrund och kritisk granskning.* Stockholm: Skolverket.

UNICEF. (2013). *Child Wellbeing in Rich Countries: A Comparative Overview.* Innocenti Report Cart 11. Florence, Italy: UNICEF Innocenti Research Centre.

Vuorinen, T., Sandberg, A., Sheridan, S., & Williams, P. (2013). Preschool teacher's views on competence in the context of home and preschool collaboration. *Early Child Development and Care. 184(1),* 149–159. Taylor and Francis Online. doi: 10.1080/03004430.2013.773992

Westberg, J. (2008). *Förskolepedagogikens framväxt: Pedagogisk förändring och dess förutsättningar, ca 1835–1945.* Uppsala: Acta Universitatis Upsaliensis. Studia Historica Upsaliensia.

Williams, P., Sheridan, S., & Pramling Samuelsson, I. (2016). *Barngruppens storlek i förskolan.* Konsekvenser för utveckling och kvalitet. Stockholm: Natur & Kultur.

6 Early childhood education, gender relations and equality among parents and families in Sweden

Ingegerd Tallberg Broman and Ingrid Pramling Samuelsson

Historical perspectives – a long and untoward way

From a historical perspective, it is evident that early childhood education and care (ECEC) has made a crucial impact on Swedish society, including the preconditions for parental roles and family life. The expansion of ECEC in the growth of the welfare state in Sweden has significantly influenced family and labour market policy, social equality, gender equality and the struggle for professional legitimization; as a consequence, it was met with resistance clearly relating to power relations and gender issues.

Such dramatic changes of the societal order, which have been the consequences of an institution for all children, combining care and education and offered on an everyday and full-time basis at a low cost, have of course not been smooth. As summarized by Alva Myrdal (1982) in the 1980s, "[I]t has been a long and untoward way". The resistance has mostly been related to issues concerning changing of gender relations, of the position for 'the home' in the society and of parental roles and equality. The establishment of an ECEC institution in Swedish society represents a 100-year process, but today ECEC is a highly evaluated part of ordinary family life and childhood enabling equality among different forms of families.

The ECEC history in Sweden is an example of and a part of Nordic history, with both many common and specific national and local characteristics, due to the country's earlier history concerning gender patterns, parental roles and home-society relations.

Established in Sweden in the 1890s and practiced during the first three decades of the 20th century, the more organized, Fröbel-inspired kindergarten movement gained support by the establishment of the first training colleges around 1900 by a common journal for Nordic kindergarten teachers and by a special interest association. These networks and associations were part of a distinct ECEC paradigm which had targets, content, working methods and pedagogical outlooks as well as expectations of parental cooperation; this paradigm's relation to schooling had a powerful impact on society which still remains today.

In the 1930s scientific argumentation became increasingly prominent as a foundation for education professionals but with an admixture of, and interaction with, discourses that had been active in earlier periods. This resulted in a period of expansion and development, but this time of growth came to an end in the 1940s due to years of economic crisis and war followed by a domestic period in the 1950s. During this after-war decade family life meant the mother stayed home with the children, while the father went to work. The male breadwinner – housewife model was the dominant discourse until the 1960s (Nauman, 2005). Despite many exceptions and criticism from social scientists and feminist theorists, the gendered division of work and care remained the dominant ideology of the time.

In the 1950s the conflict between the state's interest in increasing the labour market participation of mothers of young children and the "needs of the child" were considered by a committee on family policy (SOU, 1951, p. 15). The conclusion was that children under 3 were best cared for at home by their parents. After the age of 3, it was decided that they would benefit from more collective forms of childcare. At the same time, the committee supported society's need for labour and women's freedom to work and thus suggested the expansion of childcare institutions for all preschool-age children, although the implicit idea was limited to kindergartens.

In the 1970s, relatively large proportions of preschool children were children of single mothers and children with special needs. Working-class parents were more hesitant than middle-class parents about sending their children to preschools, and the care of working-class children was more often organized in informal ways, while shift-working parents often managed by themselves. Today, no social differences of significance are found in attendance (Skolverket, 2004). As we can see in Table 6.1, the percentage of children in ECEC settings has grown enormously during 30 years.

We can also see in Table 6.2 how the number of children in the population has decreased to some extent and how the number of children included in ECEC has increased.

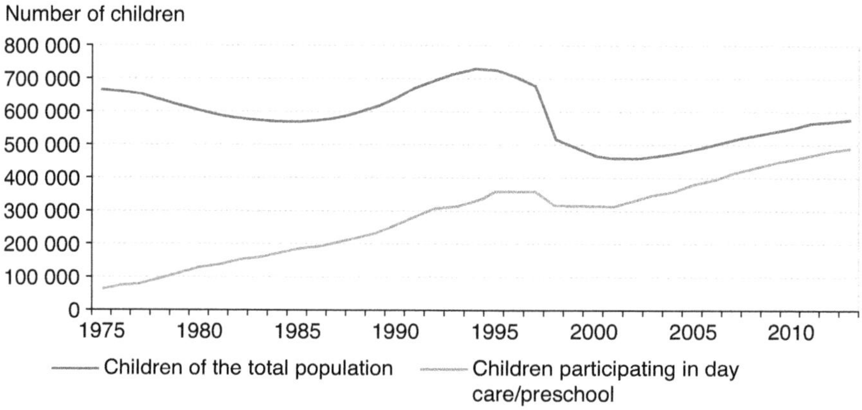

Figure 6.1 Children in the Swedish population – and in the ECEC 1975–2014

Table 6.1 Development of ECEC in Sweden 1972–2002 – proportion (%) of children 1–6 years in municipal ECEC in Sweden 1972–2002

Year	1972	1980	1990	2002
Percentage (%)	10	34	55	82

Source: SCB, 2003, Skolverket (2004)

Table 6.2 Changes in the Nordic model and areas of conflict

Change	*Areas of conflict*
Women as wage earners	Individualization, children
Father's involvement in childcare	Working life, traditions
Collectivization of childcare	Traditions, religion, parental authority
Parental leave	Individualization, working life
Childcare allowance	Gender equality, the best interest of children

The resistance to the expansion of the Swedish preschool in the 1970s consisted mostly of arguments that the responsibility for care and education of young children is not, and should not, be a public responsibility. The view of the child changed from only being a family child to become everybody's child in the sense that all citizens in society have responsibility for children. The political decision about the expansion of the preschool was a consensual decision (Jönsson, Sandell & Tallberg Broman, 2012, p. 53).

State feminism

During the 1970s the model for the modern Swedish ECEC was created, and all forms of municipal childcare increased significantly during this period. Both a kind of 'state feminism' and a need for women in the labour market supported a development and expansion of ECEC. ECEC became a policy priority in Sweden. The jurisdiction of the welfare state that was introduced in the 1960s, 1970s, and 1980s was supposed to be woman friendly. A woman-friendly state would not force harder choices on women than on men or permit unjust treatment on the basis of sex.

At an early stage, the dual earner/carer model attracted broad political support, especially in Sweden and Denmark, and since the 1980s these countries offer day care to a higher proportion of children than other Nordic countries (Eydal & Rostgaard, 2011a, p. 99a).

Helga Hernes, social scientist and from 1979 to 1983, director of research at the Norwegian Research Council for Science and the Humanities's Secretariat for Women and Research, developed the concept of "the woman friendly state" and "state feminism". She summarized: "There were two things we really fought for in the 70s. One was kindergartens, to enable women to enter the labour market, and the other was the legalisation of abortion" (http://kjonnsforskning.no/en/2015/12/helga-hernes-mother-state-feminism-and-gender-quotas).

Shared responsibility and social investment

A significant aspect of the Swedish and Nordic ECEC policy is the idea of sharing child education and care between families and public institutions (Karila, 2012). The professional and political struggle for the legitimization of early childhood education is based on the acceptance of shared responsibility for the socialization and education of young children.

In the European Union (EU) the target was set 2009 for 90% of children over the age of 3 to be in preschool. This target was reached in many Western member states, but most of the eastern states still lagged behind (COM, 2011). However, it was not specified how many hours per day the children should be in preschool, and in many of the countries, childcare is only offered on a part-time basis. This creates problems for the working parents of young children.

Contemporary reforms point to increased expectations of preschool as part of lifelong learning and preparation for school. Such ideas are included in the social investment strategy which is supported on the EU level and by international organizations such as the Organisation for Economic Co-operation and Development (OECD). According to White (2009), the social investment strategy implies a positive relationship between early childhood development and early childhood education programs and children's success later in life, which is related to a country's economic success (Jönsson et al., 2012, p. 48).

International actors

For quite some time, the issue of ECEC has been on the European political agenda, for example, through the network for the reconciliation of work and family responsibilities from 1986 to 1996. The recommendation from the European Council of Ministers (2002) aimed at improving women's access to the labour market and advocated services, which combines "reliable care" with "a pedagogical approach" (Jönsson et al., 2012).

Other international actors (especially the OECD) have contributed to the fact that childcare has appeared on the political agenda in many countries. Ideas about lifelong learning are developed within the framework of new social risks of the post-industrial society. Ageing populations, the increase of female employment and new family formations (smaller families, later marriages, increasing rates of divorces and separations, etc.) have contributed to insecure incomes and to uncertainties about how to arrange the care of children and the elderly. A care gap is expected to appear in most European countries.

In this context, ECEC is expected to play an important role for the future of the child and for society as a whole. The return of investments in preschool is calculated as much higher than investments in schooling or job training (Heckman, 2006; Esping-Andersen, 2008).

> Early childhood education and care are often promoted as both a way to care of children while their parents – that is mothers – work, and as an investment in prevention, to reduce the chance of social failure and therefore the need for basic skills training later in life as well as the likelihood to encounters with the criminal justice system.
>
> (Jensen, 2006, p. 30)

The importance of gender perspective

A general preschool which combines care and education and is offered to all families at an affordable cost entails a thorough transformation of gender and power relations in a society. A deeply grounded notion in Swedish society, as well as in many others in the 19th century, of women and children as belonging to the private domestic sphere and men as belonging to the public sphere, has influenced attitudes on this issue and on the development of institutions for education, mostly for boys and men on all levels. On an EU-level you can still see how questions about young children and their care and education often are related to labour market questions.

The emergence of high-quality preschools which combine care and education and that possess an extensive legitimacy can be said to have fundamentally changed the relationship between mother, father and child. During the time when the field was initiated, society was controlled by a patriarchal order and strictly divided according to class and gender, especially in the middle and upper class.

Women at the end of the 19th century were excluded from many fields of education, professions and jobs. For a bourgeois woman, being a homemaker was, in general, the only possible sphere of work. Motherhood and the home were greatly idealized, and this was seen as where women were in their so-called natural place. The main principle was that the sexes were essentially different, and this applied to the more privileged classes in particular. Women and men were perceived differently and had to be kept separate, with moral and hygienic arguments to support this (Fröbel, 1982/1826).

The kindergarten movement did not challenge this directly rather more indirectly by broadening the concepts of a social and pedagogical home to include a wider social, societal and spiritual form of motherhood (Key, 1914; Allen, 1991). An example of this can be found in the terms given to female teachers, which were clearly related to the concept of family, such as *skolmoster* (school aunt), *skolmamsell* (school mademoiselle) and *fröken* (miss).

Through their social and educational tasks in care, nursing and education, free zones of a kind were created for women. These gradually developed into occupations and semi-professions mostly by middle-class women. The women created social and pedagogical areas which were affected by their cultural and class gender.

A feminist issue

In several countries, with Sweden as a leading example, the question of public involvement in childcare became a feminist issue with support from many quarters, and the matter was pursued by feminists both outside and inside organizations. It is worth noting that this was an issue chiefly for liberal and socialist feminists, not radical feminists, as Randall (1995) points out. Bottom-up cooperation among feminists, along with the support of the trade unions, chiefly LO, the Swedish Trade Union Confederation (although that was two edged due to the support of 'femocrats' in the political and administrative bureaucracy), was of crucial significance for the construction of the Swedish model. Another central factor in the development of the 'equality project of preschool' was the collaboration of political lobby groups, trade unions, active parents and preschool teachers. This made the project of establishing a preschool for all children in Sweden possible. Todays the norm has been feminism, and we can see that the leading parties in the government talk about themselves as feminist parties.

Individualization, defamiliazation, democratization and radical changes in family life

In Sweden, the ECEC, as it is known today, has contributed to the individualization of man, woman and child alike. Women's dependence on the welfare state, which took the place of an earlier dependence on the husband or relatives, has been problematized using Scandinavian evidence (Hernes, 1987).

The expansion of preschool has, to a large extent, been affected and obstructed by the fact that it was an equality project which enabled both women and men to work outside the home. This has been relevant both in the history of preschool from a Swedish perspective and in the international discussion in recent decades (Letablier & Jönsson, 2005; Scheiwe & Willekens, 2009). Occasionally in the course of debating gender equality there is the accusation that we tend to forget about the children. Gender equality work has largely focused on equality in working life (Gislason, 2011).

The ECEC and the expansion of a social service state resulted in radical changes within family life and the conditions of childhood. It changed gender relations in society and influenced the transformation of the male breadwinner model into that of dual-income families with more shared parenting.

The professionalization of the care and education of young children meant the institutionalization of childhood, and the expansion of the public sector led to the transition of Sweden into a social service state. This resulted in the defamilialization of the care of children as well as that of elderly persons (Anttonen, 1990; Lister, 1990).

The democratization and social investment in ECEC increased expectations on parents' participation and responsibilities as citizens. In Sweden, democratic civil rights as citizens and as parents became more emphasized at the beginning of the 21st century, and the emphasis on responsibilities is even more apparent now in the second decade (Harju & Tallberg Broman, 2013). Increased expectations on, and inclusion of, parents (especially immigrant parents) are accentuated as strategies for supporting children and professionals in reaching the aims of the preschool. Parents participation is important, both as democratization and for support and better outcomes (Tallberg-Broman, 2009).

Equality for different kinds of families

As a result, the expansion of ECEC has created better conditions for equality for different kinds of families, a high birth rate (1.92) and a high rate of employment for both women and men. As of 2014, 75.9% of women and 78.5% of men between the ages of 20 and 64 were in the workforce. Further, due to both parents' participation in the workforce, as well as in regard to household and parental responsibilities, the meaning of motherhood and fatherhood has slowly been changing in Sweden. The relations between state and family, the state and the single parent, parent and child, and mother and father have been greatly influenced by the development and expansion of readily available preschool services. ECEC has been a part of equivalence for all kinds of families.

But a gender squeeze?

As editor to the book *Parental Leave, Childcare and Gender Equality in the Nordic Countries*, Gislason (2011) comments that "the Nordic model has been characterized by a high rate of labour participation of both men and women, efforts to achieve equality between women and men and by society´s concerted investments into care and education of children." In recent years, however, signs of stagnation have emerged – what has sometimes been describes as a "gender squeeze" – and unless we balance the distribution of parental leave and other care duties, the devaluing of women in the labour market will continue (p. 13). Even though the 'Nordic model' has been relatively successful in advancing equality between women and men, mothers and fathers, there are still areas where the situation is very bad, such as the gender pay gap (p. 16).

Changes in the 'Nordic model' and areas of conflict

In Table 6.2 the changes that have taken place in the recent decades, and the areas of conflict that have been ensued, are summarized by Gislason (2011, p. 15).

The tradition of seeing mothers as main caregivers of children continues to be strong, but there are many signs in all Nordic countries, stresses Gislason, that fatherhood is beginning to influence fathers' participation in wage earning in that they are trying to increase their share of care responsibility (p. 20).

As we have recognized, *democratization and social investment* have been and are central in policy and practice in ECEC (because preschool is the official name for all settings before the school age in Sweden, we will use this notion from now on). Some of these questions that are obvious in society are equality between men and women as well as parents' participation in their child's everyday life in preschool.

Part of the efforts to boost gender equality in recent decades has been to encourage parents to share their parental leave and in other ways to promote a new kind of role for fathers. Most Nordic countries have moved toward individualization in the use of parental leave. The operative premise has been that parental leave is important for gender equality (Gislason, 2011). Studies show that the childcare allowance seems to cement traditional parental gender roles and that it also is used in a class-segregating way.

Today parents have 480 days of parental leave for each child, of which 390 days are around 80% of the regular salary and 90 days with lower compensation. They can also stay at home 120 days per year with sick children; this compensated by the government to 80%. But although the parental leave reform is 40 years old, only 25% of the time is utilized by men. That is why the government last year decided that 90 days have to be utilized by the other partner (men), or these months will be lost. So although Sweden is considered to be one of the most equal countries in the world, there is still a long way to go when it comes to taking care of and fostering children (Björnberg, 2002). With the slow improvement of change, it will take until 2040 before parents share equally. But even if men do not take equal parental leave, they are much more involved in their children's everyday lives than ever before, which influence family life and by that women's situations. Not the least it is as common that men take care of sick children as women.

The fertility rate in Nordic countries has, in a European comparison, been rather high, a fact that partly can be related to affordable childcare and a right to day care and ECEC institutions on a full-time basis. In Sweden the birth rate was 1.9 in 2012, whereas many countries, e.g. Lettland, Ungern, Germany, Italy and Spain, show much lower rates, below 1.5.

Almost all children are today in preschool

The coverage for younger children in all Nordic countries is well above the EU average, and a unique Nordic feature is the provision of full-time care for younger children (Eydal & Rostgaard, 2011a).

Almost all children are in preschool today. Already from 2 years of age, 88% participate in preschool. There have been two main reforms for ensuring every child's right to an equal start of education in Sweden: 1) to give all children from 3 years of age access to at least 15 hours preschool a week without cost. Children can however stay longer, paid by parents in what is called 'a maximum fee', which is at the most about 140€ per month. There is also a suggestion in the government right now to lower the age from 2 years for 15 hours of free preschool. This reform can be seen as making it possible for all parents to send their children to preschool whatever their economic situation looks like. All children, also asylum seekers, have the right to a place in preschool within a few months from parents asking for it. 2) The other equality factor is a national curriculum that is supposed to secure that all children get a similar start in the education system, of which preschool is part of according to laws (SFS, 2010: 800). Whether it is sufficient to participate 3 hours a day or not is a matter of debate (Kultti, Pramling Samuelsson & Harju-Luukkainen, 2016).

In the curriculum for preschool (National Agency for Education, 2011), it is clearly stated the cooperation with parents in terms of "preschool should supplement the home by creating the best possible preconditions for ensuring that each child's development is rich and varied" (op. cit., p. 13). It is also stated that parents should have opportunities to be involved in the preschool and influence activities there. The responsibility of the staff is to make sure that parents can practice this right, as there is an ongoing dialogue between parents and preschool staff, and that parents are involved in assessing the work of the preschool. This is shown to be a unique right for parents compared to other European countries (Pramling Samuelsson & Cojocaru, 2016). The close relationship between preschool and home is also shown in research to be a key factor for children's success later in school (Sylva, Melhuish, Sammons, Siraj-Blatchford & Taggart, 2010).

Kristjansson (2006) has also shown how democracy is a central topic with young children in Nordic countries, a topic that has to be a concern for every generation and never taken for granted, according to him. Eydal and Rostgaard (2011b) also emphasize that Nordic countries share this ideal – that the child should be involved in the decision-making process. They also stress the idea that the ECEC system shares responsibility for the child with the parents but also independently helps the child evolve into a responsible citizen who is aware of the importance of democratic values (p. 70).

It is also shown in a comparative study between Scandinavian parents and Mayan parents in Guatemala that democracy and children's rights are an evident part of life by many parents from Scandinavia, whereas this is heavily questioned in the Mayan parents' views (Pramling Samuelsson, Sommer & Berger González, 2016). In parallel with parent's rights are children's rights to be active participants and learn responsibility as important goals in the preschool curriculum. In the curriculum is it formulated that children should develop the ability to express their thoughts and views, influence their own situations, accept responsibilities, and understand and act according to democratic principles and decision-making (National Agency for Education, 2011, p. 12). To foster democracy education has to begin early in life and can never be taken for granted. It is also stated in the curriculum that preschools should work towards challenging traditional gender roles.

Parents in general are very positive about preschool for their children, but an interesting change has taken place. In the 1960s parent demonstrated for access to preschool (Klinth & Johansson, 2010), but today they demand high quality (Pramling Samuelsson, Sheridan, Williams & Nasiopoulou, 2014). A reason for this may be that this generation of parents has a higher degree of education than any earlier generation has had. In a way they take for granted that society has a responsibility for children.

Is the family good enough?

An explorative study (Sandell i Jönsson et al., 2012, p. 55–56) of two preschools situated in two different socio-economic areas in a city in southern Sweden shows that school-like activities preparing for school are strongly supported by the interviewed parents in the preschool recruiting children from immigrant and low socio-economic families, whereas middle-class parents in another area are more ambivalent. They underline the importance of the children remaining children and being able to play while simultaneously being anxious that their children should participate in organized activities. Parents in both areas define learning in a traditional way, that is, what is taught in schools and taught in organized forms, and that differs from the preschool teachers' ideas of learning. The preschool teachers also emphasize that values other than school preparation are important. Both groups of parents use the preschool to enable them to work or study. They also trust that planned activities are supplementing 'babysitting' or care of their children. The parents support the idea of the *educare* model.

The study showed that the cooperation between preschool and parents still was to some extent based on the old idea that the family as not a good enough socialization environment (Donzelot, 1980; Gleichman, 2004). Parental involvement was organized in different ways at the two preschools; the preschool functions as a social meeting point in the area with many immigrants, and the parents are notified that they *must* attend meetings, whereas parents in the middle-class preschool have organized themselves in a parents' organization and cooperate with the preschool teachers through this organization. The preschool teachers in the former preschool arrange parents' education and include parents in the fostering of children to become 'good' (Swedish) citizens. It has resulted in less social isolation among immigrant parents, and the preschool helps create social cohesion in addition to fulfilling the goals of an educational and welfare institution (Sandell in Jönsson et al., 2012, p. 55–56).

Increased expectations of inclusion of parents is something preschool teachers are aware of, but still there is no self-evident way to deal with this cooperation because parents are a very diverse category and so are preschool staff. Not the least, it is a challenge with all immigrant parents; research shows that parents know the intentions of the curriculum, but in practice they try to educate the parents about Swedish preschool culture and what they are expected to do rather than staff listening to parents (Kultti & Pramling Samuelsson, 2016). Many immigrant parents have other expectations for their children's learning and different norms of gender than native parents have (Tobin, 2009).

Challenges of today

Research on Swedish preschools shows a great interest in gender equality, participation and democracy. Preschool as an educational system for equality, and equal opportunities is highlighted in both theses: research surveys and research projects (Tallberg-Broman, 2009). The issues and research questions are discussed both as central goals and values and as essential aspects of learning and a prerequisite for active learning.

ECEC, in the 'Nordic model', has had a great impact on the conditions for equality between parents and among families. But research shows big challenges within the ECEC and describes gender discrimination and reinforcement of gender stereotypes rather than the intended gender equalization (Eidevald, 2009). The research also shows stereotyped gender expectations related to various subject areas of knowledge.

The research on 'the pre-school family' and on the relationships between preschool and the family/the parents is very limited, especially from gender and diversity perspectives (Lunneblad, 2013). The interest and research priority has been more directed to how the preschool can contribute to gender equality and to non-segregating gender roles and positions for the children and on staff composition from a gender perspective. This focus has also been supported by several government investigations and a larger number of gender projects. There is a great need for stimulating research on the relationship between the ECEC and different kinds of families.

Parents' perceptions of preschool have been identified in various national studies (Skolverket/National Agency for Education, 2013; Skolinspektionen/School Inspectorate, 2016) and are also on a regular basis studied locally, but few studies goes behind the survey data. We know very little about the parents' perceptions and relationships to preschool; we know very little about how they perceive the preschool and about how it affects their parental roles and their family life. This seems very important to explore further and to know much more about for the preschool staff, especially in relation to the increasing variety of parents and families in the globalized society.

The challenges we face, beside more solid research in Sweden related to gender and equality are mainly two: 1) to meet the global world of people and 2) to foster the next generation into gender equality.

The global world of people

With change in the global world as well as in Swedish society, there are great challenges. The two main challenges related to preschool are: 1) to integrate all children and families coming from other ethnic backgrounds and 2) to develop a preschool of high quality for all children and still keep the values of democracy, equality and rights to influence high on the agenda. Some time back there was an interview with a Syrian newly arrived refugee on TV, and he said, "[W]e only have to learn your language and your laws, and then we can work here". This is of course true, but it is easy to say and much more complicated in reality – where people's identities are part of the culture where we grow up. The same cultural encounters take place in preschool!

The situation in Sweden is that we in the last years have received a tremendous amount of immigrants and asylum seekers (in 2015, 160.000 came to Sweden, of which one-third is children) who have changed the situation and created new challenges in society and in preschool. In some cities half the population of children has a mother tongue other than Swedish. One cannot expect all parents to just accept and fall into the Swedish way, which has a very long history. Fighting for a preschool for all has been a joint effort for the teachers' union and for people in political positions in the government. There is a number of strong people, both men and women, who have meant a lot for the development of preschool. Also, the state supported media for educating parents about the benefit of preschool for their children (Lindgren, 2011).

To work against traditional gender patterns and gender stereotypes in preschool

Because preschool now is counted as the first step in the education system, there is also a curriculum for this first stage. The first national version of the curriculum was published 1998, two years after the Ministry of Education had taken over the responsibility for preschool from the Ministry of Social Welfare and Health. The curriculum is, however, based on the preschool tradition and is open and allowing for interpretations. It is 20 pages long, and it only states the mission of preschool, the theoretical perspective on children's learning and development, and Swedish values and goals to strive for. There is, however, nothing about how to work with children because the professionals are expected to have knowledge about that. The curriculum was revised in 2010, and language and communication, mathematics, science and technology goals were strengthened. But there was also more focus on following up, evaluating and developing the quality of preschool. It can be interpreted as if we get a more knowledge-oriented preschool, at the same time it is stated that preschool should be play oriented and thematically organized (National Agency for Education, 2011). Democratic values are central with an obvious intention to work against traditional gender roles already in preschool (Hellman, 2010). The School Inspection (2012) has done evaluations about how the work proceeds towards the revised curriculum, and it is shown that there are three different results: excellent preschools where they work according to the new guidelines; a large group of teachers struggling with how to change what they have been doing, which means that they in a way are 'on their way'; and finally the group that does not see any difference from what they always have done – that is, they are not aware of the change that has taken place. These three categories can also be compared to excellent, medium and low-quality preschools in Sweden that were evaluated in a study by Sheridan, Pramling Samuelsson and Johansson (2009).

The challenges to meet the new demands from the government are large, not the least as there is such a lack of educated preschool teachers. It has decreased to 43% on a national level (Skolverket, 2014) at the same time as there is an expectation to raise the quality in preschool in general. Sylva et al. (2010) show that it is the quality that makes the difference for children, and part of quality is the cooperation with parents.

Another challenge in the Swedish system of preschool is the increased number of children attending, which has led to more children in each group, something that worries both parents and preschool staff. The opinion in media and from professionals has got the government to launch new direction of smaller numbers of children in each group (Skolverket, 2016). These directions are not mandatory, only recommendations; we do not know what will happen, because the number of children are related to money and facilities. Williams, Sheridan and Pramling Samuelson (2016) have shown how quality in preschool is a complex issue related to the number of children, the competence of the staff, the environment, which children are participants (toddlers, older preschoolers, native Swedish children or a mix of children with many cultural backgrounds). This means that raising the quality for all children is a larger question than number of children in the group, and the quality is of course related to teachers' time available and the possibility of focusing on gender questions and equality.

References

Allen, A. T. (1991). *Feminism and Motherhood in Germany 1800–1914*. New York: Rutgers University Press.

Anttonen, A. (1990). The feminization of the Scandinavian welfare state. The welfare state in transition: From the social insurance state towards the social service state. In L. Simonen (Ed.), *Finnish Debates on Women's Studies: Women's Worlds, Realities and Choices*. Tampere: University of Tampere.

Björnberg, U. (2002). Ideology and choice between work and care: Swedish family policy for working parents. *Critical Social Policy*, *22*, 33–52.

COM. (2011). 66 final. Communication from the Commission. *Early Childhood Education and Care: Providing All Our Children With the Best Start for the World Tomorrow*. Brussels: Commission of the European Communities.

Donzelot, Jacques. (1980). *The Policing of Families*. Baltimore: Johns Hopkins University Press.

Eidevald, C. (2009). *Det finns inga tjejbestämmare: Att förstå kön som position i förskolans vardagsrutiner och lek*. Dissertation. Högskolan i Jönköping, Jönköping.

Esping-Andersen, G. (2008). Childhood investments and skill formation. *International Tax and Public Finance*, *15*, 19–44.

European Council of Ministers. (2002). *Presidency Conclusions From the Barcelona European Council 15–16 March. http://ec.europa.eu/invest-in-research/pdf/download_en/barcelona_european_council.pdf Downloaded 16-04-15*

Eydal, G. B., & Rostgaard, T. (2011a). Day-care schemes and cash-for-care at home. In I. Gislason & G. B. Eydal (Eds.), *Parental Leave, Childcare and Gender Equality in the Nordic Countries*. TemaNord 2011:562, 65–107. http://ffdd.ru/activity/attach/information/182/parental_leave_childcare_and_gender_equality_in_the_nordic_countries.pdf

Eydal, G. B., & Rostgaard, T. (2011b). Toward a Nordic childcare policy – The political processes and agendas. In I. Gislason & G. B. Eydal (Eds.), *Parental Leave, Childcare and Gender Equality in the Nordic Countries*. TemaNord 2011:562, 147–178. http://ffdd.ru/activity/attach/information/182/parental_leave_childcare_and_gender_equality_in_the_nordic_countries.pdf

Fröbel, F. W. A. (1982). *Kommt, lasst uns unsern kindern leben*. Band 1–3. Berlin: Volk und Wissen. Volkseigener verlag.

Gislason, I. (2011). Introduction. In I. Gislason & G. B. Eydal (Eds.), *Parental Leave, Childcare and Gender Equality in the Nordic Countries*. TemaNord 2011:562, 13–30. http://ffdd.ru/activity/attach/information/182/parental_leave_childcare_and_gender_equality_in_the_nordic_countries.pdf

Gleichman, L. (2004). Föräldraskap mellan styrning och samhällsomvandling: En studie av syn på föräldrar och relationen mellan familj och samhälle 1957–1997. *Studies in Educational Studies*, *72*, Stockholm, HLS förlag.

Harju, A., & Tallberg-Broman, I. (2013). *Föräldrar, förskola och skola. Om mångfald, makt och möjligheter*. Lund: Studentltteratur.

Heckman, J. (2006). Skill formation and the economics of investing in disadvantaged children. *Science*, *312*, 1990–1902.

Hellman, A. (2010). *Kan Batman vara rosa?* Göteborg: Acta Universitatis Gothoburgensis.

Hernes, H. (1987). *Welfare State and Woman Power: Essays in State Feminism*. Oslo: Norwegian University Press.

Jensen, J. (2006). The LEGO™ paradigm and new social risks: consequences for children. In J. Lewis (Ed.), *Children, Changing Families and Welfare States*. Cheltenham: Edward Elgar Publishing Ltd., 27–50.

Jönsson, I., Sandell, A., & Tallberg-Broman, I. (2012). Change or paradigm shift in the Swedish preschool? *Article Journal Sociologia, Problemas e Práticas*, *69*, 47–62.

Karila, K. (2012). A Nordic perspective of early childhood education and care policy. *European Journal of Education*, *47*(4), 2012.

Key, E. (1914). *Missbrukad kvinnokraft och Kvinnopsykologi* (4:de upplagan). Stockholm: Bonniers.

Klinth, R., & Johansson, T. (2010). *Nya Svenska fäder* [*New Swedish Fathers*]. Umeå: Borea förlag.

Kristjansson, B. (2006). The making of Nordic childhoods. In J. Einarsdottir & J. Wagner (Eds.), *Nordic Childhoods and Early Childhood Education*. Greenwich, CT: Information Age Publishers.

Kultti, A., & Pramling Samuelsson, I. (2016). Investing in home–preschool collaboration for understanding social worlds of multilingual children. *Journal of Early Childhood Education Research*, *5*(1), 69–91. Retrieved from http://jecer.org/fi

Kultti, A., Pramling Samuelsson, I., & Harju-Luukkainen, H. (2016). *Rapport av pilotstudien: Förskolan som resurs för barns välbefinnande och lärande*. I samarbete med Västra Götalandsregionen. Göteborgs universitet: Institutionen för pedagogik, kommunikation och lärande. Retrieved from http://hdl.handle.net/2077/42470

Letablier, M.-T., & Jönsson, I. (2005). The logic of public action. In U. Gerhard, T. Knijn, & A. Weckwert (Eds.), *Working Mothers in Europe: A Comparison of Policies and Practices*. Cheltenham: Edward Elgar Publishing Ltd., 41–57.

Lindgren, A.-L. (2011). Statlig utbildningsteve saluför idén om en förskola för alla. In J. Westberg (Ed.), *Förskolans aktörer. Stat, kår och individ i förskolans historia*. Uppsala: Opuscula Historica Upsaliensia 44, s 67–87.

Lister, R. (1990). Women, economic dependency and citizenship. *Journal of Social Policy*, *19*(4), 281–298.

Lunneblad, J. (2013). Tid till att bli svensk: En studie av mottagandet av nyanlända barn och familjer i den svenska förskolan. *Nordic Early Childhood Education Research Journal*, *6*(8), 1–14.

Myrdal, A. (1982). *Förskolan segar sig fram. I A. Myrdal m fl. Förskolan, 80-talets viktigaste skola. s. 9–18*. Stockholm: Tiden.

National Agency of Education. (2011). *Curriculum for Pre-school.* Lpfö 98. Revised in 2010.

Nauman, I. (2005). Child care and feminism in West Germany and Sweden in the 1960s and the 1970s. *Journal of European Social Policy, 15*(1), 47–63.

Pramling Samuelsson, I., & Cojocaru, S. (2016). Diverse perspectives of participation. Denmark, Greece, Germany, Hungary, Iceland, Romania, Sweden. In K. Fisher, I. Kaschif-Haude, & J. Schneider (Eds.), *Strengthening Activity Oriented Interaction and Growth in the Early Years and in Transitions.* Life Long Learning Programme. www.signals-eu.com/documents/Signals-Compendium.pdf

Pramling Samuelsson, I., Sheridan, S., Williams, P., & Nasiopoulou, P. (2014). Stora barngrupper I förskolan – ett medieperspektiv. In J. Balldin, J. Dahlbeck, A. Harju, & P. Lilja (Eds.), *Om förskolan och de yngre barnen – historiska och nutida nedslag* [*About Preschool and the Youngest Children – Historical and Contemporary Strikes*]. Lund: Studentlitteratur, s. 101–114.

Pramling Samuelsson, I., Sommer, D., & Berger González, M. (2016). Children's rights to participation in two cultures: Guatemala Mayan and Scandinavian parent views of young children. In A. Ferrell & I. Pramling Samuelsson (Eds.), *Diversity in the Early Years.* Oxford University Press.

Randall, V. (1995). Feminism and child daycare. *Journal of Social Politics, 25*(4), 485–505.

Scheiwe, K., & Willekens, H. (2009). Introduction. In K. Scheiwe & H. Willekens (Eds.), *Childcare and Preschool Development in Europe: Institutional Perspectives.* Basingstoke: Palgrave.

SFS. (2010:8000). Skollagen. Regeringskansliet [The Act of School Law]. Stockholm: The Swedish Government.

Sheridan, S., Pramling Samuelsson, I., & Johansson, E. (Eds.). (2009). *Barns tidiga lärande. En tvärsnittsstudie om förskolan som miljö för barns lärande* [*Children's Early Learning. A Cross-Sectional Study of Preschool Environment for Children's Learning*]. Göteborg: Acta Universitatis Gothoburgensis.

Skolinspektionen. (2016). *Förskolans kvalitet och måluppfyllelse 2015–2017.* Delrapport 1. Regeringsrapport 2016. Dnr: 2015:3 364.

Skolverket (2004). *Statistik.* Stockholm: Skolverket.

Skolverket. (2013). *Föräldrars val och inställning till förskola och fritidshem: Resultat från föräldraundersökningen 2012.* Stockholm: Skolverket.

Skolverket. (2014). *PM.* Stockholm: Skolverket, Enheten för utbildningsstatistik Dnr. 2014: 00036.

Skolverket. (2016, 12 februari). Nya riktmärken ska bidra till mindre grupper [*New Benchmarks Are Going to Contribute to Smaller Groups*]. Retrieved from www.skolverket.se/om-skolverket/press/pressmeddelanden/2016/nyheter-2016-1.244816/nya-riktmarken-ska-bidra-till-mindre-barngrupper-1.245981

SOU. (1951: 15). *Daghem Och Skolor. Betänkande om Barnstugor och Barntillsyn. Avgivet av1946 års Kommitté för den Halvöppna Barnavården.* Stockholm: Socialdepartementet.

Sylva, K., Melhuish, E., Sammons, P., Siraj-Blatchford, I., & Taggert, B. (2010). *Early Childhood Matters: Evidence From the Effective Preschool and Primary Education Project.* London: Routledge.

Tallberg-Broman, I. (2009). "No parent left behind": Föräldradeltagande för inkludering och effektivitet. *Educare, 2–3,* 221–240.

Tobin, J. (2009). *Children Crossing Borders: Including the Voices of Migrant Families in ECEC Programmes.* Working Paper submitted to The Bernard van Leer Foundation.

White, L. A. (2009). *The Internationalization of Early Childhood Education and Care (ECEC) Issues: Implication for Gender Equality*. Paper prepared for the RC19 Conference "Social Policies: Local Experiments, Travelling Ideas", 20–22 August 2009, Montréal.

Williams, P., Sheridan, S., & Pramling Samuelsson, I. (2016). *Barngruppens storlek i förskolan. Konsekvenser för utveckling och kvalitet*. Stockholm: Natur & Kultur.

7 Divorce, families and children

Per Arne Rød

Introduction

As in other countries, the traditional family in Nordic countries is patriarchal, with the man as its head and with the ideal of lifelong monogamy. This structure is expressed through divorce legislation and legal practice. Around 22% of all families in Nordic countries have children (Nordic Statistical Yearbook, 2014). Of these families, 77% consist of married or cohabiting couples. Because many couples are living together without being formally married, the number of those married and divorced does not give a complete picture of the range of people that move in together or move apart from each other. Since 1995, the number of marriage settlements has increased in all Nordic countries, except in Denmark, where there has been a reduction. Norway and Finland have seen a reduction in the number of divorces during the same period. Looking at the number of marriages and divorces in 2013 in relation to the population, Denmark had the highest proportion of divorces. In Denmark, the proportion of those divorced was 3.4 per 1,000 inhabitants, whereas for the Nordic region as a whole, the average was 2.6 per 1,000 inhabitants. The increase in the figures for Denmark must be seen in relation to the fact that since 2013, the law there allows for divorce without prior legal separation.

The modern family types are in many ways a break with the patriarchal tradition, and the position of lifelong monogamy has been weakened. 'The divorced family' is a family type that is not dissolved by divorce but reorganized. Some authors, such as Ahrons (1980), use the term 'binuclear family' to describe this. In the various languages of Nordic countries, the following family types are registered: married couple with children, father with children, mother with children and cohabiting couple with children (Statistics Norway, 2015). The type of family that is increasing most rapidly is that of 'mother with children'– single mothers. In Nordic countries, families with children are increasingly less based on parents who have entered into a contract of marriage. As early as in 1992, for example, it was equally usual for first-born children to come into the world outside marriage as within marriage. The likelihood of children experiencing family dissolution while growing up has notably increased in recent decades, from one in seven in the 1970s (Jensen, 1999) to one in two 30 years later (Thuen, 2004). There is reason to believe that we would find equivalent figures for the other Nordic countries.

Public debate and research in recent decades have shown a marked increase in interest in what divorce means for the children involved. Research has been underway in the United States in particular, and here a number of studies has demonstrated that children of divorced parents as a group score more poorly on various psychosocial factors than children who grow up without experiencing parental divorce (Emery, 1999; Størksen, Røysamb, Holmen & Tambs, 2006; Wallerstein, Lewis & Blakeslee, 2000; Amato, 2014). Amato summarizes the consequences of divorce for children as follows: "Divorce leads to disruptions in the parent-child relationship, continuing discord between former spouses, loss of emotional support, economic hardship, and an increase in the number of other negative life events" (Amato, 2000, p. 1282). Surveys from Nordic countries have also reached a similar conclusion when it comes to aggression and antisocial behaviour, school achievement and mental health problems (Hansagi, Brant & Andreasson, 2000; Nævdal & Thuen, 2004; Breivik & Olweus, 2006). Some research has concluded that these problems may improve after parents move away from each other (Moxnes, Haugen & Holter, 1999).

According to several provisions of the Norwegian Children Act (1981), children are subject to their parents' rights and duties to make choices for them, yet at the same time they should be heard and their opinions taken into account. The consideration of the child's own wishes is strongly emphasized both here and in the Child Welfare Act of 1992. These acts imply an ideal process of meeting children as independent citizens with claims on decent and respectful treatment. Marital breakups contrast the child's position as an independent individual, capable of making choices, with the child's need to be protected by adult caregivers. In cases where children's interests coincide with their parents' decisions about daily care and visitation arrangements, there will usually be fewer challenges. Several scientists, such as Lamb, Sternberg and Thompson (1997), have concluded that the various care and non-resident arrangements can work well for children when their parents are able to work together. But in those situations where there is *conflict* between the children's parents about the care and visitation arrangements, there is extensive evidence that this imposes a difficult burden on children and hampers their development (Emery, 1999; Kelly, 2000; Rød, Ekeland & Thuen, 2008). Children who experience conflict-ridden breakups are therefore likely to be referred to as a vulnerable group, where their life experience involves the risk of mental health problems. Conflicts not only characterize the parents' cohabitation and cooperation both before and after the separation, but also the family atmosphere, and with it, the children's development. Parents with high levels of conflict often underplay the level of conflict and tend to involve themselves with their children. When the children need their parents to be emotionally available, parents are often little involved and distance themselves or ignore their children's needs (Ary, Duncan, Duncan & Hops, 1999; Rød et al., 2008). As adults, children who have grown up with significant parental conflicts have an increased risk of mental illness, social difficulties and poorer adaptation to working life (Paradis, Reinherz, Giaconia, Beardslee, Ward & Fitzmaurica, 2009). Studies of behavioural issues suggest that about one-third of the children who grow up with significant parental conflicts develop behavioural problems (Ware, Jouriles, Spiller, McDonald, Swank & Norwood, 2001). It also appears that the children's behavioural problems (and this is especially true in families with extensive parental problems) can cause parents' conflicts to escalate (Jenkins, Simpson, Rasbash & O'Connor, 2005). The concept of conflict is central to the themes discussed here and will therefore be described in detail.

The basis for the theme

As a social worker in the field of child protection, child psychiatry and family therapy, I have met many children with experiences from conflict-ridden breakups. As a scientist, I have had the opportunity to interview the children and their parents about their experiences from the time before their parents' separation, the time around the litigation related to residency and visitation arrangements and the children's present situation. I have also interviewed child welfare workers to obtain knowledge about the reviews and the choices they have made when encountering the concerns of children in such situations. It is important to emphasize that all children are different and that they respond differently to similar events and experiences. The strength of children's stories and that of their experiences, little known until recently, has led to concern regarding the life situations of children who live with long-running parental conflicts.

Children's experiences, understanding and responses to conflict-ridden breakups

I will first describe some results from my own research. These are children's experiences analyzed in the light of the theory of emotions (Ben-Ze'ev, 2000). Their stories are also analyzed in the light of the Norwegian Child Welfare Act (1992). Results from this research are discussed in relation to understanding the conflicts, theory of emotions and social responsibility for the protection of minors.

Aggressive feelings

For a majority of the children, aggressive feelings were directed mainly against one of the parents. A 19-year-old boy had learned that his mother took his younger brother with her when she moved out of the home. The boy missed his brother and reacted strongly to his mother's behaviour:

> He does not feel like my brother anymore, but he's there. She should have done a lot to get in touch again, but she is my mother. She has infected him with all sorts of painful thoughts about us. It is my mother who has simply poisoned him. My brother has no reason to feel anything against me. I cannot see that my mother has a good effect on my little brother.

The boy's aggression involves a negative assessment of his mother's actions. Her actions shock him, and he feels them to be unfriendly and highly undeserved. The boy has learned that the mother stopped him from having any contact with his brother and that his brother has been manipulated to foster a negative perception of his father and brother. The boy's feelings towards his mother tend towards hatred. Although anger is a direct response to an action, hatred is generally associated with a view of the other as a bad person (Ben-Ze'ev, 2000). Anger means that we want to hit back and avenge the action we are exposed to. Hatred leads to the wish that someone did not exist. Hatred can be characterized as a general negative attitude to someone. When we hate people, we experience that negativity in a basic way.

Other children had aggressive feelings, both towards one of the parents and towards the judge, as this statement from a 14-year-old girl shows:

> I realise how bad it is before I go to stay with him. But then I just think . . . it is only weekends when I go over there. But it is always just as horrible. So can a judge make a decision, who has never met us, has never spoken to us, just heard two adults telling their story? He didn't trust the psychologists. It is very, very unfair. It's the kids' words that should count the most. It's what it's all about.

Several of the children described how angry they had been after the court's decision and about how unfair they felt it was. They had expressed aggression towards the judge and the court through words and drawings, for example, *"imprison the judge in the forest, so he never comes out"* (boy, 11 years). The feelings against the court's decision were related to resentment against the sole companionship of one parent. The children highlighted that contradicting claims threaten the relationship with one parent when they themselves have not wanted visitation from the other. The aggressive feelings described towards the parent were a result of the contact arrangements which they considered disagreeable. The children were annoyed by the parent's unwillingness to change visitation arrangements that represented a considerable strain for the kids. Whereas several of the children expressed their support of the resident parent, the non-resident parent was defined as not being considered a part of the child's family. As one boy of 11 years stated:

> It seems, we don't like how he is, but we like to go over to his place. But not when he is at home. With him, I don't feel that I can be myself. If you are in a proper family, then you should be able to be yourself. I will not be like family with my father.

The children who showed aggressive feelings toward the non-resident parent and when facing the judge felt doubly violated: by the parent and by the court and the judge. The children found it deeply unfair that the judge instructed them on visitation with a parent they despised. They found the court's decision to be unfair in that the judge had not listened to their opinions. The children considered themselves overlooked in a case where they themselves were the main protagonists. When the judge also did not believe the psychologists, they felt that they were believed by one part of the judicial system but that another part did not believe them. Their aggression may be viewed as a sense of hope that was replaced by a sense of betrayal. Their aggressive feelings towards the judge were demonstrated by the children through words, drawings and complaints against the parental caregiver. The aggression towards one of the parents was demonstrated by children excluding them from the family. Some of the children had violent feelings towards one parent that took the form of a general negative attitude, in other words tending towards hate. The feelings appeared not as a spontaneous reaction to any specific action that the children were trying to retaliate against but showed a desire to create the maximum distance from one parent.

Anxiety

Most children described the situation regarding the relationship breakup as one where they had been worried and afraid. One of the boys said he had often had trouble sleeping. This suggests emotions that have to do with anxiety. And some of the children related incidents where they had been very anxious. Situations that created anxiety, however, were different from the children's physical presence in the conflict between the parents. Therefore, several of the children's experiences may be referred. Some of the anxiety had the character of acute fear, an intense discomfort in connection with specific situations. A girl of 12 years spoke about a conflict situation that arose after the court had made a particular contact arrangement:

> Dad didn't come and get us. We had packed and were ready. Dad called from the police station: "If he did not get the kids that weekend, the police would come and get us." I was scared; it was I who took the phone. Afterwards my dad beat my mum; he was very angry. I shouted: "Do not turn on my mum". Out in the yard, I was afraid that my dad would run over my mum with the car.

The same girl also remembered previous quarrels between the parents. The parents had cried and slammed doors. When the girl asked them to make up, she was told not to interfere. She also told me about episodes where her father had shut her in a room, turned off the light and locked the door.

Another girl of 16 years had also learned that she was directly involved in the dispute between the parents. She had stood weeping between the parents, but they had ignored her. She still relives these events through nightmares. She told me that every time she was sick, she heard her parents arguing.

Whereas Emery (1999) in his investigations found that children were worried about their parents and even feared being abandoned, this survey describes the children's anxiety in connection with the conflict situations before, during and after their parents' divorce. Conflict experienced from the time the parents lived together left a mark on the children, and they experienced that the conflicts were repeated or appeared in new ways after the relationship breakup. Several of the children had attacks of anxiety outside conflict situations. They even explained the anxiety as being related to their parents' relationship conflict. Some of the children registered where and when the feelings of anxiety occurred but felt powerless to avoid them. The reports from these children, pointing in the direction of the reaction, seem to corroborate the conclusions of Wallerstein and her colleagues, namely that the discomfort and uncertainty in connection with divorce leads to anxiety and psychological problems in the majority of children (Wallerstein & Kelly, 1980; Wallerstein et al., 2000).

In this survey, several children said that the emotional discomfort was repeated. Their descriptions suggest discouragement and resignation, which in turn indicate emotional feelings and reactions of a more depressive nature.

Depressive feelings

Several of the children said that they cried when their parents bickered. They said that it made them sad or upset. A girl of 15 years related her experiences of all the fighting between her parents and how sorry she felt. Even though the parents argued a lot, she and her sister were upset when their parents told them that they were going to end the relationship. The girl said that she was so upset in the period that followed that she didn't come to school. She was sick and felt that everything had gone wrong. Now she, like several of the other children, was sorry to act as a messenger between the parents.

A boy of 12 years was asked to describe how he had felt when his parents told him that they were going to end their marriage:

> I thought that this was a little sad and upsetting. My parents said that they noticed that I was sorry, that my voice was a little bit different. It was just like I had a lump in my throat. Or a fur ball in a way. Mum was often present when I cried.

When the boy was asked about how he felt now, he said:

> It's almost like before. Apart from that I have been a little sadder than before they moved out, or when the trial began. Sadder on occasions where, for example, I'm talking about this to mum or dad. I get a kind of lump in my throat. Then I start to cry.

The children were asked if they had any advice to give other children in similar situations. Several of the replies were characterized by a resigned attitude insofar as they could not influence the situation. Because the parents' relationship was so acrimonious, the children's actions and opinions had no effect. Like the children in Emery's (1999) surveys, the children in this survey are, in part, characterized by hopelessness for the future. But these children associate their emotions directly with the conflict between the parents, a conflict to which they see no resolution.

Sadness and happiness are polar opposites but are nevertheless within the same emotional domain (Ben-Ze'ev, 2000). Happiness is the most general of all positive feelings and involves an overall perception of life or central aspects of life. Unlike compassion, which is directed towards other people, we are concerned by the sadness that affects us or someone who is close to us. The sad children in this survey are primarily concerned with the negative effect on them. But some of the children are also sad because of negative effects on a brother or a sister or on one of the parents.

Central to the feeling of sadness is the experience of loss. The survey by Emery (1999) found that the children mourned the dissolution of the family. The children in our study have experienced loss of conflict-free communication between their parents, and they are sad because they don't see any end to the conflict. They are tormented because they are regularly involved. The negative experiences are also exacerbated by the children's inability to see opportunities to change the situation. This was also shown when they were asked what they would do if they had a magic wand. Almost all said that they wanted their parents to get back together. However, most of them probably had no hope that this could happen. Several of the children turned to their own or a sibling's confirmation ceremony as a specific example of a parental conflict's assumed strength and its unreasonable repercussions. The confirmations either entailed a situation in which each of the two families had a separate celebration or in which only one of the families celebrated. There were also examples where one part of the family wanted to attend a confirmation ceremony but did not receive an invitation to the celebration or get to meet the child who was being confirmed. The children's perception was that the sole person who excluded one parent from the celebration was the other parent.

Shame and guilt

Although the children were aware that the conflict over custody arrangements was the parents' responsibility, many of them displayed guilt for various reactions by the parents as a consequence of the situation. Guilt is caused by regret for past or present actions. Actions that are considered negative will result in guilt. Actions that are deemed positive, on the other hand, result in a feeling of pride.

A boy of 17 years was asked what he remembered from the time of the trial:

> What I remember best from that time was that my mum was ill. It really got to us siblings. We sat there, we sat at every meal, when she ran out and threw up. Maybe my brother reacted the most to it. He was often with my mum. The difference between us was that he showed that he cared, while I did not show it at all.

The guilt stemmed from not having shown that he cared, even though his mother said that her health problems were not the children's fault. Their guilt implied that the children did not believe what she said. The same boy confessed to having stayed home from school for a period after one of the custody hearings. Following the court's decision he had moved to his mother's but was bored there and hated school. The boy described this period in retrospect as the basis on which he became known as a weaker person with a lower pain threshold and more concerned with his own illness. He felt that his health deteriorated because of the time he lived with his mother. He accused himself of having been stupid and not tough enough to cope with the difficult period.

At the end of the interview with a boy of 12 years, it was clear that he felt guilt regarding what he could say to his parents and his way of talking with them: *"It was nicer to talk to you than it was with mum and dad'*. When asked why he felt that way, the boy replied: *'It may be that I'm not so afraid of hurting the other parent"*.

Guilt refers to a specific action or non-action that implies some kind of violation, usually of a moral character. Shame is connected with the idea that we think of ourselves as bad people but is not primarily based on what we do (Ben-Ze'ev, 2000). For several of the children, it was that they blamed themselves for something they had done or for something they should have done. Their actions were visible proof of their loyalty to their parents. Children's negative assessments of their own actions mean that they regretted how they had behaved. None of the children expressed pride at what they had done.

To not be heard

Common to the four emotional expressions are children's experiences of not being heard. Both in the context of acute conflict situations and in relation to the conflicts that had persisted for several years, the children felt that the adults had not placed importance on what the children had said. This triggered aggressive feelings that were often succeeded by resignation, insecurity or sadness. Both directly and indirectly, the children expressed a hopelessness resulting from not being heard. In the same way as adults who invest their emotions in most intimate relationships, children are hurt most when they are failed in these relationships. In these situations where the children's opinions were not sought, the conflict between the parents took priority. Representative of the children's experience of not being heard was the statement from a 15-year-old boy when he was asked what advice he would give to other children in similar situations:

> They have to say where they want to stay, say what they mean. But it's not something they can do, for there will be a custody hearing anyway. For parents disagree anyway. So there is nothing you can do.

The concept of conflict

A number of authors through the ages have been concerned with conflict and its meaning. It was also considered to be important in social development, as emphasized by the great thinkers of antiquity. Gradually, conflict theories were also used in studies of families. The theory of conflict has been described partly as an independent theory and partly as a foundation for other theories.

Van der Vliert (1998) developed a conflict model in which both the structure and process items are included. The model distinguishes between what might trigger the frustrations between the parties and what conflicts between them can be about. Ekeland (2004) points out that the conflict itself is not negative or positive. What matters is what we do with it. He refines the academic understanding of the concept of conflict by analyzing seven assumptions he believes must be present for a situation to be referred to as a conflict. The assumptions he points to are differences, dependency, power, interests, needs, tensions and emotions.

> We can talk about a conflict when the differences between people who are dependent on each other, are experienced as irreconcilable and menacing in relation to their own needs and interests, and when it created tensions and emotions because one of the parties finds that the other party is using the power to influence the situation to their own advantage.
>
> (2004, p. 88)

Conflicts between parents

Amato and Keith (1991), Borrine, Handal, Brown and Searight (1991) and Emery (1999) are central family researchers from the United States and the UK. They point out that all conflicts are dynamic; they evolve. Scholars agree that parental conflicts pose a clear risk for children's psychosocial development.

Ekeland and Myklebust (1997) found in a study of mediation in family counselling offices that conflicts were highest in child custody cases. They found that the proportion of high-conflict cases was between 10 and 15%. The survey by Ådnanes, Pile, Jensberg, Husum and Rantalaiho (2011) suggests that the conflict level has changed little since 1996.

Child welfare workers' understanding of conflict can have a bearing on their encounter with parents in conflict and what they consider to be a risk for the children (Saini, Van Wert & Gofman, 2012). Child welfare workers lacked training in dealing with parents who argued when questioned about their relationships. The researchers concluded that much greater attention must be paid to how social services can help children who find themselves locked in a care situation characterized by parental conflicts about who the children will live with after a relationship breakup.

In my own survey, which takes a child welfare perspective on children's experiences with conflict-ridden divorce, a central finding is that parental conflicts deprived the children of necessary development support (Rød, 2010). Lack of development support is an important basis for action by child protection services. Some of the children found that they had to choose between moving to live by themselves or living without the necessary support of the residential parent. Further research would be needed to clarify whether the situation was so bad that the child should be taken into care.

Discussion

Most children in this survey were characterized by negative feelings along four different emotional ranges: aggressive, anxious and depressive feelings and a feeling of shame and guilt. The strength of what they express is indicative of how important parental conflict is for them. There is consistent emphasis on the children's experiences as stressful for their life situations even many years after the actual relationship breakup. Aggression towards one of the parents, aggression towards the judge who had not believed their narrative, horror and guilt for hurting their parents, as well as sadness and resignation for not being able to change the situation, are recurrent emotions. Most children emerged as vulnerable up to 8 years after the court proceedings, as evidenced by emotional strain. The fragility shows up as a combined result of the children's life experiences and level of resilience. The children have experienced parents who, over the years, have had and still have ongoing conflicts. The lessons apply to the critical events and conflict-ridden interaction patterns before, during and after child custody cases. Traumatic conflicts between the parents caused the anxiety to stick, and adolescents emerging from such childhood experiences primarily manifested the aggressive or depressive feelings that they had as children. The conflicts affected children who were still acting as messengers between their parents, having to weigh their words and actions so as not to be perceived as disloyal.

The children's experiences are reflective of a situation in which the parents' rights as adults in conflict take precedence over the parents' duties as parents. The traditional Protestant attitude places an emphasis on duty, and an attitude of self-sacrifice was considered most worthy. The ethics of rights has largely superseded the ethics of duty that prevailed in former times, and the situation of children in this survey is compared with that of other groups. A question that can be raised in this context is whether the children have had sufficient periods of stable and good care, implying that the law on child protection services (The Child Welfare Act, 1992) can be the basic criterion for daily care. Another question is whether the parents in such periods have practiced what family sociology defines as functional parenthood (Holter, 1975). Some of the features of this dimension are, for example, socialization of children to enable them to fulfil tasks and roles in the family and society, the transfer of knowledge and cultural values and norms, and the exercise of social control. The conflict between the parents may have resulted in the failure of some or all of these dimensions. For, as Rønbeck (2006) concludes, the lesson learned is that in a child, issues related to conflict will easily overshadow all other themes.

Because the pressures that children experience vary in scope and intensity, we can choose to minimize the risk of strain, or we can overdramatize it. The question is, what do the children's descriptions of their experiences convey about this risk? Are the experiences so intrusive that they affect and change children's development? And are the descriptions given by children such that we can decline to say anything certain about why child development is damaged by conflict-ridden breakups? Furstenberg and Cherlin (1991) maintain that it is worth caring about the negative long-term effects for children whose parents divorce but claim that these are significant only for a minority. Half of the children whose parents reported high conflict levels in connection with relationship breakups needed professional help as a result (Thuen, 1997). In contrast, for parents who were not prone to having conflicts between themselves, this figure was about 10%. Although a majority of the children in this study had aggressive feelings towards one of the parents, they experienced being caught in a conflict of loyalties between both parents. Buchanan, Maccoby and Dornbusch (1996) conclude from their research that such conflicts are particularly harmful to children. Based on this assumption, the children in our survey represent a group who are at greater risk of developing psychosocial problems.

The conflict between the parents was difficult to cope with while the parents lived together. Children subsequently act as the link between the parents, a link that needs to carry descriptions of and accusations against the parents. Whereas Buchanan et al. (1996) emphasize the different rules and boundaries set by parents as the basis for the development of antisocial behaviour, the children in our study were additionally characterized by the fact that they were the focus of the disagreement between the parents. The children's aggressive feelings are predominantly directed towards one parent. At the same time they embody an attitude of resignation and bitterness over the fact that their situation does not seem to change. On this basis the emotions from the depressive spectrum may be particularly applicable to these children. Repeated situations where children's unwelcome emotions are activated increase the opportunities for events over time that have an adverse effect on their development. The strong feelings emerge as reactions to the blocking of their basic psychological needs.

The children's feelings and reactions can also be explained by the fact that they had little or no information about the basis for the conflict between the parents. The conflict appeared meaningless to the children. Requesting the children's knowledge and assessment of the situation was even less common than providing the children with information. The children had little influence over questions such as how the contact arrangements should be adapted to their wants and needs. The aggressive feelings can be seen as a result of the children fundamentally perceiving that what they experienced was overlooked.

Their efforts to obtain attention for themselves and their needs were perceived by the children as being unimportant to their parents. Often, the children's aggressive feelings were related to sadness and dissatisfaction. Sadness is a passive emotion that has more to do with loss than with harm. The perception that the conflict is pointless can therefore add to the children's sense of being sad and upset.

The children frequently perceived that they were not being heard. The UN Convention on the Rights of the Child (CRC) (35), article 12, and the Norwegian Children Act (1981) sections 31 and 33 stipulate that children should be heard and that their opinion should be given weight. In 2003, the Norwegian government adopted the provisions of CRC into Norwegian law. When children are not heard, this is in conflict both with the provisions and the intentions of the current legislation. In the spirit of the times, where the CRC forms the legal basis in areas where the child's interests are affected, this finding may give rise to significant concern. When adult conflicts are sufficiently serious, it appears that the interest in decentration and care of one's own children is reduced to the extent that it threatens their development and health.

In this group of children, a majority tend to have polarized positions. The tendency can be random, based on the composition of the selection. It appears that over time, the children develop a stronger loyalty to the parent they live with. They have an understanding of the parent's situation and actions and the parents' contrasting decisions in situations that are important to them. The celebration of a child's confirmation is an example of a situation where the children show an understanding of the argument that they tend to develop a stronger loyalty to the residential parent. Some children do not show the same polarized standpoints. They are primarily concerned about not being disloyal towards one of the parents. Therefore, they try consistently to balance their opinions. With some children, the loyalty is due to disagreement with the resident parent on the parent's joint financial obligations. These children are concerned about financial justice, they do not believe the resident parent's opinions, and they suspect that the resident parent's choice is governed by financial motives.

When children like these – up to 8 years after their parents' legal divorce – experience a conflict that still interferes with and affects their everyday lives, it entails a significant strain on the children's development and quality of life. For most of the children in this survey, the burden that they carry over many years is so great that they may need professional help to work through their experiences.

There is much to indicate that the experiences of the children in this study correspond to those of children in other Nordic countries. For example, Ottosen, Stage and Jensen (2011) found that children subject to different child custody arrangements were highly dependent on their parents' ability to cooperate and on whether they lived in proximity to each other. If this was not the case, children became tired and had problems in achieving a coherent pattern in their daily lives. Parental conflicts led to difficulties in making arrangements with friends or participating in leisure activities. The authors emphasize that children react differently to the stress that shared custody arrangements necessarily entail and that it is therefore important to relate to the individual child.

Conclusion

This survey indicates that children cannot protect themselves against their parents' conflicts, even though the court has taken formal responsibility regarding the decision on child custody. For some children, the court process has contributed to the experience of being overlooked in questions that have a great impact on their quality of life and future prospects. Most children experience the court's treatment of the conflict and the actual decision as less important than the ongoing conflict between the parents. It is this that children are concerned with and from which they cannot escape. The parents' right to be in conflict has been given precedence over their duties as parents. The children find that they are scarcely seen and heard by their parents.

It is not the case that 'time heals all wounds'. On the contrary, several of the children developed more aggressive feelings towards one of the parents as the years passed so that, for them, each day was more characterized by sadness and resignation. Their feelings can be regarded as reactions to the blocking of their basic psychological needs, which over time is detrimental to their development and quality of life. It is therefore most important that the parents are able to handle disagreements in a constructive way. Although based on this survey we cannot reach a conclusion on what is the cause and what is the effect, there is reason to question whether the legal process is at all appropriate in parental conflicts. A custody case invites parties to behave in a competitive manner, which may be devastating to the relationship between the parties, even if the case is resolved. Because parenthood cannot be dissolved, it is important to facilitate ways to handle conflicts, which take account of both this and the child's dependence on functional parenthood. One solution might be to strengthen the arbitration scheme so that custody cases become rarer. Training courses for parents have been found to be helpful (Borren & Helland, 2013). Such courses after breakups are less prevalent in Norway, but studies from other countries show that they can have positive effects in assuaging the conflict.

For children in Nordic countries who find themselves in a situation similar to that of these children, meeting other children with similar life experiences can be helpful in processing their experiences. Today such groups exist in a few Norwegian municipalities. This service should involve systematic testing and evaluation. Also, research is needed on how parents manage to deal with disagreements among themselves while still managing to focus on children's psychological needs. For children, long-running parental conflicts are a persistent strain that increases the risk of developing problems and illnesses.

Norway needs to intensify alternative measures in at least two areas. First, it is important that as many parents as possible receive help in managing disagreements so that the child's daily life is characterized by care and stability. One promising method is family counselling through the Family Counselling Service, which has been given a positive assessment in high-conflict cases (Slettebø, Flacké, Flon, Negård & Oterholm, 2016). This method may also appear to have transfer value to less conflict-ridden relationships between couples. Second, a modification of the Family Counselling Service's mandate, whereby families would have to report to the service after 6 months or 2 years, for example, to assess whether visitation and residential arrangements were functioning in the child's best interests. This could provide better stability in the child's life, and arrangements could be changed that were not functioning well.

References

Ådnanes, M., Pile, G. M. D., Jensberg, H., Husum, T. L., & Rantalaiho, M. (2011). What characterizes the difficult issues in parenting mediation, and arbitration is the scheme well enough custom? *Focus on the Family*, *2*, 85–115.

Ahrons, C. (1980). Redefining the divorced family: A conceptual framework for post-divorce family systems reorganizations. *Social Work, 25*, 437–441.

Amato, P. R. (2000). The consequences of divorce for adults and children. *Journal of Marriage and Family, 62*, 1282.

Amato, P. R. (2014). The consequences of divorce for adults and children: An update. *Društvena istraživanja: Journal for General Social Issues, 1*, 5–24.

Amato, P. R., & Keith, B. (1991). Parental divorce and well-being of children: A meta-analysis. *Psychological Bulletin, 110*, 26–46.

Ary, D. V., Duncan, T. E., Duncan, S. C., & Hops, H. (1999). Adolescent problem behavior: The influence of parents and peers. *Behaviour Research and Therapy, 37*, 217–230.

Ben-Ze'ev, A. (2000). *The Subtlety of Emotions*. Cambridge, MA: The MIT Press.

Borren, I., & Helland, S. S. (2013). *Interventions to Allay Parents' Conflict*. Rapport 2013:6. Oslo: Folkehelseinstituttet.

Borrine, M. L., Handal, P. J., Brown, N. Y., & Searight, H. R. (1991). Family conflict and adjustment in intact, divorced, and blended families. *Journal of Consulting and Clinical Psychology, 59*, 753–755.

Breivik, K., & Olweus, D. (2006). Adolescent's adjustment in four post-divorce family structures single mother, stepfather, joint physical custody and single father families. *Journal of Divorce & Remarriage, 44*, 99–124.

Buchanan, C. M., Maccoby, E. E., & Dornbusch, S. M. (1996). *Adolescents After Divorce*. Cambridge, MA: Harvard University Press.

Ekeland, T. J. (2004). *Konflikt og konfliktforståelse for helse og sosialarbeidere*. Oslo: Gyldendal Akademisk.

Ekeland, T. J., & Myklebust, V. (1997). *Parental Mediation: User Perspective*. College: Møre Research.

Emery, R. (1999). *Marriage, Divorce and Children's Adjustment*. London: Sage.

Furstenberg, F. F., & Cherlin, A. J. (1991). *Divided Families. What Happens to Children When Parents Part?* Cambridge, MA: Harvard University Press.

Haagensen, K. M. (2014). *Nordic Statistical Yearbook 2014*. København: Norden.

Hansagi, H., Brant, L., & Andreasson, S. (2000). Parental divorce: Psychosocial well-being, mental health and morality during youth and young adulthood. A longitudinal study of Swedish conscripts. *European Journal of Public Health, 10*, 86–92.

Holter, H. (Ed.). (1975). *The Family in Class Society*. Oslo: Pax Forlag.

Jenkins, J., Simpson, A., Rabash, J., & O'Connor, T. G. (2005). Mutual influence of marital conflict and children's behavior problems: Shared and nonshared family risks. *Child Development, 76*(1), 24–39.

Jensen, A.M. (1999) Barn og samboerskap: Et uutforsket minefelt? *Tidsskrift for Velferdsforskning*,2 (2), 116-125.

Kelly, J. B. (2000). Children's adjustment in conflicted marriage and divorce: A decade review of research. *Journal of the American Academy of Child & Adolescent Psychiatry, 39*, 963–973.

Lamb, M. E., Sternberg, K. J., & Thompson, R. A. (1997). The effects of divorce and custody arrangements on children's behavior, development, and adjustment. *Family and Conciliation Courts Review, 35*(4), 393–404.

Lov om barneverntjenester/The Child Welfare Act. (1992). https://lovdata.no/dokument/NL/lov/1992-07-17-100

Lov om barn og foreldre/The Children Act. (1981). https://lovdata.no/dokument/NL/lov/1981-04-08-7

Moxnes, K., Haugen, G. M. D., & Holter, T. (1999). *Skilsmissens virkning på barn. Foreldres oppfatning av skilsmissens konsekvenser for deres barn.* Trondheim: Allforsk.

Nævdal, F., & Thuen, F. (2004). Residence arrangements and well-being: A study of Norwegian adolescents. *Scandinavian Journal of Psychology, 45*, 363–371.

Ottosen, M. H., Stage, M. H. S., & Jensen, H. S. (2011). *Børn i deleordninger.* København: SFI. Det Nationale Forskningscenter for Velfærd.

Paradis, A. D., Reinherz, H. Z., Giaconia, R., Beardslee, W. R., Ward, K., & Fitzmaurica, G. M. (2009). Long-term impact of family arguments and physical violence on adult functioning at age 30 years: Findings from the Simmins Longitudinal Study. *Journal of the American Academy of Child & Adolescent Psychiatry, 48*, 290–298.

Rød, P. A. (2010). High-conflict parental divorce – The venue for child protection? *Focus on the Family, 2*, 92–114.

Rød, P. A., Ekeland, T. J., & Thuen, F. (2008). Barns erfaring med konfliktfylte samlivsbrudd: Problemforståelse og følelsesmessige reaksjoner. *Tidsskrift for Norsk Psykologforening, 5*, 555–562.

Rønbeck, K. (2006). Parents in conflict-negotiation-based case kyndighets work by children's law. *Tidsskrift for Norsk Psykologforening, 43*, 338–346.

Saini, M., Van Wert, M., & Gofman, J. (2012). Parent-child supervised visitation within child welfare and custody dispute contexts: An exploratory comparison of two distinct models of practice. *Children and Youth Services Review, 34*(1), 164–168.

Slettebø, T., Flacké, A., de Flon, H., Negård, I. L., & Oterholm, I. (2016). *Familieråd i familievernet. Evaluering av et pilotprosjekt 2013–2015.* VID, Rapport 2016/3.

Statistisk Sentralbyrå (SSB), Norge. (2015). https://www.ssb.no/befolkning/artikler-og-publikasjoner/dette-er-norge-2015

Størksen, I., Røysamb, E., Holmen, T. L., & Tambs, K. (2006). Adolescent adjustment and well-being: Effects of parental divorce and distress. *Scandinavian Journal of Psychology, 47*(1), 75–84.

Thuen, F. (1997). *Life After the Divorce: Psychological Reactions to the Breakups.* Report No. 1. Bergen: Department of Social Psychology, University of Bergen.

Thuen, F. (2004). *Livet som deltidsforeldre.* Bergen: Fagbokforlaget.

United Nations. (1989). *Convention on the Rights of the Child. http://www.ohchr.org/EN/ProfessionalInterest/Pages/CRC.aspx*

Van de Vliert, E. (1998). Conflict and conflict management. In P. H. D. Drenth, H. Theierry, C. J. de Wollf (Eds.), *Handbook of Work and Organizational Psychology: Personnel Psychology.* East Sussex: Psychology Press, s. 351–376.

Wallerstein, J., & Kelly, J. B. (1980). *Surviving the Break Up: How Children and Parents Cope With Divorce.* New York: Basic Books.

Wallerstein, J., Lewis J., & Blakeslee, S. (2000). *The Unexpected Legacy of Divorce: The Twenty-Five Years Landmark Study.* New York: Hyperion.

Ware, H. S., Jouriles, E. N., Spiller, L. C., McDonald, R., Swank, P. R., & Norwood, W. D. (2001). Conduct problems among children at battered women's shelters: Prevalence and stability of maternal reports. *Journal of Family Violence, 16*, 291–307.

8 "We have this family 'under the microscope' so to speak"

Schools, child abuse and family support

Ylva Odenbring, Thomas Johansson and Johannes Lunneblad

Introduction

Sweden was the first country in the world to ban child abuse in 1979 (Save the Children, 2014), yet research shows that approximately one-fifth of Swedish children still experience child abuse (Annerbäck, Wingren, Svedin & Gustafsson, 2010). The school is one of the institutions in society that should ensure children's and adolescent's health and well-being. This means that schools in Sweden are required by the Social Services Act (*Socialtjänstlagen*) to report any suspicion of students being exposed to domestic violence, maltreatment or lack of parental care (Socialstyrelsen, 2014). Furthermore, the national curriculum states that it is the principal's responsibility to ensure that students' health develops in line with their needs and that they get all the support needed (Skolverket, 2011). If the student has any problems or difficulties, it is also the school's responsibility to establish a dialogical relation with the parents.

In this chapter the aim is to explore how three Swedish secondary schools define and classify students exposed to violence and/or abuse. The study extends the literature about youth victimization by examining school officials' narratives about how schools involve and collaborate with families, social services or the police to support students who are suspected of having been exposed to domestic violence. The following research questions have guided the study:

- How do school officials classify students as suffering domestic violence?
- What experiences do school officials have from their collaboration with families, social services or the police?

Child abuse and school

Harassment and violations often have negative effects on youth and children, increasing their risks of adverse outcomes such as school dropout, drug use and criminal behaviour (Koo, Peguero & Shekarkhar, 2012). The research literature has shown that there is a strong connection between the school environment and school violence. Effective and safe schools are characterized by clear goals, positive expectations of students' achievements and close collaboration with parents (Sprague & Walker, 2005).

The research literature on abused children and school shows that maltreated children often have more academic and behavioural problems in school than other children. Teachers, meeting the children on a daily basis, consequently have a unique opportunity to identify problems in children's lives (Jonson-Reid et al., 2007). However, other findings indicate that cases of abuse reported by teachers are considerably less likely to be substantiated than reports from other professionals (King & Scott, 2014). Cases reported by teachers also differed in focus from those reported by other professionals. Teachers tended to report the physical, emotional and behavioural problems of the child, whereas other professionals reported risk factors associated with the performance of the family and the primary caregiver. In serious cases concerning child abuse in families with documented problems, however, teachers were as likely as other professionals to report risk factors associated with the family.

The research literature on parental involvement in schools suggests that trust is a key to engaging parents and building good relationships among students, parents, teachers and other school authorities (Halgunseth, 2009; Durand, 2011; Jeynes, 2012). Frequent opportunities to interact and meet are necessary conditions to build this trust and to provide parents with some influence in the school (Adams, Forsyth & Mitchell, 2009). Research also indicates that parental involvement is essential for children's learning and familial well-being (Halgunseth, 2009). Furthermore, schools' support of and positive relations with parents have positive outcomes for the future and well-being of vulnerable students (Weitz Spånberger, 2011). Schools' support is essential to both parents and students because families and children can receive social and emotional support, which also can protect children from being neglected (McWilliam, 2003; Lareau, 2011).

Research also shows that families' social background is essential to what kind of support they are offered by the school. Especially disadvantaged families may not be aware of the support that the schools and social services can provide (Lareau, 2015). Research also shows a lower level of tolerance in schools of abuse committed by foreign-born people. Parents born outside of Sweden were reported with less visible evidence, such as skin wounds or other physical damage to the child, than parents born in Sweden (BRÅ, 2011). Several factors can intervene in the collaboration between schools and parents, and there are different mechanisms that can disturb and threaten the trust relation between parents and the school. The relationship between ethnic minority parents and schools reveals a complex and ambivalent picture. Scandinavian research indicates that children growing up in minority families are considered particularly problematic by school officials at schools (Lunneblad & Johansson, 2012; Kryger, 2015). As a result minority parents are often marginalized and ignored when trying to discuss their children's situations in school. For example, it is common that parents with immigrant backgrounds and their family problems are framed in relation to culture and ethnicity, whereas the parents of majority backgrounds are discussed in terms of social problems (Lunneblad & Johansson, 2012).

Research focusing on the school context within the wider institutional context of domestic violence and abuse is still lacking. This chapter hopes to contribute with new knowledge on how children at risk of suffering in their home environments are identified and supported in schools and how school officials involve and collaborate with parents and other professionals to support these students.

Method, sample and methodology

This study was designed and constructed as a case study of three Swedish secondary schools located in southern Sweden. Data were drawn from interviews with principals, school nurses, counsellors and other key school officials in the schools' student health team meetings. The three schools selected for the study are located in different geographical and socio-economic areas. These schools were selected to allow us to examine how narratives emerge in different urban contexts of social, ethnic and economic inequalities as well to achieve variation in the school officials' responses and strategies (Bunar, 2011). The differences found between the schools will only be highlighted when they help us further develop our analysis of the empirical material. The schools are given the pseudonyms Tulip school, Water Lily school and Hogweed school in the study.

Tulip school is located in a smaller town with a population of 20,000. The school is located in a relatively mixed neighbourhood of families with different socio-economic and cultural backgrounds. Water Lily school and Hogweed school are both located in one of Sweden's major metropolitan areas. Water Lily school is located in a white, middle-class area, whereas Hogweed school is located in a socially disadvantaged, multicultural neighbourhood. A majority of the students at Hogweed school has a foreign background with ancestry in countries such as Eritrea, Lebanon, Iran, Iraq, Palestine, Somalia, Syria, Pakistan or the Balkan states.

Methodologically, we start by taking a discourse analytical perspective on the different stories and narratives (Foucault, 2000; Laclau & Mouffe, 2001). The study is influenced by discourse theory in a broader sense, but we also try to place the different narratives and discourses within a sociological framework (Wodak & Krzyzanowski, 2008). We are interested in theoretically exploring how the professionals' narratives connect to general societal and cultural discourses on violence, victimization and social welfare and how the key professionals' categorize situations related to domestic violence. We also want to explore how key professionals describe their collaboration with families, social services or the police.

To contextualize and place the narratives into an institutional framework, and to analyze and explain policy enactment in the investigated schools, we use the contextual dimensions proposed by Ball, Maguire, Braun, Hoskins and Perryman (2012): *situated context*, *professional culture*, *material context* and *external context*. Situated context refers to contextual aspects such as school setting and intake. Professional culture refers to teachers' shared values and commitments within the school and how they shape policy enactments. The professional culture also refers to norms, values and school climate and to what kinds of 'problems' the school has to face. Material context refers to place, space and segregation, and it also relates to aspects such as school buildings, budgets, levels of staffing and infrastructure. The external context includes aspects such as legal requirements and responsibilities and the degree and quality of support from local authorities. These four dimensions sometimes overlap and interconnect. In this chapter we focus on three of the contextual dimensions: professional culture, external context and material context.

Dealing with violence entails involving other professionals from different agencies. We are especially interested in how these different systems collide and form the ground for how school officials talk about child abuse. We also want to explore how key professionals describe their collaboration with families, social services or the police. We are also interested in what kinds of explanations are given for parents' neglect or violent behaviour. In our analysis of the professionals' narratives, two main themes related to domestic violence emerged in the empirical analysis. The results will be organized according the following themes: *domestic abuse and child neglect* and *honour violence*. In our analysis, we discuss how these discourses appear in the key officials' narratives and how different categories are related to more general societal discourses.

Results: narratives of domestic violence and contexts

This part of the chapter will use the empirical material to examine school officials' narratives about how they involve and collaborate with families, social services or the police to support students who are suspected of having been exposed to domestic violence. The school officials talked about child abuse on two different levels: a more general level, which included lack of adequate parental care, physical violence, child labour or expulsion from the home and a more specific level centred on honour violence.

Domestic abuse and child neglect

School officials' narratives of children beaten by their parents were often related to an external context and a more general societal discourse about child abuse, which includes both physical and psychological abuse (Harter & Taylor, 2000). The participants talked about the different forms of child abuse that students were exposed to and the various ways child abuse came to the schools' attention. Sometimes the pupils told the school counsellor or a teacher what had happened to them and asked for help; in other cases an adult (whether at the school or not) reported that a child had been abused. The counsellor at Water Lily school told about an incident when a girl asked him for help after she had been beaten by her mother with a broomstick and had bruises on her legs and the soles of her feet. The school immediately contacted social services, who contacted the parent: "They [the social services] talked to the mom and they agreed that she was going to get in touch with the social services and get family support" (Counsellor, Water Lily school). The school nurse at the same school said that another girl had been hit by her father, and again the school decided to contact the social services and file a report.

SCHOOL NURSE: There was another child who told us and she was removed from her family. Her teacher or some assistant took care of her during the weekend. And after that she was removed to her grandparents in another town. . . . The dad had beaten her and she had to clean the house, she was more or less a maid. But, it was mainly because of the child abuse that we filed a report. The girl lives at home today, but we have this family 'under the microscope', so to speak.

In these cases the children told someone at the school about their home situation, but the school officials said social services also sometimes makes home visits to families such as single parents, lonely parents, families in financial difficulties or newly arrived refugees to check on how they are doing and offer them support. At Water Lily school, families can also get extra support through a family worker who also does home visits and works with a special program called family check-up. Based on research from the United States, this program offers families the opportunity to be video-recorded in their homes and then watch the video recordings together with the family worker and discuss how they can solve any problems in the family. Consequently the external context, that is, local authorities such as the social services, are related to and interconnect with the professional culture in school, offering support to certain families to prevent domestic maltreatment (Ball et al., 2012).

The narratives about children who were physically hurt often overlapped with those about parental neglect. Some schools in Sweden have a school assistant who meets and socializes informally with the students in the school cafeteria, in the corridors and in the canteen. At Tulip school, the school assistant and school nurse both mentioned one boy who had been beaten, and although social services had been involved in the case several times, nothing happened. Both participants expressed general resignation with the social services and the lack of support for abused children.

SCHOOL ASSISTANT: He was beaten with wooden handles at home. This was what happened. Sometimes it feels hopeless. Once we had a boy who slept in a cellar and in staircases and on park benches

SCHOOL NURSE: He was living with his foster dad who had thrown him out. We drove to the social services office and brought this boy there, but nothing really happened.

SCHOOL ASSISTANT: We filed a big new report because I had been in touch with him during the weekend, and he had said that he was going to throw himself in front of a truck on the expressway. This really set things going.

SCHOOL NURSE: He was then removed from the foster home and stayed somewhere else for a short period of time.

The narratives also contain situations when the school discovers alcoholism or drug problems in the children's home. In most cases, the teachers discover that something is wrong, for instance, when a parent arrives at the school smelling of alcohol, but in some cases the children tell the teacher themselves. Sometimes parents of other children discover that something is wrong in the children's home environment, as expressed by the counselor at Tulip school.

> COUNSELLOR: There was actually a mother who went to the social services and filed a report on another family. Her child was at this family's house and when she went there to pick up her child there was a he . . . yes it was noisy, there was almost fighting, and there was a lot of alcohol on the tables and the mother and father were pretty wasted, so she filed a report, no, she phoned the head teacher there, who filed a report. They brought this friend to their home . . . She couldn't stay there [with the parents], so this mother took the responsibility . . . After that they filed a report to the social services and after that they made an investigation. I don't know what happened after that, but the mother who filed the report is not very popular with the other family, although it was the school that made the official report.

In this example the parents noticed that something was wrong in another family, which induced the school to make a report. This resulted in an investigation by social services. The girl stayed at home and was not removed from her home, but the family is now monitored by social services. These results correspond with results from those of Weitz Spånberger (2011). According to this study only a few children are removed from their homes because of lack of adequate parental care or domestic violence. The majority of children who are placed in foster homes are removed because of their own psychosocial health or because of conflicts with the parents.

In line with the law and the Social Services Act, schools must contact social services as soon as they suspect that something is wrong in the home. Respondents at Tulip school say they always contact social services before they contact the police in these cases. However, the kind of support individual students and families receive varied. At Water Lily school, the families were given family support or were introduced to the family check-up program, but at Tulip school the school officials described that the cooperation with social services does not work very well, and the individual child's right to support from social services seemed more or less absent.

In our material hardly any of the professionals express uncertainty about whether they should file a report to social services. Nor do the professionals talk explicitly about what they have done to help children exposed to maltreatment, besides trying to develop good relations with the parents. One possible explanation is that school professionals conceptualize domestic child maltreatment as an issue for social services and consider that the school's responsibility is fulfilled when a report is made. Our results suggest that there is a clearer boundary in secondary school between the school's responsibility and social service's responsibility. However, the secondary school professionals also wanted more information about what had happened with the report they made.

Swedish researcher Blomqvist (2012), who has investigated the collaboration processes among school, family, social services and child and youth psychiatric care (BUP), showed similar findings. Both school and social services professionals report that BUP seems to engage in endless investigations and mappings of problems and planned action plans. They feel that everyone is constantly waiting for something to happen. Professionals at BUP, on the other hand, are satisfied with their collaboration with the school and social services. According to Blomqvist (2012), these results must be understood in the light of schools' and social services' limited opportunities to influence BUP. Moreover, BUP has a form of veto over whether or not to offer psychiatric care to a particular child. This means that children are sometimes on a waiting list to get medical help.

The collaboration between the school and social services in the present study should also be understood in the light of the social services' requirement to protect confidentiality. When social services takes over a case, the school has no access to information about the progress of the case. Several respondents in the study expressed frustration with this lack of information and said they sometimes file another report in an effort to ensure that something would actually happen, even when social services was still working on the case. Hence, the narratives indicate that the external context sometimes obstructs and counteracts an effective professional culture in school (Ball et al., 2012).

Thus, domestic abuse and child neglect are seen to be framed within a discourse on school control and/or support of the family. The focus is mostly directed towards the parents and their 'problematic' behaviour. In one way, this contributes to an externalization of the 'problem'. Consequently, the problem has to be solved in collaboration with social services and sometimes also with the police. The next section focuses on how one particular category of violence, honour violence, is framed and dealt with.

Honour violence

At Hogweed school and Tulip school the informants talked about pupils with parents who have origins in western Asia, south-western Asia and eastern Africa being exposed to honour violence. Common in these narratives of honour violence was the impression that these students were more controlled by their families than their peers. These narratives were often related to a common discourse on violence and crimes committed to protect or re-establish the so-called honour of a family and/or a community (Elakkary, Franke, Shokri, Hartwig, Tsokos & Püschel, 2014). These narratives were also connected to the professional culture and the material context as they refer to problems the schools have to face: pupils positioned within discourses on honour crime cultures and general urban segregation (Ball et al., 2012).

In 2011 the Swedish government assigned the county administration in Östergötland to contribute information and education about honour violence among young people. This assignment extended over 2 years. The aim was to inform and educate youth as well as schoolteachers about these issues (Länsstyrelsen Östergötland, 2012, 2013). Today, several schools in Sweden send their professionals to attend courses and programs that focus on honour-related violence. At Tulip school and Hogweed school staff members have participated in similar courses and programs, putting the issue of honour violence on the agenda, framing certain types of violence as a specific social problem important to counteract and influencing the professional culture at school (Ball et al., 2012).

Hogweed school has been part of a similar program. One part of this program aims to engage immigrant parents through the use pictures of families. Intended to be quite neutral, the pictures illustrate aspects of family such as the family tree, the three-generation perspective and the nuclear family versus a larger or extended family and are meant to symbolize the norms, beliefs and expectations of a family in the new society. This method generates different discussions on families, norms and values, often leading to questions around the control of girls and how to maintain family honour in the new country.

COUNSELLOR: Quite a few are controlled in their life, the girls. It's considered to be so normal that there is a certain openness about it. Even I, as staff, get questions like, "but what kind of parents wouldn't arrange a marriage, what parents let their daughter go out with anyone and someone you don't know, what kind of parents would accept their children to live in a homosexual relationship and what kind of parents would let their daughters to be out after school without keeping track of where she is?"

Respondents said that younger siblings expressed concern when their older siblings were dating and had secret boyfriends and girlfriends. The siblings gained considerable insights about their older sibling's secrets lives through Facebook and Instagram, which created an ethical dilemma for them. "Am I going to keep it a secret, or do I have to tell Mum and Dad?"

COUNSELLOR: When pupils have contacted the teacher or me and tell me about it, it is often at a stage when they can't keep it to themselves anymore. There have been occasions when pupils have come here with a packed suitcase, because they can't go home. Quite often there has been a secret boyfriend involved, and they have been living a double life.

According to the respondents, in situations such as this, the school immediately contacts social services. When a girl is considered to be in danger, social services sometimes removes her from her home. Often this is unexpected for the classmates and the teachers, and no one knows where the girl is located after that, which makes it difficult to talk about what actually happened. There is a silence about these girls. However, the counsellor at Hogweek school told us that social pressure often leads these girls to return home and to deny what they had earlier told the school and the social services.

COUNSELLOR: Although young people can be very spontaneous and impulsive, I've never experienced that a girl has taken this step impulsively. When we've seen it coming it is well thought out. Then, it is quite common that the girls take everything back shortly afterwards, that you become very ashamed and feel guilty that you have broken the loyalty to the family. So, when you are sitting there with the social workers they just say "[N]o, no, no, I don't know where you got this from."

At Tulip school the narratives of honour crimes were not as frequent, but the school assistant described a similar incident when the school had to call the police.

SCHOOL ASSISTANT: We had a father who stepped in here and beat his daughter . . . This is the only time we have had this kind of crime, honour crime that we know of . . . She was taken into custody and lived in a protected accommodation somewhere, but then she decided to move back home. She was most certainly attracted to both the one and the other. She was allowed to go to the prom and graduation together with her Swedish boyfriend. After that the Swedish boyfriend was threatened and she was sent to her home country and got a boyfriend from that country . . . It was really important that she had this, a boyfriend from Lebanon, it was put on Facebook and everything.

The school assistant described how this girl went to Lebanon with her mother during the summer break and returned to Sweden after that. She continued her studies in upper-secondary school but had to break up with her Swedish boyfriend. Moreover, the Swedish boyfriend was threatened several times by her brothers and had to cut off all contact with his ex-girlfriend. The school assistant was also threatened, but she never made a police report. Despite several witnesses stating that this girl had been beaten by her father at the school cafeteria, on the stairs at the school's main entrance, and in their car, both the father and the girl denied everything when the case went to court.

According to some researchers, families from honour-based social networks – afraid of jeopardizing their membership in a specific group and in relation to the material context that is marginalized in the new country – sometimes feel that they have to continue with or even strengthen the cultural practices situated in their former homeland (Meetoo & Mirza, 2007). In honour-based social networks women are considered to be a man's property and are therefore the symbol of the family's honour. In most cases honour-based violence is committed against a female by her male relatives (Elakkary et al., 2014). Contemporary research, however, is critical of the one-sided assumptions that honour violence is based on Islamic values and/or is distinguishable from other forms of domestic violence against women (de los Reyes, Eduards & Sundevall, 2013). Honour crimes and killings have no religious basis and have been condemned by several Islamic leaders. This kind of violence has been committed in Druze, Christian and Muslim communities and sometimes also in Jewish communities (Elakkary et al., 2014). Honour crimes have been documented in several countries around the world: Afghanistan, Bangladesh, Brazil, Ecuador, Egypt, India, Iran, Israel, Italy, Jordan, Lebanon, Morocco, Norway, Pakistan, Peru,

Sweden, Turkey, Uganda, the UK and the United States (Meetoo & Mirza, 2007; Elakkary et al., 2014).

As Meetoo and Mirza (2007) argue, domestic violence cuts across ethnicity, class, religion and age, and violence against women expresses a system of power. Psychological dimensions also have to been taken into consideration to understand the relationships among values, family, masculinity and violence. Of course, not all fathers and families within a specific cultural environment support and defend these kinds of criminal acts (Johansson, 2009). In our data there are also examples of what the respondents frame as issues around honour that also can be understood as parents simply asking for advice, as expressed by the counselor at Hogweed school.

> COUNSELLOR: Sometimes families make a compromise [about the secret relationship] . . . A girl's father came to the school and said "I know that my daughter is no longer a student here, but now I do not know how to handle this, can you advise me? After all you know my daughters." This shows, in a way, that you somehow want to make a change.

This parent's wish to receive advice and support his daughter can be understood in light of institutional parental involvement in which the relationship between the parent and school is formalized. This marks new modes of governing the child, the family and education.

In this section we have looked more closely at cases understood in terms of the category of honour violence. Although this category also includes different forms of violence against children, such as abuse and severe neglect, it clearly stands out as a distinct explanation for some parents' violent behaviour. This violence, however, is understood and framed in terms of cultural explanations. When Swedish parents abuse and neglect their children, it is understood and explained in terms of social problems, or psychological and psychiatric problems, whereas immigrant parents' behaviours are framed and explained in terms of culture or ethnicity and often as honour violence.

Discussion

Regardless of the form of child abuse, professional culture and external context dominated the informants' narratives. The schools' *professional culture*, that is, the school officials' values and commitments to the students' well-being, shapes and frames their policy enactments. The results reveal how schools work with various authorities to support pupils who are victims. But the collaboration with other authorities, such as social services, also meant that officials at school lost insight into the situation and that they lost the initiative to act. This was something that was perceived as a disadvantage by the officials at school and that made collaboration with other authorities difficult. The professional culture overlaps with the dimension of *external context* by including parents, social services, the police and the justice system. Laws and policy constitute the documents of the professional culture. The Social Service Act, the national curriculum and the Convention of the Rights of the Child (United Nations, 1990) clearly influence the content of the narratives.

The key officials' talk about controlled children had a clearly gendered focus. Only girls were mentioned as being at risk of honour violence, although boys are also sometimes subject to this kind of violence. Our results indicate that general societal understandings of violence against women and women's vulnerability are strengthened in the narratives about honour violence. This discourse connects to *material context* and relates to aspects such as place, space and segregation. Moreover this discourse also connects to the *professional culture* as it refers to problems the schools have to face. School officials at Tulip school and Hogweed school account that they have students who are positioned within discourses on honour crime cultures. This might also explain why the participants in those schools stress this form of child abuse.

This also shows the importance of considering how the material context influences the relation between parents and school. Previous research has revealed that the relationship between ethnic minority parents and schools in Sweden is complex. There are indications that minority parents have specific difficulties in relation to their children's schooling. The situation these parents face is, however, better understood in light of their socio-economic position, their social status and limited knowledge and use of the majority language than in relation to ethnicity as a single factor. Research also shows that minority parents feel marginalized and ignored in their communication with schools (Lunneblad & Johansson, 2012).

All three schools related to the external culture, involving, for example, families in one way or another when children had been exposed to child abuse. Tulip school and Hogweed school worked with family support or family involvement programs to collaborate with and involve the families. At Water Lily school narratives about families were articulated through discourses about vulnerable families. What we can see here is how the discourse of the vulnerable family is articulated through nodal points such as the single parent, the lonely parent and the refugee family (Laclau & Mouffe, 2001). Surprisingly, the picture material that is used in Hogweed school's family involvement program portrays the nuclear family as the only family form, presenting what could be understood as normative aspects of how a family should be constructed and understood. Family researchers are critical of this one-sided picture of family because many children grow up in different family constellations (Johansson, 2009).

Conclusion

This chapter has examined how school officials label and categorize students in need of support and protection. The results show that the professionals' narratives revolve around two main themes: *domestic abuse and child neglect* and *honour violence*. Domestic abuse and child neglect are often framed within a discourse on parents and their 'problematic' behaviour. This framing contributes to an externalization of the 'problem'. Consequently, the problem has to be solved in collaboration with social services and sometimes also with the police. When parents categorized as Swedish abuse their children, it is understood and explained in terms of social or psychological problems, whereas parents' categorized as immigrants behaviours are framed and explained in terms of culture or ethnicity and as honour violence. Employing discourse analysis we understood this as a contradictory discourse in regard to schools' obligations to prevent ethnical and cultural stereotypes. Without wishing to diminish the seriousness of the oppression of the individual in the name of honour, there is a risk that the discourse on honour-related violence locates gender oppression in specific cultural places, where it is said to constitute a legitimate practice. Furthermore, there is also a risk that the violence and control among people identified as Swedes are made invisible and normalized as an exception to a general rule, whereas violence among immigrants is connected to and constructed as an aspect of their culture.

References

Adams, C. M., Forsyth, P. B., & Mitchell, R. M. (2009). The formation of parent-school trust: A multilevel analysis. *Educational Administration Quarterly*, *45*(1), 4–33.

Annerbäck, E. M., Wingren, G., Svedin, C. G., & Gustafsson, P. A. (2010). Prevalence and characteristics of child physical abuse in Sweden–Findings from a population-based youth survey. *Acta Paediatrica*, *99*(8), 1229–1236.

Ball, S. J., Maguire, M., Braun, A., Hoskins, K., & Perryman, J. (2012). *How Schools do Policy: Policy Enactments in Secondary Schools.* London: Routledge.

Blomqvist, C. (2012). *Samarbete med förhinder: om samarbete mellan BUP, socialtjänst, skola och familj* [*Collaboration With Counterchecks: On Collaboration Between Child Psychiatry, Social Services, School and the Family*]. Gothenburg: PhD dissertation, Gothenburg University.

BRÅ. (2011). *Den polisanmälda barnmisshandeln: utvecklingen fram till 2009* [*The Police Notficated Child Abuse: Developments Up to 2009*]. Stockholm: Brottsförebyggande rådet.

Bunar, N. (2011). Multicultural urban schools in Sweden and their communities: Social predicaments, the power of stigma, and relational dilemmas. *Urban Education*, *46*(2), 141–164.

de los Reyes, P., Eduards, M., & Sundevall, F. (Eds.). (2013). *Internationella relationer – könskritiska perspektiv* [*International Relations – Gender Critical Perspectives*]. Stockholm: Liber.

DePanfilis, D. (2006). *Child Neglect: A Guide for Prevention, Assessment, and Intervention.* U.S. Department of Health and Human Services Child Abuse and Neglect User Manual Series. Retrieved on 8 September 2015, from www.childwelfare.gov/pubs/usermanuals/neglect/neglect.pdf

DePanfilis, D., & Dubowitz, H. (2005). Family connections: A program for preventing child neglect. *Child Maltreatment*, *10*(2), 108–123.

Durand, T. M. (2011). Latina mothers' cultural believes about their children, parental roles and education: Implications for effective and empowering home-school partnerships. *The Urban Review*, *43*, 255–278.

Elakkary, S., Franke, B., Shokri, D., Hartwig, S., Tsokos, M., & Püschel, K. (2014). Honor crimes: Review and proposed definition. *Forensic Science, Medicine, and Pathology*, *10*(1), 76–82.

Foucault, M. (2000). *The Archaeology of Knowledge*. London: Routledge [Original published in 1969].

Halgunseth, L. (2009). Family engagement, diverse families, and early childhood education programs: An integrated review of the literature. *YC Young Children*, *64*(5), 56.

Harter, S. L., & Taylor, T. L. (2000). Parental alcoholism, child abuse, and adult adjustment. *Journal of Substance Abuse*, *11*(1), 31–44.

Jeynes, W. (2012). A meta-analysis of the efficacy of different types of parental involvement programs for urban students. *Urban Education*, *47*(4), 706–742.

Johansson, T. (2009). *Familjeliv* [*Family Life*]. Stockholm: Liber.

Jonson-Reid, M., Kim, J., Barolak, M., Citerman, B., Laudel, C., Essma, A., & Thomas, C. (2007). Maltreated children in schools: The interface of school social work and child welfare. *Children & Schools*, *29*(3), 182–191.

King, C. B., & Scott, K. L. (2014). Why are suspected cases of child maltreatment referred by educators so often unsubstantiated? *Child Abuse & Neglect*, *38*(1), 1–10.

Koo, D. J., Peguero, A. A., & Shekarkhar, Z. (2012). Gender, immigration, and school victimization. *Victims & Offenders*, *7*, 77–96.

Kryger, N. (2015). Barndomskonstruktioner i skole-hjem-relationen i Danmark – et kritisk blik [Constructions of childhood in the school and home relation in Denmark – A critical perspective]. *Barn*, *1*, 9–23.

Laclau, E., & Mouffe, C. (2001). *Hegemony and Socialist Strategy. Towards a Radical Democratic Politics*. London: Verso [Original published 1985].

Länsstyrelsen Östergötland. (2012). *Våga göra skillnad* [*Dare to Make a Difference*]. Report 2012:24. Linköping: Länsstyrelsen Östergötland.

Länsstyrelsen Östergötland. (2013). *Gift mot sin vilja* [*Married Against Your Will*]. Report 2013:10. Linköping: Länsstyrelsen Östergötland.

Lareau, A. (2011). *Unequal Childhoods: Class, Race, and Family Life*. Berkeley: University of California Press.

Lareau, A. (2015). Cultural knowledge and social inequality. *American Sociological Review*, *80*(1), 1–27.

Lunneblad, J., & Johansson, T. (2012). Learning from each other? Multicultural pedagogy, parental education and governance. *Race Ethnicity and Education*, *15*(5), 705–723.

McWilliam, E. L. (2003). The vulnerable child as a pedagogical subject. *Journal of Curriculum Theorizing*, *19*(2), 35–44.

Meetoo, V., & Mirza, H. S. (2007). There is nothing 'honourable' about honour killings. Gender, violence and the limits of multiculturalism. *Women's Studies International Forum*, *30*(3), 187–200.

Save the Children [Rädda barnen]. (2014). Förbjud aga i alla länder [*Ban Child Abuse in All Countries*]. Retrieved on 12 December 2014, from www.raddabarnen.se/barnaga/

Skolverket. (2011). *Läroplan för grundskolan, förskoleklassen och fritidshemmet 2011* [*Curriculum for the Compulsory School, Preschool Class and the Recreation Centre, 2011*]. Stockholm: Skolverket.

Socialstyrelsen. (2014). *Anmälan till socialnämnden vid kännedom eller misstanke om att ett barn far illa* [*Reports to the Social Services at Knowledge or Suspicion that a Child Is Being Abused*]. Retrieved on 2 July 2014, from www.socialstyrelsen.se/barnochfamilj/barnsomfarilla/anmalanarbarnfarilla.

Sprague, J. R., & Walker, H. M. (2005). *Safe and Healthy Schools: Practical Prevention Strategies.* New York: Guilford Press.

United Nations. (1990). *Convention of the Rights of the Child.* New York: United Nations.

Weitz Spånberger, Y. (2011). *Ungas erfarenheter av skola, samhällsvård och vuxenblivande: en studie av fem livsberättelser* [*Young People's Experiences of School, Out-of-Home Care and Transitions to Adulthood: A Study of Five Life Stories*]. PhD dissertation, Stockholm University.

Wodak, R., & Krzyzanowski, M. (2008). *Qualitative Discourse Analysis in the Social Sciences.* New York: Palgrave Macmillan.

9 Economic, social and cultural status (ESCS) and mathematics performance of immigrant students in the Finnish metropolitan area in PISA 2012

Heidi Harju-Luukkainen, Mirja Tarnanen, Kari Nissinen and Jouni Vettenranta

Introduction

Student's educational achievement is partly related to how well the educational system functions. For students with an immigrant background, educational achievement is associated with how well the educational system succeeds in integrating them in the host country. In Finland, immigrant students have performed lower than their non-immigrant peers, even after controlling for socio-economic factors. A similar trend has also been observed in several countries (see, e.g., OECD, 2014; Kuusela et al., 2008; Levels et al., 2008; Kilpi, 2010; Dustmann et al., 2011; Harju-Luukkainen, Nissinen, Sulkunen & Suni, 2014). This is alarming, given that lower educational achievement is often associated with poorer opportunities for further education, economic development and social life (OECD, 2006; Teräs et al., 2010).

Apart from school, family also plays an important role in students' educational achievement. In fact, family-related factors are among the most commonly analyzed background factors. However, despite ample findings on family background, we still know little about the different channels through which this social and cultural capital affects students' educational outcomes (see Jaeger, 2009). According to Bernelius (2011), family background plays a central role among younger children in particular, whereas peer group influences are stronger among older students. Israel, Beaulieu and Hartless (2001), for their part, found that both process and structural attributes of a family's social capital have a strong impact on high school students' educational achievement.

The area in which one lives is also of importance. Finland has a long history of welfare and has long enjoyed relatively homogenous socio-spatial development. However, during the last years the different areas of Finland have started to differentiate. This segregation is reflected, among others, in growing gaps in students' educational achievement in different parts of Finland.

In sum, student's educational achievement is affected by a variety of factors having to do with school, family and society. Based on these premises, two research questions were formulated with regard to students with an immigrant background. Firstly, we will study to what extent students' economic, social and cultural status (ESCS) affects their mathematics performance. This will be done by regression analysis. Secondly, we will take a deeper look at the two variables (mathematics performance and ESCS) using the Kriging method. The method can be used to illustrate regional accumulation of educational variables (McCoy & Johnston, 2001). Kriging is a geostatistical interpolation method based on spatial autocorrelation, the statistical relationship among measured points. The method is new to educational sciences and helps identify geographical distributions (see Vettenranta & Harju-Luukkainen, 2013; Harju-Luukkainen & Vettenranta, 2013, 2014; Harju-Luukkainen, Vettenranta, Ouakrim-Soivio & Bernelius, 2016). In sum, the aim of this study is to highlight the effect of ESCS on students' mathematics achievement and to visualize possible regional accumulations of these variables. This is done to deepen our understanding of how students' family-related factors affect educational attainment and how they are distributed from a geostatistical perspective.

Students with an immigrant background in Finland

In Finland, the number of students with an immigrant background in basic education has increased steadily over the last decades and will continue to do so, given the flow of asylum seekers across Europe since 2015. From 2007 to 2012, the number of students studying Finnish as a second language in basic education increased by a total of 58% (NBE, 2014). However, in Finland the number of migrants has been small compared to the other Nordic countries. In 2014, for the first time in Finland's history, the number of registered mother tongue speakers of languages other than the two national languages, Finnish and Swedish (293,540, or 5.4%), exceeded the number of Swedish speakers (290,760, or 5.3%) permanently living in Finland (Statistics Finland, 2015). Russian-speaking immigrants make up the largest immigrant group, followed by those speaking Estonian, Somali, English and Arabic (Statistics Finland, 2014). In 2013 the number of students with an immigrant background in education from the preschool level to the secondary level was 42,411 (4.3%) (Hietala & Ouakrim-Soivio, 2015).

Schools have traditionally been one of the most important actors when integrating students with an immigrant background into a host country. Learning outcomes play an essential role when judging how successful schools have been in this. However, both on a national and on a global scale, there is extensive research-based evidence showing that students with an immigrant background perform lower than their non-immigrant peers and, as a consequence, are much more often selected for academically less demanding secondary tracks (e.g., OECD, 2006; Kuusela et al., 2008; Levels et al., 2008; Kilpi, 2010; Dustmann et al., 2011; Harju-Luukkainen et al., 2014). As far as first-generation students with an immigrant background are concerned, this is no surprise because it takes, on average, 5 to 7 years to learn a new language at the level needed to succeed academically in school (Cummins, 2000). Also, many of these students migrate at school age or are so-called late arrivals. However, as shown by the PISA 2012 assessment, the same tendency can also be seen among second-generation students (Harju-Luukkainen et al., 2014), which suggests that the integration of these students into Finnish society has not been completely successful.

When discussing schools' success in integrating students with an immigrant background, several factors having to do with both policy and operating levels need to be considered. From the policy level point of view, Finnish legislation and the Finnish school system guarantee equal opportunities for education to all Finnish residents. The current curriculum for basic education (ages 7–16) underlines the importance of language awareness and multilingualism in school communities and across the curriculum, the aim of basic education being to support each pupil's linguistic and cultural identity and the development of his or her mother tongue (NBE, 2004b, p. 12). Thus, in Finland, unlike many other European countries, students whose mother tongue or one of whose family languages is a language other than Finnish, Swedish or Sámi may take part in the instruction of their own mother tongue, provided under separate funding and complementing basic education. There is also research-based evidence that enhancing L1 literacy instruction promotes equality in language education policy on the school level and that the L1 ability of immigrant students has a positive effect on their linguistic, educational and identity development and predicts their second language development (e.g., Cummins, 2001; Markose & Hellstén, 2009; Dooley, Exley & Comber, 2013). However, the L1 instruction of immigrant students is based on free choice by municipalities and is thus not compulsory for students (NBE, 2014). Therefore, the teaching arrangements and qualifications of teachers differ significantly from one municipality/area to another, as do the language skills and age groups of students (Youssef, 2007; Tarnanen & Kauppinen, 2015).

In the study documented in the report "Learners with an Immigrant Background within the Finnish Education System – Evaluation on the Access to Education and the Support Given During Studies" by the Finnish Education Evaluation Centre, education providers in Finland estimated themselves to be relatively well aware of the support needed by students with an immigrant background and also able to meet these needs reasonably well (Pirinen, 2015). However, only a little over half of them (56%) had objectives concerning students with an immigrant background or multiculturalism in their teaching or educational strategies or equivalent plans, and slightly less than a half (46%) were exercising practices aimed at students with an immigrant background, such as teaching Finnish/Swedish as a second language or teaching the learners' native language (Pirinen, 2015). When education providers do not have any strategic policy, students' needs may be tackled on a case-by-case basis, which does not necessarily work in schools with larger numbers of students with an immigrant background, neither does it help develop practice in a systematic way.

Based on the evaluation results, it was recommended that education providers' vision and strategy lean on the principles of multiculturalism and multilingualism.

Also, it was emphasized that appreciation of cultural diversity and multilingualism as well as the development of language awareness need to be established as part of the operating culture of schools and educational institutions and across the curriculum (Kuukka, Ouakrim-Soivio, Pirinen, Tarnanen & Tiusanen, 2015). Evidently, as discussed, language proficiency in both L1 and L2 has an impact on educational achievement. However, teachers may not be able to differentiate between everyday language skills and the language of schooling. Cummins (2000) makes a distinction between two types of language proficiency: basic interpersonal communication skills, referring to the 'surface skills' of listening and speaking, which are typically acquired quickly by many students, and cognitive academic language proficiency, referring to students' abilities to cope with the academic demands placed upon them in various subjects. To be able to support students' learning and development of academic skills across the curriculum, teachers need to be aware of the kind of language proficiencies their students have.

Multicultural awareness is also important when we want to improve the educational achievement of students with immigrant backgrounds. Gay (2010) argues that if cultural factors are recognized, acknowledged and used in the instructional process, educational achievement will improve radically, not the least because culture determines how we think, believe and behave, and these, in turn, affect how we teach and learn, even without our being consciously aware of it (see also Banks, 2006). Also, Finnish teachers themselves at all educational levels have emphasized the need for competence development in how to tackle cultural and linguistic diversity and for further education in how to teach and learn in multicultural settings (Kuukka, Ouakrim-Soivio, Paavola & Tarnanen, 2015). More culturally responsive teaching would mean "using the cultural knowledge, prior experiences, frames of reference, and performance styles of ethnically diverse students to make learning encounters more relevant to and effective for them" (Gay, 2010, p. 31). Obviously, pedagogy and the ways of working in schools should be developed because students with immigrant backgrounds are highly motivated and enjoy being in school more than do their non-immigrant peers, and yet this well-being and motivation do not translate into better learning outcomes (Räsänen & Kivirauma, 2011; Leinonen, 2013; Harju-Luukkainen et al., 2014).

In addition, the cultural capital provided by parents and transmitted to their children has been shown to have an impact on immigrant children's educational achievement (Brizi, 2006). Thus, there is a need to identify and align home and school literacies and practices to improve educational achievement and to promote identity investment, as noted in a number of studies (e.g., Cummins, 2001; Markose & Hellstén, 2009). This means that cooperation between schools and homes needs to be active and open because Epstein states (2011) that two-way communication between school and home is vital to student success. The importance of developing L1 academic skills and the significance of L1 for students' academic achievement and identity work seem to be unfamiliar not only to guardians with immigrant backgrounds but also to L1 teachers (Tarnanen & Kauppinen, 2015). Usually schools do not organize separate parent-teacher meeting events for guardians with immigrant backgrounds. However, there have been diverse experiments on how to support cooperation between school and home, such as school for parents and personal meetings (Antikainen, Paavola, Pirinen, Salonen, Tiusanen & Sirkka Wiman, 2015). However, there is variation in how mainstream parent-teacher meeting events reach guardians with immigrant backgrounds. For example, in the capital area of Finland, approximately half of 13-to16-year-old students with Somali or Kurdish backgrounds reported that their guardians participated in parent-teacher meeting events sometimes, and slightly less than a half said they participated often (Wikström, Haikkola & Laatikainen, 2014). To involve parents, schools should view parents as valuable resources that can be used to help students succeed, and they should develop systematic practices (e.g., regular report cards, translators and home meetings) for this. Also, if parents are supported by schools, they can create a positive home environment which will enable their children to thrive and grow as students (Epstein, 2011; LaRocque, Kleiman & Darling, 2011).

Students with immigrant backgrounds in PISA 2012 and ESCS

PISA is an international assessment organized by the Organisation for Economic Co-operation and Development (OECD). The first PISA study was conducted in 2000. After that there have been five assessments with a new study administered every three years. The focus of the assessments rotates among three core domains: reading literacy, mathematical literacy and scientific literacy. In PISA 2012, in addition, a new domain was introduced – problem solving.

In PISA 2012, students with immigrant backgrounds in Finland were oversampled for the first time. Oversampling means that more students are selected for testing than would be their true proportion in the population. The oversampling made it possible to gain more representative data on students with immigrant backgrounds. The Finnish PISA data on immigrant students consisted of 691 first-generation and 603 second-generation students. Most of them lived in the metropolitan area. The rest of the data comprised a total of 7,535 students across the country.

A first report on these findings was published in 2014. According to Harju-Luukkainen et al. (2014), the results of students with immigrant backgrounds were alarming compared to their non-immigrant peers in Finland. As seen from Figure 9.1, in PISA 2012, students with immigrant backgrounds performed lower in all assessment domains. In mathematics, for instance, non-immigrant students received a mean score of 522 points, first-generation students with immigrant backgrounds 425 points and second-generation students with immigrant backgrounds 449 points. According to OECD (2014a, p. 16), 41 points scored equals approximately one year of schooling. First-generation students were thus lagging behind by more than two school years and second-generation students by almost two school years. The results were more or less similar also in scientific literacy and reading literacy (for more details, see Figure 9.1).

The variables that have important effects on students' educational achievement are often family related. The degree to which these family-related attributes have

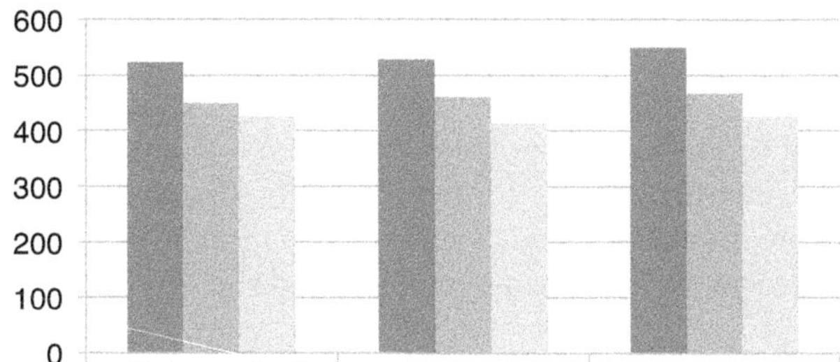

	Mathematical literacy	Reading literacy	Scientific literacy
Non-immigrant background	522	527	549
Second-generation immigrant background	449	460	467
First-generation immigrant background	425	413	425

Figure 9.1 Educational achievement of students with immigrant backgrounds in PISA 2012

Source: Harju-Luukkainen et al., 2014

an impact varies from country to country (OECD, 2010a). Several studies also show that educational achievement is associated with cultural factors (see, e.g., Carbonaro, 1998; Sun, 1999; Israel et al., 2001; Schlee, Mullis & Schriner, 2009; Castillo, Ruiz, Chillón, Jiménez-Pavón & Esperanza-Díaz, 2011; OECD, 2010a; Bernelius & Kauppinen, 2011). However, it is important to keep in mind that students' high socio-economic backgrounds do not necessarily lead to high educational achievement and that a low socio-economic background does not necessarily lead to low achievement. Nevertheless, there is a strong correlation between students' family background variables and educational achievement. In PISA, students' educational and cultural backgrounds are measured by several questions. These include, for example, parents' levels of education, parents' work status, family wealth and cultural possessions at home. Taken together, these consitute the ESCS index (the index of economic, social and cultural status). The ESCS index is an important background variable explaining variance in students' educational achievements in the different domains. According to Harju-Luukkainen et al. (2014), in PISA 2012 the ESCS index explained 11% of the variance between first-generation students, 7% of the variance between second-generation students and 8% of the variance between students without immigrant backgrounds.

Data

To answer the research questions, PISA 2012 data were used. The data consisted of 691 first-generation and 603 second-generation students. The rest of the Finnish data comprised a total of 7,535 students across the country. In the metropolitan area (Helsinki, Espoo and Vantaa), 82 schools were assessed: in Helsinki

47, in Espoo 18 and in Vantaa 17 schools. Outside the metropolitan area, 311 schools were assessed. The number of students assessed in and outside the Finnish metropolitan area can be seen in Table 9.1.

In this study, the metropolitan area was defined as the cities of Helsinki (the capital of Finland), Espoo and Vantaa. Inside Espoo there is also a small town, Kauniainen. However, this town was not included in the calculations because of the low number of students participating in PISA 2012. Figure 9.2 provides a closer view of the metropolitan area and the whole of Finland.

Table 9.1 Students assessed in and outside the metropolitan area of Finland

	Metropolitan area (Helsinki, Espoo and Vantaa)	*Rest of Finland/ outside the metropolitan area*	*Helsinki*	*Espoo*	*Vantaa*
First-generation immigrant background	282	409	153	41	87
Second-generation immigrant background	397	206	251	41	105
Non-immigrant background	1,942	5,593	1,098	422	385
Total	2,621	6,208	1,502	504	577

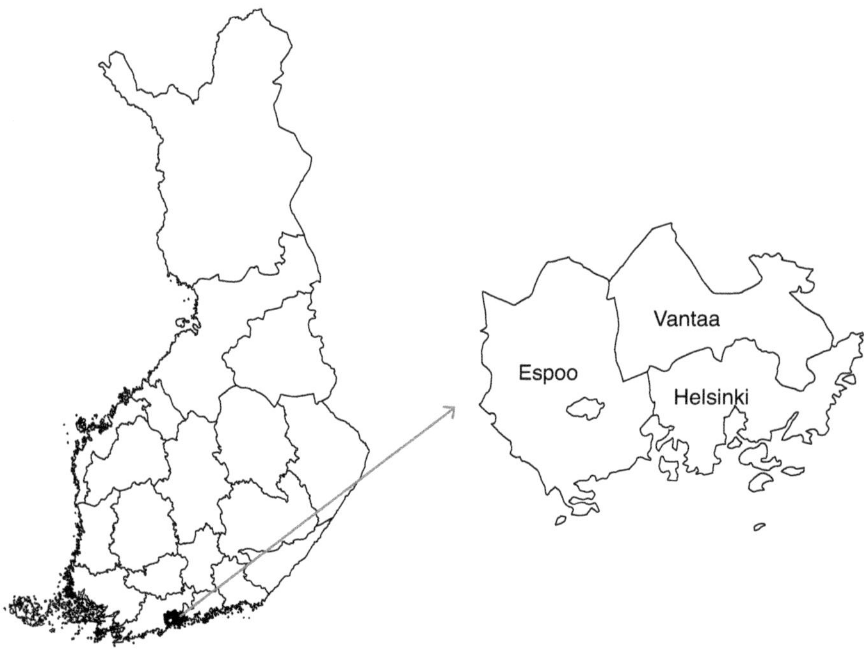

Figure 9.2 Finland and the cities Helsinki, Espoo and Vantaa

Method

This study examined students' mathematics perfromance and ESCS backgrounds. All statistical calculations were performed following the methodology recommended by the PISA consortium. Mathematics mean scores and their standard errors were estimated using the plausible value approach. All calculations were performed applying SAS software, making explicit use of the macros developed specifically for the analysis of PISA data. To get detailed information about the methodology and SAS macros, see OECD (2009). When testing statistical significance we used approximate z tests, which were obtained by dividing the estimate by its standard error. In all tests the significance level was set at 0.05.

In addition, the Kriging method was used to illustrate variation in the metropolitan area. Kriging is a geostatistical interpolation method based on spatial autocorrelation and statistical relationships between measured points. The method provides a relatively new way of illustrating spatial distributions of educational variables and enables, for instance, related analyses of regional variation (See, e.g., Vettenranta & Harju-Luukkainen, 2013; Harju-Luukkainen & Vettenranta, 2014; Vettenranta, 2015). Kriging weights the surrounding measured values to derive predictions for unmeasured locations according to the distance between the measured points, the prediction location and the overall spatial arrangement among the measurements (McCoy & Johnston, 2001). The average of the plausible values for the PISA 2012 mathematics scores and the average of students' ESCS in schools were estimated at the nodes of a square grid of 1 km × 1 km covering the three cities (Helsinki, Vantaa and Espoo) in the metropolitan areas. The estimates were made by Kriging based on values at the five nearest neighbours (schools that participated in the PISA study) weighted by distance. These geostatistical predictions were weighted by distance only, not by any student or school weights. The predictions were made separately for first- and second-generation immigrant students because the results differed clearly among the areas of Finland.

Results

In this article, we sought answers to the following two questions: (1) to what extent do students' family-related attributes (ESCS) affect their mathematics performance, and (2) is there any regional accumulation in sociocultural and economic backgrounds and mathematics performance of students with immigrant backgrounds in the metropolitan areas of Finland? To answer these questions, a two-step analysis was performed. Firstly, regression analysis was conducted for ESCS and mathematical literacy. The results of this analysis will be presented as tables and histograms. Secondly, contour geostatistical maps were produced using the Kriging method to detect possible regional accumulations.

Figure 9.3 presents students' mathematics performance in and outside the metropolitan area. The figure shows that there were small differences in mathematics performance in the metropolitan areas (Helsinki, Espoo and Vantaa). When comparing second-generation immigrant students living in the metropolitan areas (overall) with those in the rest of Finland, a significant difference (0.05) was found in favour of students living outside the area (the rest of Finland). Second-generation students in metropolitan areas thus performed poorer in mathematics compared to their peers outside the areas. Similar results were not observed for first-generation immigrant students. A comparison of the three metropolitan cities (Helsinki, Espoo and Vantaa) showed that first-generation students in Espoo performed statistically significantly (0.05) higher than their peers in the other two cities. Similar results were not observed for second-generation students.

First-generation students with immigrant backgrounds in Espoo performed statistically significantly higher than their peers elsewhere in Finland (Figure 9.3). Similarly, as shown in Figure 9.4, the standard deviation for first-generation students in Espoo was statistically significantly higher than that of their peers anywhere else. This indicates that first-generation students' mathematic performance in Espoo was spread out over a wider range of values. In the other areas there were no statistically significant differences in standard deviation.

Figure 9.5 presents students' ESCS backgrounds in and outside Finnish metropolitan areas. The PISA ESCS index had an OECD mean of 0 and a standard deviation of 1. A negative value on the index means that the value is lower than the OECD average level. The figure reveals two statistically significant differences. Firstly, first-generation students with immigrant backgrounds had higher values on the ESCS index in Espoo than students elsewhere in Finland. Secondly, first-generation students in Espoo had statistically significantly higher values than students in the other groups. In the other areas or student groups observed (whether in or outside the metropolitan areas), there were no statistically significant findings.

These results indicate that in Espoo, the group of first-generation students with immigrant backgrounds differed somewhat from those in the other metropolitan cities. They had higher values on the ESCS index and better average mathematics performance compared to the other student groups in the other cities. This makes one question to what extent ESCS affects students' educational achievements in all these different areas. This is because Harju-Luukkainen and Vettenranta (2014) have shown that the association between student performance and, for example, family background (ESCS) is by no means straightforward. In some areas or even parts of the world, the impact of family background on educational achievement is stronger and in some others weaker.

The results of the regression analysis help explain the impact of ESCS on students' mathematics performance. In Table 9.2 the regression coefficients represent the mean change in the response variable for a one-unit change in the predictor variable while holding the other predictors in the model constant. This means that it provides statistical control and isolates the effect of one variable from all variables in the model. As seen from Table 9.2, the coefficients of determination for first-generation and second-generation students in metropolitan areas were smaller than those for their peers in the other parts of Finland. This means that the impact of ESCS on mathematics performance was smaller in

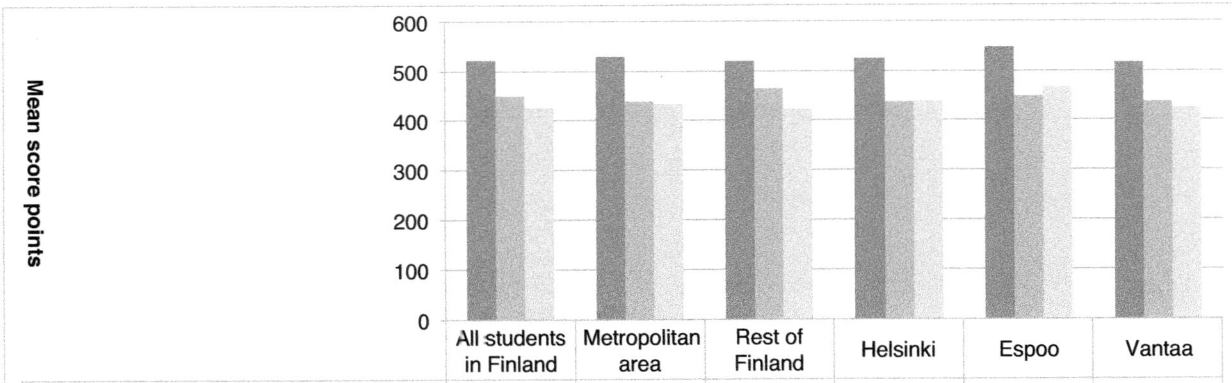

	All students in Finland	Metropolitan area	Rest of Finland	Helsinki	Espoo	Vantaa
Non-immigrant background	522	529	520	525	547	517
Second-generation immigrant background	449	438	464	437	448	437
First-generation immigrant background	425	432	422	438	465	424

Figure 9.3 Mathematics performance in and outside the metropolitan areas of Finland

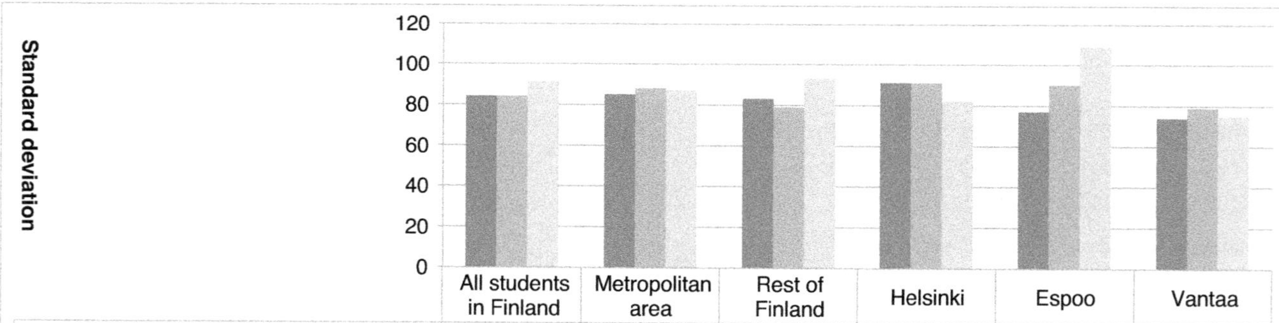

	All students in Finland	Metropolitan area	Rest of Finland	Helsinki	Espoo	Vantaa
Non-immigrant background	84	85	83	91	77	74
Second-generation immigrant background	84	88	79	91	90	79
First-generation immigrant background	91	87	93	82	109	75

Figure 9.4 Standard deviation of mathematics performance in and outside the metropolitan areas of Finland

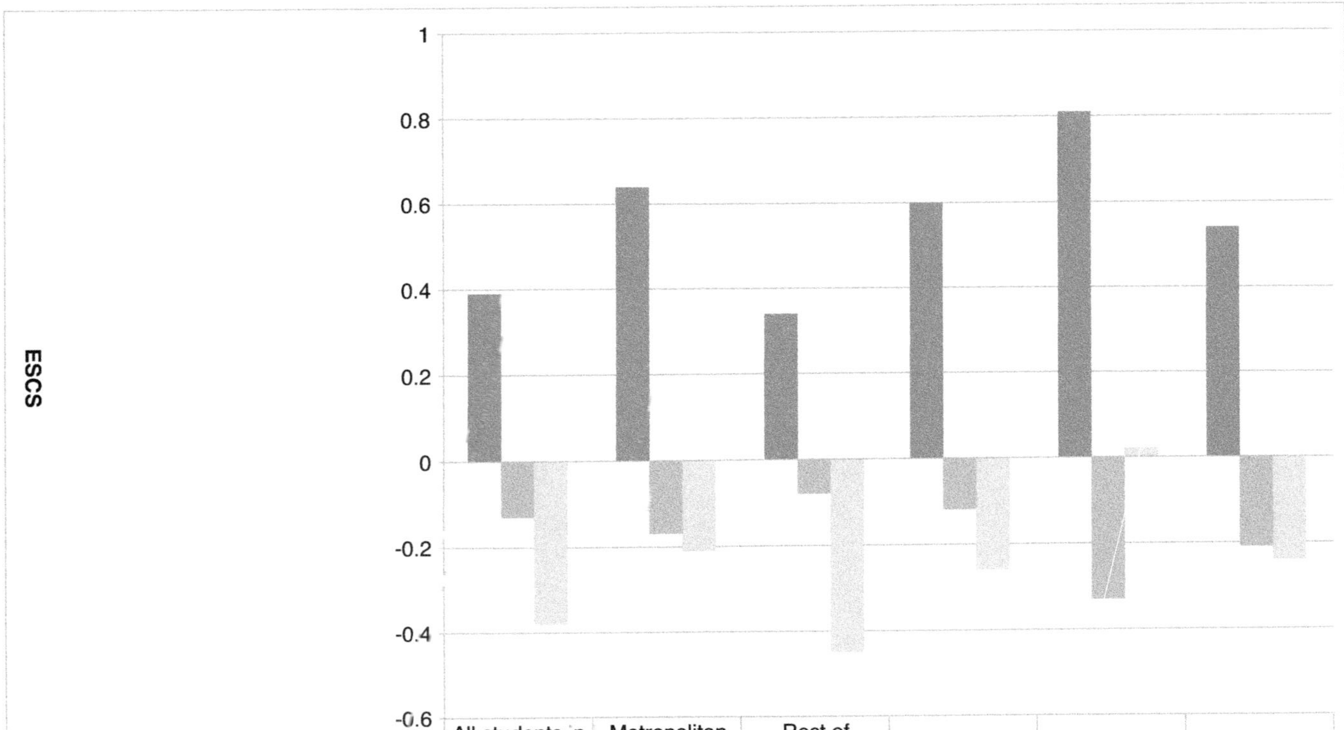

	All students in Finland	Metropolitan area	Rest of Finland	Helsinki	Espoo	Vantaa
Non-immigrant background	0.39	0.64	0.34	0.60	0.81	0.54
Second-generation immigrant background	-0.13	-0.17	-0.08	-0.12	-0.33	-0.21
First-generation immigrant background	-0.38	-0.21	-0.45	-0.26	0.02	-0.24

Figure 9.5 Students' ESCS outcomes in and outside the metropolitan areas of Finland

Table 9.2 Regression coefficients, standard errors and coefficients of determination for ESCS in and outside metropolitan areas of Finland by immigrant status

	Metropolitan areas			*Rest of Finland*		
	Regression coefficient	*Standard error*	*Coefficient of determination (%)*	*Regression coefficient*	*Standard error*	*Coefficient of determination (%)*
First generation	26.1	5.6	10	31.2	5.8	12
Second generation	25.2	6.4	7	24.7	9.0	8
Non-immigrant background	37.0	3.5	10	30.3	2.0	8

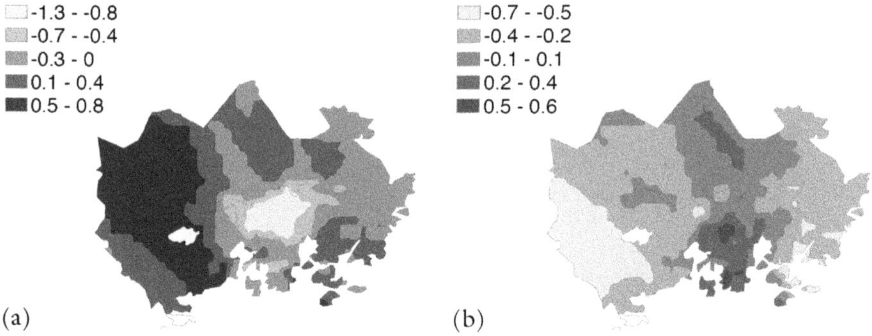

Figure 9.6 Student's family backgrounds in terms of economic, social and cultural status (ESCS) among (a) first-generation and (b) second-generation students with immigrant backgrounds

metropolitan areas than it was elsewhere. In Table 9.2 the regression coefficients for all student populations are statistically significant.

The Kriging method provides us a better visual understanding of the regional accumulation of students' economic, social and cultural backgrounds (ESCS) and their mathematics performance (see Figures 9.6 and 9.7, respectively). Figures 9.6a and 9.6b show that there were regional differences in students' values on the ESCS index among first-generation and second-generation immigrant students: among first-generation students the highest values on the index were found in Espoo (Figure 9.6a), whereas among second-generation students the values were highest closer to Helsinki central city (the southern parts of Helsinki; see Figure 9.6b).

Figures 9.7a and 9.7b show the geographic distribution of mathematics performance of first- and second-generation students with immigrant backgrounds, respectively: among first-generation students mathematics performance was

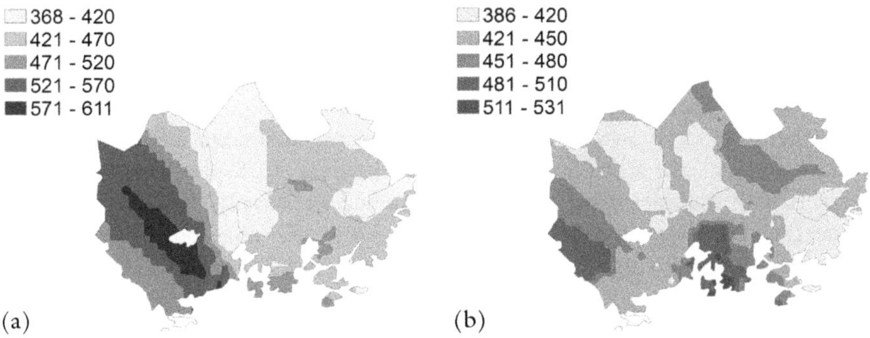

Figure 9.7 Students' mathematics performance among (a) first-generation and (b) second-generation students with immigrant backgrounds

highest in Espoo (Figure 9.7a), whereas among second-generation students the best performance was found in the southern parts of Helsinki (Figure 9.7b). These results reflect in an interesting way the above results for ESCS (Figures 9.6a and 9.6b). This means that the highest educational outcome in mathematics can be found in the same areas where the highest ESCS is also found.

Conclusion and final words

Over the last decades, the Finnish educational system has seen many changes, one of them being the increasing number of immigrant students and the number of students speaking languages other than the national languages. In PISA 2012 in Finland, students with immigrant backgrounds were oversampled for the first time. This oversampling made it possible to gain more representative data for further analysis and increase our knowledge of this particular group of students. In this article the focus was on students' educational achievement and family backgrounds – measured by their ESCS – in metropolitan areas of Finland (the cities of Helsinki, Espoo and Vantaa). Regression analysis was conducted to examine the effect of ESCS on students' mathematics performance, and geostatistical maps were produced to get a better idea of regional variation in the area.

It is a well-known fact that adolescents are closely connected with their environments, which influences their lives and learning in many ways. According to Harju-Luukkainen and Vettenranta (2014), the connection between students' family background (ESCS) and educational achievement is by no means straightforward. In some areas ESCS plays a more important role than in others. However, we know that these connections exist, and students from more advantaged backgrounds generally perform better (see, e.g., OECD, 2010a). In light of the results of this study, ESCS could explain 7 to 10% of students' mathematics performance in the metropolitan area and 8 to 12% outside the area, depending on the student group (see Table 9.2). This means that if a student from an immigrant background lives in a metropolitan area, his or her ESCS does not explain his or her educational achievement as strongly as it does for his or her peers outside the area. At the moment these differences are still small, but if they grow, reconstructive actions are needed. This is because Finnish education policy relies on equality. All students, regardless of social background or language, should have the same educational opportunities.

Furthermore, as shown by this study, there is regional accumulation of mathematics performance and ESCS in metropolitan areas. In Espoo, first-generation students with immigrant backgrounds performed statistically significantly (0.05) higher than their peers in other cities in the area. Also, the values on the ESCS index of these students were significantly higher than they were in the other cities. Similar results were not observed for second-generation students. This suggests that the city of Espoo may attract families with a high value on the ESCS index (first-generation immigrants), which in turn, has an effect on students' educational performance. Interestingly, a similar effect could not be found among second-generation students. This study does not provide an explanation for this discrepancy. However, previous studies have shown that in Espoo, there are among migrants experts in the electrical industry and information technology (Munter, 2009). Most likely these families have come to Finland because of work, which means that in general, their educational and socio-economic levels are relatively high. It is possible to detect other accumulations of educational issues in the geostatistical maps. For example, as seen in Figure 9.7b, among second-generation students, educational achievement was highest in the southern parts of Helsinki. Figure 9.6b, for its part, showed that the value on the ESCS index was highest in this same region.

These results raise questions about educational equality end equity in Finland. Further, what could be done to improve the educational achievement of students living in metropolitan areas, where achievement and ESCS are not that high? It is important to find ways to answer this question because we know from previous studies that students' educational achievements are associated with their future prospects (OECD, 2010b). However, if we only look at histograms, many important geographical accumulations may go undetected. Therefore, there is a need for studies looking at these variables that affect students' educational achievement from various perspectives but also for studies defining the size of these effects. Geostatistical studies can provide important information. For example, maps produced using the Kriging method give decision makers more in-depth information about local circumstances. By combining several methods (statistical and geostatistical), we can better identify regional characteristics. This, in turn, can help, for example, local educators and administrators when planning reconstructive action. Also, before taking any reconstructive action, it is important to gain a full understanding of each area. To gain such an understanding, both regional and scientific data are needed.

References

Antikainen, M., Paavola, H., Pirinen, T., Salonen, M., Tiusanen, M., & Sirkka Wiman, S. (2015). Maahanmuuttajataustaisten oppijoiden muu oppimisen tuki.

In T. Pirinen (Ed.), *Maahanmuuttajataustaiset oppijat suomalaisessa koulutusjärjestelmässä – koulutuksen saavutettavuuden ja opiskelun aikaisen tuen arviointi.* Helsinki: Kansallinen koulutuksen arviointikeskus, 131–179.

Banks, J. A. (2006). *Cultural Diversity and Education: Foundations, Curriculum, and Teaching* (5th ed.). Boston: Allyn and Bacon.

Bernelius, V., & Kauppinen, T. M. (2011). School outcomes and neighbourhood effects: A new approach using data from Finland. In M. Ham, D. Manley, N. Bailey, L. Simpson, & D. Maclennan (Eds.), *Neighbourhood Effects Research: New Perspectives.* London: Springer, 225–247.

Bernelius, V. (2011). Osoitteenmukaisia oppimistuloksia? Kaupunkikoulujen eriytymisen vaikutus peruskoululaisten oppimistuloksiin Helsingissä. (School achievement according to postal adress? The effect of differentiation of city schools on students' learning results in the comprehensive school in Helsinki) *Yhteiskuntapolitiikka, 76*, 479–493.

Brizic, K. 2006. The secret life of languages. Origin-specific differences in L1/L2 acquisition byimmigrant children. *International Journal of Applied Linguistics 16*(3) 339–362.

Carbonaro, W. (1998). A little help from my friend's parents: Intergenerational closure and educational outcomes. *Sociology of Education, 71*(4), 295–313.

Castillo, R., Ruiz, J., Chillón, P., Jiménez-Pavón, D., & Esperanza-Díaz, L. (2011). Association between parental educational/occupational levels and cognitive performance in Spanish adolescents: The AVENA study. *Psicothema, 23*, 349–355.

Cummins, J. (2000). *Language, Power and Pedagogy: Bilingual Children in the Crossfire.* Clevedon: Multilingual Matters.

Cummins, J. (2001). Tests, achievement, and bilingual students. Teoksessa C. Baker & N. H. Hornberger. *An Introductory Reader to the Writings of Jim Cummins.* Clevedon: Multilingual Matters, 139–147.

Dooley, K., Exley, B., & Comber, B. (2013). Leading literacies: Literacy teacher education for inclusion and social justice. In C. Kosnik, J. Rowsell, P. Williamson, R. Simon, & C. Beck (Eds.), *Literacy Teacher Educators: Preparing Teachers for a Changing World.* Rotterdam, Netherlands: Sense Publishers, 65–78.

Dustmann, C., Frattini, T. & Lanzara, G. (2011). Educational achievement of second generation immigrants: An international comparison. NORFACE MIGRATION Discussion Paper No. 2011-25.

Epstein, J. L. (2011). *School, Family, and Community Partnerships: Preparing Educators and Improving Schools.* Boulder, CO: Westview Press.

Gay, G. (2010). *Culturally Responsive Teaching: Theory, Research, and Practice.* New York: Teachers College Press.

Harju-Luukkainen, H., Nissinen, K., Sulkunen, S., & Suni, M. (2014). Avaimet osaamiseen ja tulevaisuuteen: Selvitys maahanmuuttajataustaisten nuorten osaamisen tasosta ja siihen liittyvistä taustatekijöistä PISA 2012 –tutkimuksessa [Keys to Competence and Future. A Report on PISA 2012 Results and Related Underlying Factors for Students With an Immigrant Background]. Jyväskylä: Finnish Institute for Educational Research.

Harju-Luukkainen, H., & Vettenranta, J. (2013). The influence of local culture on students' educational outcomes. In K. Tirri & E. Kuusisto (Eds.), *Interaction in Educational Domains.* Rotterdam: Sense Publishers, 77–90.

Harju-Luukkainen, H., & Vettenranta, J. (2014). Social capital and local variation in student performance in Swedish-speaking Ostrobothnia in Finland. In E. Hyry,

E. Estola, & M. Hiltunen (Eds.), *Place and Education*. Oulu: University of Oulu, 127–143.

Harju-Luukkainen, H., Vettenranta, J., Ouakrim-Soivio, N., & Bernelius, V. (2016). Differences Between Students' PISA Reading Literacy Scores and Grading for Mother Tongue and Literature at School: A Geostatistical Analysis of the Finnish PISA 2009 Data. *Education Inquiry, 7*(4), 463–479. DOI: 10.3402/edui.v7.29413

Hietala, R., & Ouakrim-Soivio, N. (2015). Maahanmuuttajataustaisten oppijoiden määrä alueittain. In T. Pirinen (Ed.), *Maahanmuuttajataustaiset oppijat suomalaisessa koulutusjärjestelmässä – koulutuksen saavutettavuuden ja opiskelun aikaisen tuen arviointi*. Helsinki: Kansallinen koulutuksen arviointikeskus, 47–50.

Israel, G., Beaulieu, L., & Hartless, G. (2001). The influence of family and community social capital on educational achievement. *Rural Sociology, 66*(1), 43–68.

Jaeger, M. (2009). Equal access but unequal outcomes: Cultural capital and educational choice in a meritocratic society. *Social Forces, 87*(4), 1943–1972.

Kilpi, E. (2010). The education of children of immigrants in Finland. DPhil. Oxford University, UK.

Kuukka, K., Ouakrim-Soivio, N., Paavola, H., & Tarnanen, M. (2015). Kulttuurisen monimuotoisuuden edistäminen ja kehittämistarpeet. In T. Pirinen (Ed.), *Maahanmuuttajataustaiset oppijat suomalaisessa koulutusjärjestelmässä – koulutuksen saavutettavuuden ja opiskelun aikaisen tuen arviointi*. Helsinki: Kansallinen koulutuksen arviointikeskus, 181–199.

Kuukka, K., Ouakrim-Soivio, N., Pirinen, T., Tarnanen, M., & Tiusanen, M. (2015). Maahanmuuttajataustaisten oppijoiden kielen oppimisen tuki. In T. Pirinen (Ed.), *Maahanmuuttajataustaiset oppijat suomalaisessa koulutusjärjestelmässä – koulutuksen saavutettavuuden ja opiskelun aikaisen tuen arviointi*. Helsinki: Kansallinen koulutuksen arviointikeskus, 85–130.

Kuusela, J., Etelälahti, A., Hagman, Å., Hievanen, R., Karppinen, K., Nissilä, L., Rönnberg, U., & Siniharju, M. (2008). Maahanmuuttajaoppilaat ja koulutus – tutkimus oppimistuloksista, koulutusvalinnoista ja työllistämisestä.

LaRocque, M., Kleiman, I., & Darling, S. M. (2011). Parental involvement: The missing link in school achievement, preventing school failure. *Alternative Education for Children and Youth, 55*(3), 115–122. doi:10.1080/10459880903472876

Leinonen, E. (2013). *Perheen sukupolvisuhteet ja kotoutuminen nuorten näkökulmasta*. Helsinki: Helsingin kaupungin tietokeskus.

Levels, M. & Dronkers, J. (2008) Educational performance of native and immigrant children from various countries of origin. *Ethnic and Racial Studies, 31*(8), 1404–1425.

McCoy, J., & Johnston, K. (2001). *Using ArcGis™ Spatial Analyst*. New York: ESRI.

Markose, S. & Hellstén, M. (2009). Explaining success and failure in mainstream schooling through the lens of cultural continuities and discontinuities: two case studies. *Language and Education, 23*(1), 59–77.

Munter, A. (2009). *Ulkomaalaistaustaiset työmarkkinoilla*. Tietoisku 3/2009. Espoo: Espoon kaupunki.

National Board of Education (NBE). (2014). *Koulutuksen seurantaraportit 2014:10*. Helsinki: Opetushallitus.

National Board of Education (NBE) (2004). *Perusopetuksen opetussuunnitelman perusteet 2004*. Helsinki: Opetushaliitus.

OECD. (2009). *PISA 2009. Assessment Framework – Key Competencies in Reading, Mathematics and Science*. Paris: OECD.

OECD. (2010a). *PISA 2009 Results: Overcoming Social Background – Equity in Learning Opportunities and Outcomes (Volume II)*. OECD: Paris.

OECD. (2010b). *PISA Pathways to Success. How Knowledge and Skills at Age 15 Shape Future Lives in Canada*. Paris: OECD.

OECD. (2014) PISA 2012 results: What students know and can do - Student performance in mathematics, reading and science. Volume I. Paris: OECD

Pirinen, T. (ed.). (2015). *Maahanmuuttajataustaiset oppijat suomalaisessa koulutusjärjestelmässä – koulutuksen saavutettavuuden ja opiskelun aikaisen tuen arviointi [Students with an immigrant background in Finnish education. Assessment of dducational vailability and support during studies]. Julkaisut* 17:2015. Helsinki: Kansallinen koulutuksen arviointikeskus.

Räsänen, M., & Kivirauma, J. (2011). Oppilaana monikulttuurisessa koulussa. In K. Klemelä, A. Tuittu, A. Virta, & R. Rinne (Eds.), *Vieraina koulussa? Monikulttuurinen koulu oppilaiden, vanhempien, opettajien ja rehtoreiden kokemana. Kasvatustieteiden tiedekunnan julkaisuja A:211*. Turku: Turun yliopisto, 39–95.

Schlee, B., Mullis, A., & Schriner, M. (2009). Parents' social and resource capital: Predictors of academic achievement during early childhood. *Children and Youth Services Review*, *31*, 227–234.

Sun, Y. (1999). The contextual effects of community social capital on academic performance. *Social Science Research*, *28*, 403–426.

Teräs, M., Niemi, E., Stein, D. & Välinoro, M. (2010). *Muunkieliset nuoret siirtymävaiheessa peruskoulusta toiselle asteelle Helsingissä*. Helsinki: Helsingin kaupungin maahanmuutto-osasto.

Tarnanen, M. & Kauppinen, M. (2016). Oman äidinkielen tekstikäytänteet huoltajien ja opettajien näkökulmasta. In. H.-M. Pakula, E., Kouki, H., Silfverberg & E. Yli-Panula (Eds.), *Uudistuva ja uusiutuva ainedidaktiikka*. Turku: Suomen ainedidaktiksen tutkimusseuran julkaisuja 11, 291–308.

Vettenranta, J. (2015). Koulutuksellinen tasa-arvo Suomessa [Educational equality in Finland]. In J. Välijärvi & P. Kupari (Eds.), *Millä eväillä tulevaisuuden peruskoulu nousuun? Opetus-ja kulttuuriministeriön julkaisuja 2015:9*. Helsinki: Opetus-ja kulttuuriministeriö.

Vettenranta, J., & Harju-Luukkainen, H. (2013). *A New Way of Recognizing the Spatial Distribution of Educational Issues: Regional Variation of Science Literacy in the Finnish TIMSS 2011 Data*. 5th IEA International Research Conference. TIMSS and TIMSS Advanced. Retrieved on 13 August 2013, from www.iea.nl/fileadmin/user_upload/IRC/IRC_2013/Papers/IRC-2013_Vettenranta_Harju-Luukkainen.pdf

Wikström, K., Haikkola, L., & Laatikainen, T. (Eds.). (2014). *Maahanmuuttajataustaisten nuorten terveys ja hyvinvointi. Tutkimus pääkaupunkiseudun somali-ja kurditaustaisista nuorista*. Työpaperi 17/2014. Terveyden ja hyvinvoinnin laitos.

Youssef, Y. (2007). Maahanmuuttajien äidinkielen opetus: nykytilanne ja tulevaisuus. In S. Pöyhönen & M.-R. Luukka (Eds.), Kohti tulevaisuuden kielikoulutusta. Kielikoulutuspoliittisen projektin loppuraportti

10 Coming and staying or coming and going? Immigrant families in Denmark

Challenges and opportunities for integration

Annette Hilton

Introduction

This chapter draws on case studies that examine different families' experiences since moving to Denmark. It highlights the factors that impacted on families' decisions to migrate and remain and the challenges faced in terms of integrating into and feeling accepted within Danish society, and it considers some of the implications of these challenges for the families. It is hoped that the chapter will give voice to the many '*udlændinge*' (foreigners) and their families who live and work in Denmark.

The impetus for the chapter grew out of personal experience and interactions with other newcomers to Denmark. While living in Denmark, I gained an insight, both personally and through conversations with language school classmates and work colleagues, into the various challenges associated with moving to Denmark. Some challenges, such as limited employment possibilities or language barriers, might be expected; others relate more to one's own perceptions of, for example, Danish society's values or Danes' expectations of newcomers. Such experiences and feelings may be more complex for parents with children or may vary among family members. Despite these challenges, many choose to remain in Denmark, hoping for a better future for themselves and their families (Jensen & Pedersen, 2007; Olwig, 2011).

The life experiences of foreigners whether migrants or expatriates in a new context are influenced by numerous factors including cultural experiences, social connections and changing personal relationships (Bodolica & Spraggon, 2008). Often the acquisition of language skills is necessary for everyday functioning and to interact with the local population (Bodolica & Spraggon, 2008; Froese, 2012). Bodolica and Spraggon identified other challenges, including not attaining social status in the host country, losing touch with the home country's ways, difficulties in adjusting to a new culture, struggling for acceptance by locals and a "double identity strangeness" (p. 553) – the feeling of being "torn between two realities" (p. 552), that of the home country and that of the host country. Many of these challenges impact on the ability of newcomers to a country or culture to integrate (to participate and function in the new country). According to Cerdin, Diné and Brewster (2014), the motivation to integrate is influenced positively by the degree of alignment between expectations and reality and the degree to which their experiences in their new country are positive or negative. The extent to which newcomers can integrate often influences their decisions to remain in the host country, repatriate or move to a third country (Jensen & Pedersen, 2007; Tharenou & Caulfield, 2010).

Olwig (2011) argued that the discourse and Danish policies surrounding immigration and integration have a significant influence on public perceptions of and general attitudes towards immigrants. Schmidt (2011) contended that the media also impacts on public perceptions by portraying immigrants as a threat to a culturally homogenous Danish society. Baig and Dağdelen (2013) suggested that in recent times, the 'othering' of newcomers to European communities has grown and is becoming a challenge to integration. The extent to which these discourses and perceptions are played out in the case of immigrants and expatriates from within Europe is not made clear in the literature. According to Beach and Lunneblad (2011), differences between home countries and the new country can present particular challenges for migrant families, for example, differences between schooling systems and expectations can be difficult for migrant families to navigate. They may lack confidence in the new school system, which can lead to concerns regarding whether or not children are receiving appropriate education. It is important to help migrant parents access schooling systems to learn about how they function as a means of enhancing their understanding of the new system and building trust in it (Vesely & Ginsberg, 2011). It is also important to help parents become more involved at their children's schools (Lunneblad & Johansson, 2012).

The literature on European migrant families within Europe is limited; however, in a study of Polish migrant families to Scotland, Sime and Pietka-Nykaza (2015) investigated the influence of intergenerationality on migrant children's cultural practices and the challenges for both parents and children. According to Sime and Pietka-Nykaza, migration has an impact on children's experiences of culture and their cultural identities and consequently on their acculturation. Such research has also shown that language and cultural differences present greater challenges for parents than they do for young children, who generally acquire cultural and linguistic knowledge more rapidly than their parents and often become language experts in the family. This increased knowledge and understanding allows children to engage in learning and in social activities in their new environments. In contrast, parents often experience reduced social networks, and sometimes the roles of children and parents in the family can shift (Kenner, Ruby, Jessel, Gregory & Arju, 2007; Phua & Kaufman, 2008). It is not clear how children navigate between two (or sometimes more) cultures and the ways in which this impacts on tensions within the family; however, children's attainment of social and cultural capital can lead to children mediating their parents' own access to social opportunities (Sime & Fox, 2015).

The research literature on immigrant families in Europe, and Northern Europe in particular, is largely focused on non-European migrants or refugees, and these migrants comprise the largest proportion of migrants to European countries. At the same time, global demand for skilled employees is increasing, and highly educated people are now moving between countries, including self-initiated expatriates – people who choose to move to another country for work – and people transferring to a new country within their company (Cerdin & Selmer, 2014). Regardless of their motivations for moving to a new country, research about migrants' and expatriates' experiences in their host countries are often focused on organizational or work-related aspects (e.g., Froese, 2012; Froese & Peltokorpi, 2013), on their reasons for expatriation (e.g., Froese, 2012; Selmer & Lauring, 2010) or reasons for repatriation (e.g., Tharenou & Caufield, 2010). Far less literature focuses on the personal or social challenges faced by expatriate foreigners and their families in their new milieu and how these influence decisions to remain or leave (Bodolica & Spraggon, 2008; Cerdin et al., 2014). Further, much of the existing literature about migrant families in Europe has been conducted with families from non-European backgrounds. In contrast, this chapter draws on findings from a small study that explored the experiences of European expatriate families in Denmark.

Method

My position as researcher

In this study, my position was one of insider – I too was a relative newcomer to Denmark having lived there for two years, and like those whom I interviewed, I came to Denmark for employment. Insider research refers to the situation of researching within a group of which the researcher is also a member (Kanuha, 2000). This shared experiential base and identity can be advantageous because participants are often more open with insider researchers (Corbin Dwyer & Buckle, 2009). There are some concerns about being an insider because of the potential for subjectivity; however, as argued by Corbin Dwyer and Buckle (2009), accurate representation of participants' experiences can mediate this risk. Furthermore, I was also an outsider because I was not in the same position as the others – my family was not with me, and not being European, I had fewer prospects of remaining in Denmark beyond a few years. My position as insider–outsider in this research allowed me to occupy the 'space' (Corbin Dwyer & Buckle, 2009) which provides an opportunity to adopt an approach to preserve similarities and differences. As Fay (1996) argued, there is "no self-understanding without other-understanding" (p. 241), which means that by understanding similarities with the group, the researcher is also able to identify the differences and acknowledges that even as an insider, not all experiences are shared by individuals within the group.

Participants

This research was based on 10 case studies selected using convenience sampling. The participants were either classmates from the language school at which we were all learning Danish, or they were work colleagues of classmates who were recruited through snowball sampling (Hennessey & Dionigi, 2013; May, 2001). I contacted classmates who then identified foreign work colleagues who were also interested in participating in the study. The participants were all professionals from diverse backgrounds and home countries. Their professions included research scientists, mathematicians, bankers, a dentist and engineers. Home countries were all southern, central or eastern European. In the interests of brevity, not all 10 case studies can be presented in detail. Although all case studies were used in the data analysis, two studies have been chosen for inclusion in the chapter because they reflect different journeys, and both participants have young families.

Data collection

Semi-structured interviews were conducted in English with each of the 10 participants. The interviews, which ranged in duration from 30 to 50 minutes, were audio-recorded and transcribed verbatim. They were conducted at a venue of the participant's choice. The interview questions centred on the participants' reasons for moving to Denmark, the factors that impacted on their decisions to stay (or at some future time to repatriate or migrate to another country) and the factors that the participants perceived had impacted on their integration into Danish society. They were also asked about whether these factors were the same for their family members and about their experiences and perceptions regarding their children's lives in Denmark.

The selected case studies (which use pseudonyms) are presented as narratives. The use of narrative is appropriate because it allows one to examine issues in depth and to describe the subjects' lived experiences (Trahar, 2009). It is built on the premise that through others' stories, we come to a stronger understanding and gain insights into their experiences (Connelly & Clandinin, 2006; Josselson, 2006; Andrews, Squire & Tambokou, 2008). Gertsen and Søderberg (2010) argued that using a narrative approach provides insights into expatriates' stories. As an insider, it is likely that my own experiences and perceptions might influence my ability to 'restory' the participants' accounts, so they are presented separately (Buonviri, 2015) before common themes across the 10 case studies are discussed.

Data analysis

Interview transcripts were analyzed using thematic analysis. The responses were coded to identify emerging themes relating to each of the main focus areas of the interviews (and the broader study): participants' reasons for moving to Denmark; the factors that impacted on their decisions to remain, repatriate or migrate to a third country; and the perceived factors that impacted on their ability to integrate into Danish society. The identification of themes was guided by a pragmatic approach, taking the existing literature and the research focus into account (Patton, 2002; Saldaña, 2013). Initially broad themes were identified, and coding was repeated to identify sub-themes within them. Coding was cross-checked with a research partner to ensure the internal validity of the analysis. Codes were compared and discussed and recoded where necessary until agreement was reached (Cohen, Manion & Morrison, 2000; see also Hilton, Hilton, Dole & Goos, 2015).

Selected case studies

Case study 1: Ivanka

Ivanka moved from Serbia to Denmark 5 years ago because she married a Serbian man who had lived in Denmark for more than 25 years. Their son was born soon after her arrival in Denmark. They separated after 3 years, and Ivanka now lives alone with their 4-year-old son. Before moving to Denmark, Ivanka worked in her own dental practice, but after moving to Denmark she was unable to practice as a dentist until she attained certain levels in Danish language and passed certification exams in dentistry. Consequently, she had worked outside her chosen profession for 5 years.

For Ivanka, the challenges of integrating into Danish society were related to not knowing the language and not having any Danish friends. She described her sense of isolation, noting that

> [t]he hardest part is because I didn't know the language and because I didn't have any friends. This is very important for me because here it is different – I'm very warm and loving and it is not possible to show these emotions . . . [H]ere, people think you are crazy if you show emotion. The Danes are much more reserved and I can never see what they are thinking.

Ivanka spoke further about the cultural differences between Danes and Serbs. The mutual lack of cultural understanding was perhaps the greatest challenge for Ivanka in the early years in Denmark because she felt such a strong need to be understood by those around her:

> I was very afraid because my husband was very aggressive to me, so everything confused me because I expected that people would help, but there was no one to talk to . . . and I lost two years . . . [I]t was hard because we were in Europe and we are only 2700 km apart but our cultures are so different – I thought we would be the same but we are so different.

Since her divorce, Ivanka has made new friends in Denmark, although they too are Serbian. She says life is much easier now that she has friends who can relate to her:

> They have more experience because they've lived here for 15 years – they can help me – tell me what's normal. They can be like a mirror and I can think, "Oh, that's what I was like but I'll be ok because things will get better".'

Ivanka spoke about the challenges of making Danish friends:

> People here expect you to show confidence in a way that matches their own way of thinking – it's hard. Everyone in Denmark says, "We are free and we

are very open," but they are not. I don't feel it's that way – only within their boundaries or their own ways.

We talked about the factors that might be helpful to the integration of foreign families in Denmark. Ivanka's son had recently started at a Danish kindergarten, which she said was helpful. Because Ivanka had begun to learn Danish, she felt more confident to speak with other parents at the kindergarten. She felt that this contact with Danes had allowed her to gain an insight into Danish culture:

> It's helped me to understand the ways that Danes communicate and more about what they think, or how they act in ways that they think of as 'normal'. I've learned more about the Danish culture and the Danish mentality. I started Danish and it helped me make contact with other parents – I can't understand how people can live here for 20 years and not learn the language – how can you survive, especially if you want to involve your child in the local cultural opportunities?

For Ivanka, learning Danish was important because she needed to be fluent in Danish to be able to practice dentistry and it gave her an opportunity to communicate with the parents at her son's school.

When asked about the future and whether she would remain in Denmark, Ivanka had a complex answer. She had recently been granted full custody of her son, so she is free to leave Denmark and work elsewhere. She is concerned about returning to Serbia because she would need to start again with a new practice. She described feeling trapped because her first priority is to her son, and she is concerned about remaining in Denmark because she doesn't have confidence in the Danish schooling system:

> I'm sometimes afraid I'm doing the wrong thing because I think that education is not so good here. I've heard that it is better in other Scandinavian countries, compared to Denmark – well, the *grundskole* (public elementary school) is not so good here.

Ivanka shared reasons that she felt contributed to her decision to remain in Denmark. Her son's father still lives there, and she would like her son to have some contact with him. In addition, her son has shown signs of autism, and she feels that he will receive more support in Denmark than he might in Serbia.

Although she feels like an outsider in Denmark, Ivanka has mixed feelings. Her perceptions reflect the double identity crisis and dual reality challenges described in the literature (see Bodolica & Spraggon, 2008):

> I miss being a professional so much that now I feel that I am nothing. I'm a good dentist and I loved my job and without this – it's part of my identity – I feel sad. In Serbia if one is on welfare, there is a kind of shame, I'm not that sort of person – I was a good student and I worked hard. It does seem that the Danes are more accepting if you are on welfare or divorced. I'm not sure

> if this is an accurate impression – maybe it's just what they say instead of what they really believe.

She has also begun to feel like an outsider in her native Serbia:

> It's a little strange when I go back now because the community doesn't function so well and it's started to irritate me . . . I have an apartment in Serbia and my family is there but I don't really miss it anymore and I even feel that I will never belong there. I accept this but Denmark is also not my home – sometimes I'm sad because I miss the feeling that I am 100% 'this'. Since five years ago until the end of my life, I will never again be 100% – just a little here and a little there – never the whole me. My son is more Danish than Serbian now . . . I hope that he will get more confidence from Danish society than I have.

She explained that the only reasons to leave Denmark would be to provide better opportunities for her son or if the political situation changed and she felt unsafe in Denmark. In this case, she would return to Serbia because "I don't know what would happen to people in Denmark with different nationalities so I would return to Serbia in a moment because I would feel safer there".

Ivanka has decided that for now, she will stay in Denmark to raise her son and try to gain employment as a dentist. In the future, she hopes to have another practice of her own. Just after our interview, she passed the Danish tests and was hopeful that work would help her to move on and become more settled in Denmark. Only time will tell.

Case study 2: Marta

Marta is a Polish woman in her late 30s who lives in Denmark with her German husband and their two children, a son age 4 and a daughter age 2. Marta and her husband Hans have lived in Denmark for 7 years, where they both work in finance. They work for the bank at which they worked before coming to Denmark. They transferred to the Danish branch from their respective home countries to fill positions for which there was no local expertise. Working for an international company, they speak English exclusively at work, and it is also their common language. Marta explained that she speaks Polish and English fluently and can understand some German. Hans speaks German and English fluently. Their children can understand and have begun to speak both of their parents' mother tongues, English and Danish because of their exposure to it through Danish kindergarten. Although neither Hans nor Marta need Danish in their work, they have both completed Danish language courses because their children are learning Danish and because they feel that they should learn the local language.

Marta's and Hans's situation is different from other couples who moved to Denmark together: "We met here and it is our place. We decided to stay here because it's a great place to raise kids – much better than Poland." Hans and

Marta have a sense of belonging because of their common experiences and because Denmark represents something to them that other countries cannot – it is 'their place' – the place where they met, and it has become the place where they plan to raise their children. This decision is not without challenges. Marta told me that the greatest challenge to integrating in Denmark is

> a big one – the Danes are so reserved, quite close – you need to be the one to go to them. It's hard to invite them out – they aren't really keen – you can tell that they're wondering, "What do you really want?" . . . After I joined (the bank), I wanted to join the wine club but they all spoke only Danish so at the first meeting I was completely left out. They knew I didn't understand their conversations but that didn't make any difference. I didn't go back after that because I didn't feel included or welcome . . . You always feel like a foreigner – they say they're cosmopolitan but you don't really feel it – in fact you feel very much excluded.

We talked about factors that help foreign families to gain acceptance or to integrate into Danish society. Marta explained that having children might give foreign parents reasons or opportunities to do something with Danes; however, in her experience, that hasn't been the case:

> I ended up in the international group of mothers . . . [I]f we were with the Danish mothers we could at least share our experiences – maybe if you met parents who had the same problems – you could at least speak to others – the kids could be the reason (to help people integrate).

We chatted about the likelihood that in future, the family's plans might change and what that would mean to them. Marta said they were planning to stay in Denmark but that this might change if she and Hans felt that they could provide better opportunities for their children elsewhere:

> If we ever went to Poland, it would be for the possibility to live in a more cosmopolitan city and to have that kind of life. Our children speak four languages but here we feel like foreigners. I don't think that will ever change – it's not my kind of mentality and I don't ever feel so much like I'm at home here.

Neither Marta nor Hans is obligated to remain in Denmark for work. An international company employs them both, and they could easily move to one of their home countries or elsewhere. They choose to stay because they like the lifestyle in Copenhagen. Their oldest child is in a Danish school, and he speaks very good Danish. Even so, Marta returned many times to the observation that "we will never feel at home here the way we might in our own countries".

We talked about this further, and Marta admitted that perhaps other reasons beyond their children's schooling opportunities might influence their decision to stay or leave:

> Loneliness and not having my family around is really hard. I really miss my friends and to understand the politics and culture here – even going to the theatre is harder here . . . I really miss the connection to my own culture . . . I would leave and go to Poland and I don't think there would be disadvantages to my kids or for work. Schooling and conditions are good; in fact, I think the schools in Poland are better than in Denmark.

As it was with the other participants or people I met during my time in Denmark, Marta shared the opinion that as a foreigner, even if your work does not require you to learn or use Danish, it is something that you should do:

> I think it's what you should do – I don't need it and I won't apply to stay but I still feel that I shouldn't work in a country for six years and not make the effort to learn the language or anything about the country . . . I kind of feel that if you are here to work and to have a nice life here then you should go to the effort of learning about the culture. I actually think it helps you to integrate a bit better because at least you know a bit about the politics so at least you can follow along with conversations with Danish colleagues at work.

I asked her about the perceptions of some foreigners that Danes did not welcome them. Marta responded that it depends on the circumstances, but she had friends who had experienced this.

> There are some I know who've had "why are you here – you're a foreigner?" Of course there are people who think you are taking jobs away from ethnic Danes. There are nationalistic people who resent foreigners coming and taking jobs. Usually they're the jobs that Danes don't want or aren't qualified for. I didn't come here looking for work – they asked me to come because no one in Denmark had my specialisation. It was the same for my husband . . . We didn't take Danish jobs, we were asked to come to do a job they couldn't fill.

Marta's final comments returned to her feelings that she would never quite 'fit in' in Denmark.

> You still look for people with common cultural backgrounds because it's nice to have friends who understand you and you understand them – you feel a sense of security. It's why people group together and stay with people from their own backgrounds. It's probably worse here because Danes are so closed and it's harder to get into their social groups.

Results and discussion

This section draws on all of the case studies, including those presented in detail. The results of the thematic analysis revealed a number of sub-themes related to the main themes of migration and integration. What follows is a discussion of the main themes with representative quotes from participants.

There were many similarities among the interview responses of the participants in the study.

Reasons to move to or remain in Denmark

Confirming other research about reasons for migration, in this study common reasons to move to Denmark centred on work or study opportunities and the political or economic situation in home countries. For example,

> The reason is not just to have work but also to have work in the same country so we (my family) can be together . . . I have now decided to look for work in industry. My intention is to live here for now. Highly qualified people like us are not so well paid or appreciated in Spain. I would not say it's easy here but it's better.
>
> (Manuel, Spain)

and

> The situation in my own country is quite bad and so when we had the opportunity to come here, we came. It could have been another country – we didn't choose Denmark but that's where I got the chance to study.
>
> (Viktor, Serbia)

The potential for better wages or working conditions was a common reason to move to Denmark for all participants.

> I really like the working conditions here and the way that work is organised – it's more relaxed and they give you responsibilities in your task so you have quite a lot of independence compared to Germany . . . [T]he whole approach to work is different here . . . [T]here's a work-life balance here whereas in Germany you live to work and it's always assumed it's top priority.
>
> (Gunther, Germany)

In the case of families, having children in school and who were settled into their lives in Denmark was a major consideration in staying: "Denmark is a great place to raise kids – better than Poland . . . I can see that the older the kids get the more difficult it will be to leave. Our son is in a Danish school and he speaks good Danish" (Marta, Poland). Participants who were yet to have children or whose children were not yet in school felt it would be easier to move. The majority of participants mentioned the Danish lifestyle as a contributing factor to their decision to remain in Denmark, for example, "[P]eople are happy here . . . I like the city and how I fit in here – I hate the level of noise in Spain and I love the quiet here" (José, Spain).

Reasons to leave Denmark

Influence of family

Interestingly, whereas children were an influence on their parents' decisions to remain in Denmark, they also influenced thoughts about possible repatriation or migration to a third country because of a lack of confidence in the Danish school system and a preference for the schooling systems of their home countries. For example, "I might choose to go home for him [my son] because the school system here is very different and I don't really like it" (Katerina, Russia) and "I think the schools in Poland are better than in Denmark" (Marta, Poland). My work in Denmark as a researcher in education gave me opportunities to observe classes and interview teachers in schools and gymnasiums and to teach graduates of the Danish schooling system at university. My observations led me to believe that there are some significantly positive aspects to the Danish education system. It appears that there may be a misalignment between parents' perceptions of Danish schooling and the reality, and this situation has been described in literature about migrant families in Denmark (Lunneblad & Johansson, 2012). It also appears that more needs to be done to inform foreign parents about the local school system and to include foreign parents in school activities, which affirms the arguments of Vesely and Ginsberg (2011).

Although all of the participants in the study moved to Denmark for work or study opportunities, in some cases the needs of different family members were mentioned as possible reasons to repatriate. For example, the need for children to have relationships with relatives outside Demark was a strong theme: "When we have children it would be better to have them nearer to their grandparents so they can help and the children can be with them" (Frank, Germany). In some cases, participants' partners had found it difficult to obtain work, and this was discussed as a possible reason to leave. Whereas the following participant has work he is happy with, he was anxious that his wife did not have a job in her chosen profession, and he would consider repatriation or migration to a third country for his wife's sake:

> My wife is a librarian and even though she has a Masters degree, it's very difficult to find work and when she does apply for a job, she has to compete with all the native speakers . . . [C]onditions may be worse back home but at least she would have a job . . . [I]t's not even financial – for most people you cannot be satisfied with your life if you don't have a rewarding job.
>
> (Karl, Czech Republic)

Social and political challenges

Social and political challenges were prominent reasons influencing a decision to leave Denmark. The majority of participants described the 'pull' of their home country (family, society, culture and friends) and difficulties in making Danish friends, challenges that were described by Bodolica and Spraggon (2008) in their study of Moldovian immigrants. These challenges led people to seek out members of their own culture: "My wife and I are in a kind of bubble here. We socialise with others from our home country . . . [O]ur only real contact with Danes is when we drop our son at kindergarten, but that's not much" (Viktor, Serbia); and "In social situations, they [Danes] like to speak Danish. Even if they talk with you, it's not like they want to be friends – they don't want to be your friend, they don't want to be close to you" (Katerina, Russia).

Some participants, primarily those from central or eastern European countries (such as Russia, Serbia and Poland), suggested that political changes threatening security for foreigners might cause them to leave Denmark or repatriate. For example, "If the political situation in Denmark changes and I stop feeling comfortable living here, then I would go somewhere else" (Katerina, Russia). These themes all align with the limited literature about immigrants' decision-making (e.g., Bodolica & Spraggon, 2008; Tharenou & Caulfield, 2010).

Challenges to integration

Cultural differences and perceptions of 'outsiderness'

The most consistent and recurring themes across the participants' stories related to cultural differences and misalignment of cultural expectations. These perceptions were closely aligned with those described by Schmidt (2011) and Olwig (2011). All participants mentioned difficulties in interacting with Danes, describing Danes as reserved and 'closed' rather than being open and friendly. Everyone described the challenges they had because of many Danes' preference to speak Danish in social situations, regardless of whether others can understand or not. Most of the participants felt that it was not possible to make friends with Danish colleagues, who might potentially be the Danes they had most contact with. For example,

> [i]n Germany it's easy to make friends with colleagues at work but Danes seem to really separate private life and work life so for them it's almost unthinkable to invite work colleagues to a private party or something like that – it's like an unwritten law that you must make friends outside of work.
>
> (Frank, Germany)

Lack of language is a predictable barrier to integration, but in the case of this study, the participants were able to speak at least some Danish and were willing to try to use it. They perceived Danes as being unwilling to speak Danish with them: "In Norway, they understand that you will have an accent or you will not always have the right words whereas here, it seems not to be ok to make mistakes" (Gunther, Germany); and, "It's very hard to learn Danish unless you have Danes who are prepared to speak it with you . . . [Y]ou have to be very fluent in Danish if you want Danes to speak to you" (Viktor, Serbia).

The majority of participants talked about expecting cultural similarities because of their common European backgrounds and yet being surprised that their own cultures differed so markedly from Danish culture. All participants voiced feelings of 'outsiderness', and there was a recurring perception of not fitting in or of always being the foreigner. For example,

> We are all Europeans so our cultures should be quite close . . . I have found Danes to be more closed than people in Russia and they have quite different opinions about friendship than we do . . . You know, I still don't think that after eight years we have integrated . . . [H]onestly, it doesn't matter how long you live here, you are always the outsider and you will always feel like that.
>
> (Katerina, Russia)

Such perceptions led to a feeling of 'otherness' or of being an outsider, which didn't seem to diminish over time and resulted in the participants seeking out other expatriates from their home countries with whom they shared cultural understandings. These findings again align with those described in the literature; for example, double identity strangeness and othering described by Bodolica and Spraggon (2008) were recurring themes in the challenges to integration mentioned by the participants in the study. They also reflect the research findings of Cerdin et al. (2014) that misalignment between expectations and reality in a new culture can influence their motivation and ability to integrate.

Factors that support integration

Language learning and intercultural understanding

Despite the varied challenges to integration, all of the participants recognized the importance of learning Danish and about Danish culture, believing that one is obligated to learn about one's host country. This suggests that their motivation to integrate remained high despite their experiences. It also suggests a perception that attaining this knowledge might influence or lead to enhanced opportunities to participate socially or culturally. The participants were unanimous in feeling that they had not integrated into Danish society; however, several mentioned language learning and increased cultural understanding as factors that they hoped might help them to become more integrated. They also applauded the Danish government's attempt to support newcomers to learn Danish:

> My opinion is that Denmark is very involved in helping people to learn the language – I think they are a bit scared to lose Danish . . . so I think they are making a nice effort . . . [T]his is not like my experience in other countries like France.
>
> (Manuel, Spain)

When questioned about the cultural elements of Danish language courses, all participants felt that learning more about Danish culture helped them understand the way Danish society functioned and gave them some insights into Danes' values: "It's really useful to get some cultural background because it helps you to understand why things are done and what you should expect in certain situations" (Gunther, Germany).

Children's influence

The parents' decision to persist with learning Danish even though they could function in their working lives without it was influenced by having children in Danish schools. The children were all learning to speak Danish and had made friends with Danish children. The parents felt that by learning Danish at the same time as their children, they would have a better opportunity to meet and interact with Danish parents. All of these perceptions resonate with the literature about migrant families and the differences that develop between parents' cultural, social and linguistic knowledge and that of their children (e.g., Kenner et al., 2007; Sime & Fox, 2015).

Some participants felt that integration might be improved via social contact with Danes through their children, "I think that having kids in school might help because we meet other parents" (Gunther, Germany). The notion that access might be gained to Danish society through children was, however, mixed. Some participants felt that their children's enrolment in a Danish school gave them opportunities to make contact with Danish parents, whereas others, like Marta, had not found this easy.

Conclusion

This chapter is dedicated to those who, despite the many challenges associated with moving to Denmark, find opportunities to flourish in their new lives. Even for those who may only remain in Denmark in the short term, the positive experiences and advantages appear to outweigh the negative experiences. The study examined different families' experiences in terms of their reasons for moving to and remaining in Denmark. These include employment and educational opportunities and lifestyle factors. It also highlighted the challenges faced in terms of integrating into and feeling accepted within Danish society. Beyond the obvious challenges of language differences, the study identified a number of cultural challenges that were not anticipated by the participants, including the 'closed' nature of Danish society and the feeling of remaining on the outside regardless of how long one remains in Denmark; lack of intercultural understanding; and a sense of isolation from one's own culture, friends and family.

Despite the challenges, motivation to integrate appeared to remain high for several participants, especially those with children, although for others, there was a kind of resignation to remaining 'on the outside' no matter how long they lived in Denmark. The strong influence of children on their parents' decisions to remain appeared to outweigh the negative feelings of being outsiders – the participants identified lifestyle and educational opportunities and the fact that their children could speak Danish as strong reasons to remain.

The study has numerous implications for families and for organizations that employ foreigners. Although it may be natural to assume that similarities exist among European cultures, which would make integration relatively easy, this did not appear to be the case for any of the participants in the study. Even in terms of navigating the education system, the participants all expressed doubts about the standard of schooling compared to their home countries. The Danish immigration authorities have developed some very sophisticated and helpful resources, including online materials for foreigners moving there; however, there remain challenges to interacting and integrating into Danish society, some of which may not be easily anticipated. It may prove useful for authorities that work with foreigners moving to Denmark to focus on ways to help parents better understand the Danish school system and to become more engaged in their children's schooling.

The participants in this study had young children and all were born in Denmark. Further research might focus on the implications for families over the longer term or focus on families who move to Denmark with school-age children. What might be the impact on the families in terms of potential intergenerational tensions in the future? If the children remain in Danish schools for several years and they develop a sense of Danish cultural identity and expertise in the Danish language, what might be the impact on them should their parents decide to repatriate or to move to a different country? Alternatively, if the children attend international schools or schools based on the schooling system in their parents' home country, how might this influence the children's sense of cultural identity – will they too feel a similar 'double identity' and 'otherness' to that described by the participants in the study?

References

Andrews, M., Squire, C., & Tambokou, M. (Eds.). (2008). *Doing Narrative Research*. London: Sage.

Baig, T., & Dağdelen, M. K. (2013). Re-emergence of othering in Europe: A threat to European integration. *Journal of European Studies*, *29*(1), 1–21.

Beach, D., & Lunneblad, J. (2011). Ethnographic investigations of issues of race in Scandinavian education research. *Ethnography and Education*, *6*(1), 29–43.

Bodolica, V., & Spraggon, M. (2008). Work experiences of Moldovan women in Italy: Bearing the double identity strangeness. *Equal Opportunities International*, *27*(6), 537–558.

Buonviri, N. O. (2015). Three music education majors' journeys through Aural Skills 101. *Journal of Music Teacher Education*, *25*(1), 95–106.

Cerdin, J.-L., Diné, M. A., & Brewster, C. (2014). Qualified immigrants' success: Exploring the motivation to migrate and to integrate. *Journal of International Business Studies*, *45*, 151–168.

Cerdin, J.-L., & Selmer, J. (2014). Who is a self-initiated expatriate? Towards conceptual clarity of a common notion. *The International Journal of Human Resource Management*, *25*(9), 1281–1301.

Cohen, L., Manion, L., & Morrison, K. (2000). *Research Methods in Education* (5th ed.). London: Routledge Falmer.

Connelly, F. M., & Clandinin, D. J. (2006). Narrative inquiry. In J. L. Green, G. Camilli, & P. Elmore (Eds.), *Handbook of Complementary Methods in Education Research* (3rd ed.). Mahwah, NJ: Lawrence Erlbaum, 477–487.

Corbin Dwyer, S., & Buckle, J. L. (2009). The space between: On being an insider-outsider in qualitative research. *International Journal of Qualitative Methods*, *8*(1), 54–63.

Fay, B. (1996). *Contemporary Philosophy of Social Science: A Multicultural Approach*. Cambridge, UK: Blackwell.

Froese, F. J. (2012). Motivation and adjustment of self-initiated expatriates: The case of expatriate academics in South Korea. *The International Journal of Human Resource Management*, *23*(6), 1095–1112.

Froese, F. J., & Peltokorpi, V. (2013). Organisational expatriates and self-initiates expatriates: Differences in cross-cultural adjustment and job satisfaction. *The International Journal of Human Resource Management*, *24*(10), 1953–1967.

Gertsen, M. C., & Søderberg, A.-M. (2010). Expatriate stories about cultural encounters – A narrative approach to cultural learning processes in multinational companies. *Scandinavian Journal of Management*, *26*, 248–257.

Hennessey, A., & Dionigi, R. A. (2013). Implementing cooperative learning in Australian primary schools: Generalist teachers' perspectives. *Issues in Educational Research*, *23*(1), 52–68.

Hilton, A., Hilton, G., Dole, S., & Goos, M. (2015). School leaders as participants in teachers' professional development: The impact on teachers' and school leaders' professional growth. *Australian Journal of Teacher Education*, *40*(12), 104–125.

Jensen, P., & Pedersen, P. J. (2007). To stay or not to stay? Out-migration of immigrants from Denmark. *International Migration*, *45*(5), 87–113.

Josselson, R. (2006). Narrative research and the challenge of accumulating knowledge. *Narrative Inquiry*, *16*(1), 3–10.

Kanuha, V. K. (2000). "Being" native versus "going native": Conducting social work research as an insider. *Social Work*, *45*(5), 439–447.

Kenner, C., Ruby, M., Jessel, J., Gregory, E., & Arju, T. (2007). Intergenerational learning between children and grandparents in East London. *Journal of Early Childhood Research*, *5*, 219–243.

Lunneblad, J., & Johansson, T. (2012). Learning from each other? Multicultural pedagogy, parental education and governance. *Race, Ethnicity, and Education*, *15*(5), 705–723.

May, T. (2001). *Social Research: Issues, Methods and Process* (3rd ed.). Philadelphia, PA: Open University Press.

Olwig, K. F. (2011). "Integration": Migrants and refugees between Scandinavian welfare societies and family relations. *Journal of Ethnic and Migration Studies*, *37*(2), 179–196.

Patton, M. Q. (2002). *Qualitative Research & Evaluation Methods* (3rd ed.). Thousand Oaks: Sage Publications.

Phua, V. C., & Kaufman, G. (2008). Grandparenting responsibility among elderly Asian Americans. *Journal of Intergenerational Relationships*, *6*(1), 41–59.

Saldaña, J. (2013). *The Coding Manual for Qualitative Researchers* (2nd ed.). Thousand Oaks, CA: Sage Publications.

Schmidt, G. (2011). Law and identity. Transnational arranged marriages and the boundaries of Danishness. *Journal of Ethnic and Migration Studies*, *37*, 257–275.

Selmer, J., & Lauring, J. (2010). Self-initiated academic expatriates: Inherent demographics and reasons to expatriate. *European Management Review*, *7*, 169–179.

Sime, D., & Fox, R. (2015). Migrant children, social capital and access to public services: Transitions, negotiations and complex agencies. *Children and Society*, *29*, 524–534.

Sime, D., & Pietka-Nykaza, E. (2015). Transnational intergenerationalities: Cultural learning in Polish migrant families and its implications for pedagogy. *Language and Intercultural Communication*, *15*(2), 208–223.

Tharenou, P., & Caulfield, N. (2010). Will I stay or will I go? Explaining repatriation by self-initiated expatriates. *Academy of Management Journal*, *53*(5), 1009–1028.

Trahar, S. (2009). Beyond the story itself: Narrative inquiry and autoethnography in intercultural research in higher education. *Forum Qualitative Sozialforschung/ Forum: Qualitative Social Research*, *10*(1), Article 30. Retrieved from http://nbn-resolving.de/urn:nbn:de:0114-fqs0901308

Vesely, C. K., & Ginsberg, M. R. (2011). Strategies and practices for working with immigrant families in early education programs. *Young Children*, *66*(1), 84–89.

11 Parental engagement in Icelandic preschools

Johanna Einarsdottir and Arna H. Jonsdottir

Introduction

Collaboration among practitioners, children and families is regarded as an important indicator of quality in early childhood education and care (Urban, Vandenbroeck, Lazzari, A., Peeters, & Van Laere, K., 2011). Parental engagement in early childhood education and care has also been viewed as an important factor for enhancing children's well-being and learning. Researchers have claimed that through parental cooperation, educators can obtain a greater understanding of individual children's lives and cultural backgrounds (Eldridge, 2001; Baum & McMurray-Schwarz, 2004). Parent-school collaboration has also been found to increase parental understanding of educational practices and school expectations as well as to enhance parents' ability to support their children at home and in school. Parents who are involved in their children's schooling have also demonstrated more positive attitudes toward their children's learning and have experienced increased self-confidence in their parenting (OECD, 2006). Research has furthermore revealed that children whose parents participate in and cooperate with their schools more clearly understand the value and importance of education (Epstein, Sanders, Simon, Salinas, Jansorn & Van Voorhis, 2002).

Recently, some concerns regarding the 'traditional' parent involvement paradigm have emerged, especially in regard to cultural sensitivity and power relations between parents and educators. In the light of this development, it is valuable to shed light on Icelandic parents' views on collaboration with their children's preschools, especially in terms of how they experience their own power and influence. The chapter will report on a focus group study with parents during which they discussed their perspectives on and experiences of partnership and collaboration with their children's preschools.

Challenges

In recent years, a reconceptualization and critical perspectives on the collaboration between educators and families have emerged. Although it has been noted that parental collaboration is beneficial for all children, additional evidence indicates that promoting the family-school partnership may be crucial for socially disadvantaged children (Wildenger & McIntyre, 2011). Souto-Manning and Swick (2006), for instance, propose an empowerment paradigm for parent and family collaboration that embraces diversity as a resource rather than viewing it as a deficit. They encourage educators to focus on (a) the strengths of the family and child, (b) an inclusive approach in which all families are validated and engaged in partnership, (c) the recognition and appreciation of multiple venues and formats for involvement, (d) a lifelong learning approach in which the teacher learns alongside children and families, (e) trust building through collaborative schemes and by recognizing multiple definitions and paradigms for family involvement and (f) linguistic and cultural appreciation, recognition and reflective responsiveness.

Another challenge to the 'traditional' view of the parent-educator partnership concerns issues of power and professional knowledge. A partnership that assumes cooperation on equal terms and an appreciation of parental expertise can challenge teachers' identities as professionals. Alasuutari (2010) discusses issues and challenges that relate to expertise and the expert-layperson relationship. Her study with Finnish preschool educators identified two different collaboration frames: a vertical frame and a horizontal one. The former describes a more traditional approach to the parent-professional relationship that emphasizes expert knowledge. The latter is in accordance with more recent discussions about expertise and democratic professionalism in early childhood education and care (ECEC). The horizontal frame also reflects the partnership approach and the ideals of the Finnish curriculum guidelines on ECEC in terms of its emphasis on the parent and practitioner's equal positions and in terms of valuing parental knowledge.

MacNaughton and Hughes (2011) have discussed the power relations between parents and teachers and how educators' formal and professional knowledge of children in general is often privileged over parents' informal, anecdotal knowledge about their specific children. To address this, they have developed an alternate model of knowledge-power relationships in the area of staff-parent communication. They suggest that educators can create new knowledge-power relations with parents through 'communicative collaboration' that acknowledges, respects and utilizes parents' knowledge of their children. Through such communicative collaboration, staff and parents are able to 'co-create' expertise as both the foundation and outcome of the social relations between them (Hughes & MacNaughton, 1999, 2001). Oberhuemer (2005) emphasizes that democratic professionalism is intended to determine a way to communicate with *all* parents and not least with those groups that are normally inactive in the formal discourse. Blue-Banning, Summers, Frankland, Nelson and Beegle (2004) have identified six main features of positive staff-parent partnerships: communication, commitment, equality, skills, trust and respect, which emphasize partnership that entails equality or reciprocity between families and service providers. An equal partnership encompasses a harmonious relationship and an active effort from professionals to empower families.

National curriculum guidelines

Iceland's national curriculum guidelines for all school levels were revised in 2011 (Ministry of Education: Science and Culture, 2011). One noteworthy feature of these curricula is a common chapter that introduces six pillars designated to form the essence of the Icelandic educational policy and create continuity in the educational system. These pillars comprise literacy, sustainability, health and welfare, democracy and human rights, equality and creativity. The preschool section of the curriculum stresses the importance of the learning environment and encourages preschool teachers to utilize play in a goal-directed way. The curriculum integrates and groups educational areas into the following four categories: expression and communication, health and well-being, sustainability and science, and creativity and culture. On the basis of the curriculum guidelines, each preschool is meant to write its own school curriculum guide.

The preschool curriculum guidelines emphasize cooperation with parents that is built on reciprocal understanding, trust, and respect.

> The collaboration of preschool personnel and parents should be based on mutual understanding and respect for the attitudes and knowledge of both parties. It is important that all these parties trust each other, that they are able to share their views and make collective decisions concerning individual children.
>
> (Ministry of Education: Science and Culture, 2011, p. 48)

According to the curriculum, a preschool's practices should stimulate cooperation among children, educators, parents and the local community. The guidelines mention the term *cooperation* 28 times and *interaction* four times. In this context, cooperation refers to cooperation within the preschool as well as with parties outside the school and between school levels. Cooperation among children is emphasized, as is cooperation with parents. The children's well-being in preschool is seen as inseparable from their family's welfare, and family and parental contributions to preschool activities are regarded as important factors. Sharing mutual information between parents and children is emphasized. Parents should have opportunities to become acquainted with the preschool's pedagogy and curriculum, and preschool educators should receive information concerning the children and their circumstances, experiences and interests.

The guidelines stress that educators, parents and children should all be active participants and collaborators and that they should all influence decisions concerning the preschool. The guidelines emphasize that preschool is a place where democratic values and practices are stressed, using the terms *democracy* and *democratic* frequently, in total 23 times. Additionally, the term *participation* appears 10 times, often in connection with democracy and children's opportunities to participate in democratic communities. The guidelines also stress parental participation and the fact that parent's views should be listened to and their influence should be encouraged. Furthermore, the individual preschool curriculum guidelines are intended to be written in partnership with parents and children, and the participation and cooperation of educators, parents and children should form the basis by which preschools are assessed.

Although the curriculum guidelines emphasize parental participation on the basis of the principle that families and preschools are collaborators, the guidelines also clearly express that as professionals, preschool teachers are responsible for the preschool's curriculum and pedagogy.

The study

Participants and method

The aim of the study was to explore parents' views and experiences of collaboration with their children's preschools. Focus group interviews were conducted in five groups containing 26 parents total, 19 mothers and seven fathers. The parents had children who were enrolled in five preschools located in the municipal area of Reykjavik, Iceland. All the parents were of Icelandic origin except two mothers who were immigrants from Poland. Focus groups were used because the study sought to create a non-threatening environment in which the parents could freely discuss the topic. Focus groups aim to capture the interaction among participants to produce information and insights that would be more difficult to access without the interaction found in the group. Focus groups enable group discussion, which resembles a natural conversation, which reveals group members' attitudes, opinions and perspectives. The aim of focus groups is not to have the group reach consensus. Rather, the approach prioritizes understanding participants' feelings, comments and thought processes as they discuss the issue (Morgan, 1998; Krueger & Casey, 2009). The participants in each group were similar in that they were parents of children at the same preschool and were parents of the oldest preschool children.

The interview guide had been predetermined but was flexible. The parents discussed their children's preschools and were asked about their experiences collaborating with the preschool. They were also asked if they wanted more influence over what was done in the preschool and whether they thought collaboration with the preschool would influence their children. Additionally, they were questioned about what form of collaboration they preferred and what influenced whether they collaborated with the preschool. All the parents had children who would start compulsory school the following autumn, and therefore they were also asked for their thoughts about the transition between preschool and compulsory school as well as their own roles in the process. Qualitative research recognizes the existence of multiple voices; in all the focus groups, the researchers sought to capture individual voices within the discussions as well as group interactions and group-wide discussions (Barbour, 2009).

Parents' satisfaction with preschools

The parents in all the focus groups said they were satisfied with their children's preschools. This is in agreement with studies in other countries that revealed parents' strong tendencies to rate the quality of their child's preschool highly (Cryer, Tietze & Wessels, 2002; Lehrer, Lemay & Bigras, 2015). The parents who participated in the current study expressed their contentment with the preschools' areas of emphasis. They valued the fact that democracy, equality and empathy were stressed and that the children learned to take responsibility in their preschools. In their opinions, these values were more important than teaching the children to read and write. The parents seemed to assess the preschool's quality based on their children's satisfaction and well-being. Although they may have been dissatisfied with some issues, they did not request changes if their children were content, felt well and were happy at preschool. These findings are consistent with an earlier study in Icelandic preschools that revealed that parents' main expectation of their children's preschools was that they provided support for their children's social development. The way the preschool day was organized and whether particular knowledge and skills were taught seemed to be less important. Rather, the parents from the study wanted their children to have the opportunity not only to enjoy themselves as individuals but also to learn autonomy and respect for others. The parents valued the educators' play and attentiveness (Einarsdottir, 2010).

Professionalism and participation

The parents discussed their collaboration with the educators as well as their influences on the practices of their children's preschools. In general, they were satisfied with their relationship with the preschool and said that they had always been able to communicate with their children's educators, express themselves when they wanted something to be different and make requests concerning their child. They also stated that the educators were willing to listen to their worries and accommodate them. The parents described both 'positive' and 'negative' reactions from the preschool teachers towards their requests. One mother's example of a positive reaction related to an event when she consulted the department leader after her son had been teased. He had been teased because he was wearing clothes one day that were the colour pink, his favourite colour. Another boy had asked him if he was turning into a girl, as described in the following excerpt.

MOTHER 1: I talked to them because [my son] was teased by a boy . . .
MOTHER 2: Because he was wearing pink? . . .
MOTHER 1: [He asked] if he didn't know that only old women wear pink . . . After that he totally refused to wear pink, not even a pink stripe on his socks was allowed.

After the mother's criticism, the educators decided to hold a *pink day* in the preschool during which everyone was encouraged to wear something pink, both children and educators. In this way, the preschool teachers apparently recognized the mother's knowledge and opinions. The preschool in question has a policy in place about bullying and equality, which might have influenced the speedy response to the mother's complaint.

An example of a negative reaction to a parent's criticism also emerged during the group interviews. One father had expressed his dissatisfaction with the outdoor education at his child's preschool and the amount of time the children spent outside every day. The children stayed outside from 10 o'clock in the morning until three o'clock in the afternoon. The father stated the parents had not been consulted about this. Rather, the practice was simply introduced. The father, who had earlier said that parents should not influence preschool pedagogy, recounted that he had spoken to the department leader about his dissatisfaction. The response was that the policy would not be changed.

FATHER: [I was told] this is your opinion, you can have it, but we will not change it.

R: But before you said that the parents shouldn't interfere with education too much . . .

FATHER: Yes, but I was just expressing my opinion . . . I wasn't satisfied with the reaction . . . but I won't talk about it more.

The father presented his view and apparently sought discussions with the preschool teachers about outdoors education that were based on his arguments, but a dialogue was not welcomed. He appeared to accept this and respected the teacher's professional decisions and knowledge.

Alasuutari (2010) points out that a form of partnership that assumes cooperation on equal terms and an appreciation of parental expertise can challenge teachers' identities as professionals. The findings from the study indicate that the Icelandic parents interviewed seemed to experience communication on equal terms in terms of their own expertise regarding their children. However, across all the focus groups, it was clear that the parents did not see it in their power to influence the pedagogical practices. The parents appeared to trust the preschool educators and viewed them as experts as illustrated in the following excerpt.

FATHER 1: You trust the people working here so why should you interfere . . . [Y]ou don't do that, you trust these people . . . [T]hey're professionals with so much experience . . . so if your child feels well, there is no purpose in interfering.

FATHER 2: So, if the child is feeling well, you as a parent feel well too.

Based on Alasuutari's (2010) notion of vertical and horizontal frames of parent-professional relationships, it can be argued that the frames are both vertical and horizontal in Icelandic preschools based on the parents' understanding. The vertical frames appear to be in place in terms of preschool pedagogy and the educators' ideology and educational beliefs. In these areas, the preschool teachers' authority seemed not to be questioned. They could decide and make the rules. On the other hand, when parental opinions or requests concerned individual children, the professionals strived to fulfil the children's and parents' wishes. On this dimension the collaboration seemed to be on equal, horizontal grounds on which the parents' knowledge was respected (Alasuutari, 2010).

Education of preschool staff

Iceland is experiencing a shortage of qualified preschool teachers. In 2014, only 32% of educators working in preschools had been educated as preschool teachers. Sixteen percent had some other type of pedagogical education, but 52% had no formal pedagogical education (Statistics Iceland, 2016). In praxis, this means that experienced preschool teachers take on administrative positions, devoting much of their time to the leadership and guidance of unskilled staff. Hence, most of the people who work with preschool children on a day-to-day basis are not qualified preschool teachers. The parents in this study were acutely aware of the importance of having preschool teachers who worked with their children. They mentioned the difference between collaborating with an educated preschool teacher and with an unskilled person. Not only did they recognize this difference in terms of the educators' professionalism and expertise but also their stability as employees. Across all focus groups, the parents described preschool teachers as the "support and safety" of the educators' groups. In one of the preschools that had experienced high staff turnover and a lack of trained preschool teachers, the parents claimed that the situation had affected their participation levels. They felt they were always in the beginning phase, constantly meeting new staff who only stayed for a few months. Their discussion here illuminates this experience.

MOTHER 1: These changes affect children in various ways . . .

MOTHER 2: Yes, and it also gets on our nerves, the parents . . . You could sense the changes with your child. You are always on first base . . . always interacting with someone new.

MOTHER 1: The young people that have been working here are in many ways fantastic, but they do not always understand the importance of things. Like when we arrive in the morning and the department leader welcomes you, and says "nice to see you" and so on, the others are more like, okay, the child is here, check. This has its influence.

Type of collaboration

The parents in the focus groups valued informal, verbal collaboration with preschool staff in which they could discuss their child's behaviour and development as well as their wishes and worries. This is consistent with other studies that have identified regular conversations between those working in preschools and families as highly valuable (Duncan, Bowden & Smith, 2006). The two Polish mothers in particular found it important to foster informal discussions about their children when they brought them to preschool in the morning and picked them up in the afternoon. They reported that the preschool had not especially encouraged them to participate in formal collaboration, but they were allowed to participate when they took initiative. That is, their expertise and resources did not seem to have been noticed or encouraged.

A great part of the parental participation took place through informal discussion between parents and educators and through the children. When the parents obtained information from their children, they found it valuable to have access to photos on the preschool's website or elsewhere to discuss what was going on in their daily preschool life with their children. The parents also made positive comments about formal events such as grill parties in the summer, Christmas celebrations, cultural week and graduation of the oldest children.

The parents did not reach consensus about the use of online social networking in collaboration between parents and educators. In two of the focus groups, parents preferred a closed group on Facebook where they could get information because they were "drowning in emails". They used Facebook to communicate with the compulsory schools and strongly favoured it. However, they mentioned that it was necessary to have certain group rules in terms of participation, pictures and discussions.

In the other two groups, parents opined that they did not like to collaborate on Facebook. In one of the groups, the parents preferred emails to receive information and reminders, and parents worried that their Facebook records could affect the educators' attitudes towards their children. The Polish mothers preferred Polish or English emails, saying it was unhelpful when emails were only in Icelandic because then they would have to get it translated the next day, which was sometimes too late when the emails concerned something happening the same day. In this way, these two mothers from another culture did not feel empowered by the preschool. One group discussed the pros and cons of social networking:

FATHER: I think it's fine to get information through email.

R: How often do you get emails?

FATHER: Once a week, even two weeks . . . Information about what's taking place and then there's maybe one picture attached . . . I think it's fine, I don't need a Facebook group about the preschool where people are discussing all kind of things that do not concern me.

MOTHER: Not everybody is on Facebook . . . I do agree a bit, it's good to get rid of all the comments, great, smiley . . . or maybe one negative person and everybody has to read his grumble . . . A phone book [is necessary] – it is sometimes inconvenient when they [the children] want to play with somebody and you do not meet the parents and you are always asking them [the educators] if I can get their phone number.

Hughes and MacNaughton (2001) found that formal communication between parents and staff, such as documents and formal meetings, does not improve staff-parent relationships. Staff consistently preferred informal, verbal communication because it allowed them to negotiate shared meaning and understandings with parents about who their children are and how the children should be treated. This was also the case with the parents in this research, not the least the Polish mothers, but the parents also appreciated formal cooperation and information about what was happening.

Time

The parents did not frequently raise the issue of a lack of time in their discussions about parent-educator collaboration. Only three parents (mothers) out of 26 in the focus groups complained about a lack of time and the employment market's lack of flexibility. One of them said:

> I think it is of great importance to collaborate, but I also think that it matters that society and employers do not expect parents to participate . . . It matters that you know about what's going on in the preschool, that you're present, you know, getting acquainted with the teachers, the children, other parents . . . but sometimes it feels like something extra, you know . . . [E]mployers do not expect it. Like, the other day, there was a dance show and we have two children here [in the preschool] and you have to come twice during the day . . . You cannot always participate although you would want to.

Most parents said that it was easiest for them to have meetings at the preschool in the morning. However, the foreign mothers were an exception. They worked from eight to 16 o'clock and expressed the fact it was very difficult for them to participate in the preschool's activities during working hours. The educators appeared to have adjusted the time to the majority of the parents' working hours to make it easier for them to participate. MacNaughton and Hughes (2011) have argued that parents who share educators' cultural and linguistic backgrounds may be able to use scarce time more efficiently than a parent from a different background; this may have been the case in these preschools. Therefore, as MacNaughton and Hughes (2011, p. 6) point out, educators can silence parents and vice versa when lack of time makes it difficult for them to communicate effectively with each other.

Transition to primary school

The oldest children in the preschools had already begun their journey to primary schools by visiting these schools during the school year. In general, the parents had strong opinions about the transition to primary schools. Most of them were satisfied with the transition activities and the organization of the school visits. However, others were worried and concerned about the changes imminent in their and their children's lives. In preschools where there had been scant collaboration between the school levels and few transition activities, the parents were critical. They criticized the fact that there had been only two visits to the primary school over the previous year and also believed it was difficult for the children to adjust to two institutions simultaneously, the school and the leisure centre. In one of the groups, the parents discussed the differences between preschool and primary school and were critical of the local authorities' lack of transition policy. For instance, one of the mothers said:

> I think that there should be a common policy for all pre- and primary schools . . . The oldest preschool children should already be connected to

> the primary school in the autumn. There should be consultation and collaboration . . . in their last school year . . . There is inconsistency within the municipality regarding the transition from preschool to primary schools.

In other preschools, the parents were highly satisfied with the collaboration between the school levels in their neighbourhood, and they mentioned that the preschool head teacher and the primary school's department leader played the main roles. The children had gone to 'spring school' with the preschool educators one week in April and again with their parents in May. Over the summer, the children spent time in the leisure centre with the preschool staff and moved there two weeks before school started. The children in first class in the primary school visited the preschool children, and during the school year, teenagers in ninth grade spent one day each week in the preschool.

Both those parents who were satisfied and those who were unsatisfied with the transition activities emphasized the fact that collaboration and preparation were necessary and intended to make the transition easier for the children. If it was successful, there would be less conflict, and the process would diminish anxiety and increase their well-being and safety. Thus they focused on the framework, surroundings and adjustment as the following discussion illustrates.

MOTHER 1: I am sure it will help many children with their adjustment . . . to go more often, not only to the leisure centre but to the school, see the other kids, see how they line up . . . Learn autonomy, how to find your shoes and tie your shoe-laces or use a shoe-horn, or get your overcoat on the hanger, remember where you left your overcoat and so on . . . practical things.
MOTHER 2: Yes, it's not a question about teaching . . .
MOTHER 1: No, it's adjustment.
MOTHER2: To learn to be in the school building . . .
MOTHER 1: You know, in a new environment, bigger environment.

One of the Polish mothers said she was very worried and stressed about her daughter's attending primary school and had many questions, not the least because the girl was her first child. She had questions such as: how long was the child expected to stay in school daily, what would happen on the first day, should she stay with her the first day or first week in the school or leisure centre, and what was best for the child and the school? Furthermore, she wanted the children to be introduced to the daily schedule, what they were supposed to learn, interaction in the dining room, how snack time was conducted, and if the routine was similar day to day. Furthermore, she wanted to know if the teacher would write notes to her in English. She preferred individual instruction and learning as in the preschool and was concerned about how things would happen in the primary school.

There seemed to be a large difference in knowledge levels between the Icelandic and Polish parents on the subject of the transition between school levels. Not only was the Polish mother sending her first child to primary school, but she also did not speak Icelandic, which made the process more difficult.

Discussion and conclusion

The aim of the chapter was to report on a study that focused on Icelandic parents' perspectives on and experiences of partnership and collaboration with their children's preschools. The parents who participated in the study were generally uncritical of the preschools, which is consistent with previous studies from other countries that have revealed that parents usually rate their children's preschools highly (Cryer et al., 2002; Lehrer et al., 2015). The parents seemed to define quality according to their children's happiness and well-being. They valued the preschools' emphases and pedagogical activities and were satisfied with the collaboration they experienced. If they were dissatisfied with certain things, they did not act on their feelings or do much about them. If their children were happy and content, they were content as well. The participating parents had children who were in their final year of preschool and were beginning primary school in the autumn. The main criticism they raised concerned the transition to primary school. They were concerned about how their children would be doing in primary school and wanted greater cooperation between the school levels. Although there were only two mothers of foreign origin who participated in this study, their marginalized position was clear. They lacked the background knowledge that the Icelandic parents had; what the Icelanders took for granted was unfamiliar to them. One example was knowledge about the primary school, in which one of the mothers expressed great concern about her daughter's transition to primary school and raised many unanswered questions.

When the findings are analyzed in light of vertical and horizontal frames of parent-professional relationships (Alasuutari, 2010), both a traditional approach that underscores professionals' expert knowledge and a more democratic approach are revealed. The parents emphasized the importance of having well-educated professionals work with their children. They trusted that the professionals knew best and respected their expertise in terms of pedagogical practices and curriculum. If they did not agree with the educators' practices, they did not agitate for changes but rather acknowledged the professional expertise of the professionals. They were also satisfied with the information they received about their children's daily preschool life. In this way, they respected the educators' expert knowledge and the vertical frame. The parents also provided examples of collaboration on equal, horizontal grounds during which their knowledge of their children was respected. They mentioned that they could always express their wishes and worries concerning their children to the educators, and they felt they were listened to. Hence, the parents' views illustrate a clear distinction between professional knowledge and their own knowledge of their children. These are two different types of knowledge, and it can be the subject of speculation as to which is more respected. This would be revealed if, on the one hand, the children and families had to adapt to the preschool's framework as with the father who was concerned about the amount of outdoors time or, on the other hand, depending on how much effort the preschool exerted to accommodate individual parents or children's wishes.

The participating parents valued the preschool teachers' professional knowledge, especially those parents who had experienced a shortage of educated preschool teachers and constant turnover of educators in their children's preschools. The parents valued the educators' professionalism and found that the preschool teachers were whom they could trust for their children's education and care. In light of these findings, building a democratic relationship between families and preschool teachers in which both partners' knowledge is regarded as equal might present a challenge. For this purpose, Hughes and MacNaughton's (1999, 2001) model of knowledge-power relationships in staff-parent communication is a useful resource. They suggest that educators can create new knowledge-power relationships with parents through 'communicative collaboration' that acknowledges, respects and uses parental knowledge of their children as well as the educators' professional knowledge. Through such collaboration, staff and parents 'co-create' expertise.

The study's findings provide implication for practice. The Icelandic preschool curriculum guidelines emphasize both educators' expert professional knowledge as well as parents' expert knowledge of their own children. Parents, educators and children should collaboratively develop preschool curriculum guidelines, and parents should participate in assessing preschool activities. The guidelines also state that preschool teachers are responsible for preschools' curriculum and pedagogy (Ministry of Education: Science and Culture, 2011).

Cooperation between parents and preschool teachers should be built on equal terms where the knowledge of both parties is respected. According to the parents who participated in this study, an imbalance seems to exist between parental knowledge on the one hand and educators' expertise on the other. Preschool teachers are the leaders in preschools, and it is their responsibility to encourage and recognize parental expertise and create new knowledge-power relationships with parents (Mac Naughton & Hughes, 2011). This study's findings could encourage early childhood educators to realize the value of regularly bringing parents to the table while the preschool curriculum is in the process of being developed and assessed. Children's transition to primary school is not a private issue for individual children; it is a family issue as well. The study made it clear that parents have a lot to offer in the arena of children's transition to school, and they can and should become active participants in the process.

The findings of the study demonstrate the Polish mothers' marginalized position. Educators must find a way to communicate with all parents, not least with groups that are normally inactive in the formal discourse (Oberhuemer, 2005). This is a lesson early childhood educators must learn as they must consider how to use diversity as a resource and how to focus on families' strengths rather than their weaknesses (Souto-Manning & Swick, 2006). Parent-preschool participation is not only an important component of preschool practices but also a sensitive one. It is the educators' responsibility to create a space in which the knowledge of all parents is respected.

References

Alasuutari, M. (2010). Striving at partnerships: Parent-practitioner relationships in Finnish early educators' talk. *European Early Childhood Education Research Journal, 18*(2), 149–161.

Barbour, R. (2009). *Doing Focus Groups* (Vol. 3). CA: Sage.

Baum, A. C., & McMurray-Schwarz, P. (2004). Preservice teachers' beliefs about family involvement: Implications for teacher education. *Early Childhood Education Journal, 23*(1), 57–61.

Blue-Banning, M., Summers, J. A., Frankland, H. C., Nelson, L. L., & Beegle, G. (2004). Dimensions of family and professional partnerships: Constructive guidelines for collaboration. *Exceptional Children, 70*(2), 167–184.

Cryer, D., Tietze, W., & Wessels, H. (2002). Parents' perceptions of their children's child care: A cross-national comparison. *Early Childhood Research Quarterly, 17*(2), 259–277.

Duncan, J., Bowden, C., & Smith, A. B. (2006). A gossip or a good yack? Reconceptualizing parent support in New Zealand early childhood centre based programmes. *International Journal of Early Years Education, 14*(1), 1–13.

Einarsdottir, J. (2010). Icelandic parents' views on the national policy on early childhood education. *Early Years: An International Journal of Research and Development, 30*(3), 229–242.

Eldridge, D. (2001). Parent involvement: It's worth the effort. *Young Children, 56*(2), 65–69.

Epstein, J. L., Sanders, M. G., Simon, B. S., Salinas, K. C., Jansorn, N. R., & Van Voorhis, F. L. (Eds.). (2002). *School, Family, and Community Partnerships: Your Handbook for Action.* Thousand Oaks, CA: Corwin Press.

Hughes, P., & MacNaughton, G. (1999). Who's the expert: Reconceptualizing parent-staff relations in early childhood education. *Australian Journal of Early Childhood, 24*(4), 27–32.

Hughes, P., & MacNaughton, G. (2001). Building equitable staff-parent communication in early childhood settings: An Australian case study. *Early Childhood Research and Practice, 3*(2). Retrieved on 10 May 2016, from http://ecrp.uiuc.edu/v3n2/hughes.html

Krueger, R. A., & Casey, M. A. (2009). *Focus Groups: A Practical Guide for Applied Research* (4th ed.). Thousand Oaks, CA: Sage.

Lehrer, J., Lemay, L., & Bigras, N. (2015). Parental perceptions of child care quality in centre-based and home-based settings: Associations with external quality ratings. *International Journal of Early Childhood, 47*(3), 481–497.

MacNaughton, G., & Hughes, P. (2011). *Parents and Professionals in Early Childhood Settings.* New York: Open University Press.

Ministry of Education: Science and Culture. (2011). *The Icelandic National Curriculum Guide for Preschools.* Retrieved on 15 July 2016, from www.menntamalaraduneyti.is/namskrar/leikskolar/

Morgan, D. L. (1998). *The Focus Group Guidebook. Focus Group Kit 1.* Thousand Oaks, CA: Sage.

Oberhuemer, P. (2005). Conceptualising the early childhood pedagogue: Policy approaches and issues of professionalism. *European Early Childhood Education Research Journal, 13*(1), 5–16.

OECD. (2006). *Starting Strong II: Early Childhood Education and Care*. Paris: OECD.

Souto-Manning, M., & Swick, K. J. (2006). Teachers' beliefs about parent and family involvement: Rethinking our family involvement paradigm. *Early Childhood Education Journal*, *34*(2), 187–193.

Statistics Iceland. (2016). Retrieved on 5 July 2016, from www.hagstofa.is/

Urban, M., Vandenbroeck, M., Lazzari, A., Peeters, J., & Van Laere, K. (2011). *CoRe Competence Requirements in Early Childhood Education and Care*. Report for European Commission, DG Education and Culture.

Wildenger, L. K., & McIntyre, L. L. (2011). Family concerns and involvement during kindergarten transition. *Journal of Child and Family Studies*, *20*, 387–396.

12 The importance of aesthetic activities in Norwegian kindergartens

Tona Gulpinar and Leif Hernes

In this article we are going to take a closer look at children's rights concerning art and culture in kindergarten, what kinds of expectations Norwegian parents have for the kindergarten and the pedagogical work that is being performed there. We are also going to have a closer look into what actually is happening in the kindergarten when it comes to art and culture. These two ways to understand how parents' expectations coincide with what actually happens in Norwegian kindergarten are based on two surveys to parents and kindergarten teachers, which were made possible by the Norwegian Research Council through financing the research project Searching for Qualities/Blikk for Barn through the program FINNUT. We will at the very end of this article through theoretical discourse try to justify the importance of working with the aesthetic disciplines in kindergarten.

What the Norwegian law system says about working with art and culture in kindergarten

The Norwegian Kindergarten Act (2005) gives children some rights that cannot be overlooked. It is about art and culture – both culture created by children and culture children live and express themselves through.

The Kindergarten Act states clearly that *"children shall be able to develop their creative zest, sense of wonder and need to investigate"* (The Kindergarten Act, Chapter 1, Section 1, Purpose). Further Section 1 states the following about the duties of kindergarten:

> The Kindergartens shall meet the children with trust and respect, and acknowledge the intrinsic value of childhood. They shall contribute to well-being and joy in play and learning, and shall be a challenging and safe place for community life and friendship. The Kindergarten shall promote democracy and equality and counteract all forms of discrimination.
>
> (The Kindergarten Act, Chapter 1, Section 1, Purpose)

These are the values and attitudes the society claims children should meet in kindergarten. Working with art and culture is the core activity in kindergarten.

Children's capacity be involved in the world they are a part of is the driving force in this discipline. Through their curiosity and ability to wonder, try out, experiment and explore, the children meet with, relate to and understand the world (Hernes, 2014; Juncker, 2016).

Children's understanding of the world manifests itself through interaction with other children and adults. In this universe, play is essential. It is within a community that includes play that children can unfold their genuine abilities and meet and interact with other children. Here they will meet with different attitudes, different entrances to play and the creative companionship that unfolds in meeting with different players, be it children or adults. This is pinpointed in the Norwegian Framework Plan for the Content and Tasks of Kindergartens (2006/2011), stating that

> [p]laying is at the core of children's wellbeing and self-expression, and interaction with others whilst playing is important for a balanced development. Kindergartens must allow for the children's initiative, imagination and sense of wonderment.
>
> (p. 10)

The Norwegian Framework Plan refers also to how children actively strive for and create their own preconditions for learning in togetherness with others, where it is in the context that peer relations are the point of departure for learning and creating through interactions in free play (Os, 2016). Research shows that free play where children interact with other children is an important arena for children's learning and development when it comes to language and social abilities.

The children's ability to socialize is to a great extent developed through play. Children are most of all occupied with other children, and they learn the best by being together with other children. This has been proven through international research over the last 10 years, among others: Corsaro (1997), Dencik (1994, 2002), Dencik, Bäckström and Larsson (1988), Frønes (1999), Gulbrandsen (2000), Harris (1995, 1998), and Sommer (1996).

The Norwegian Framework Plan states that one of the features of the Norwegian kindergarten tradition is that it takes a holistic view of care, formation, play, everyday activities and learning. Kindergartens help create culture, and play has an important role in promoting cultural values (p. 18).

Free play is the medium in which ideas and thoughts are exchanged in a free form. It is through interaction that children and adults together manage to create an understanding of being different, and our unique and different approaches to life become harmless and manifested. This, among other qualities, places democracy and equality on the agenda (Hernes, 2013; Greve & Kristensen, 2015).

Children shall contribute and have an effect on everyday life and their own lives. This will be executed through a respect for the children's expressed will, regardless of this being done through sound or through movement. Parents should also be able to contribute to the daily work with their own children. This creates a good flow of information from the kindergarten to the parents.

The Kindergarten Act states: "The Kindergarten shall, in collaboration and close understanding with the home, safeguard the children's need for care and play, and promote learning and formation as a basis for an all-round development" (§1, Purpose). It is within this perspective that we as researchers have wanted to look into what kind of expectations the parents have towards the kindergarten as a cultural arena and what the content and intentions of kindergarten teachers are when it comes to prioritizing this theme, which is one out of six that has specifically been challenged through the Framework Plan. We will argue for the importance of giving focus to this theme.

The reason for looking into this theme is based on several reports that have shown that the focus on and working with aesthetic subjects in Norwegian kindergartens has decreased over the last 10 to 12 years (Østrem et al., 2009; NOKUT, 2010).

Two surveys

The authors of Searching for Qualities have performed two surveys to look into the expectations from parents and what actually is happening in Norwegian kindergartens when it comes to the themes of art, culture and creativity.

We will through the answers from the surveys try to highlight the parents' expectations towards kindergarten and look at the connections between the parents' answers and what kindergarten teachers say about how important the aesthetic subjects are and how often they practice them. We will also highlight examples where the aesthetic subjects emerge. The answers in the surveys are based on parents' and kindergarten teachers' understanding of what they observe and what they define as aesthetic encounters. We will finally argue for the importance of aesthetic subjects in kindergarten and how aesthetic encounters manifest themselves as part of the memories of the body (Merleau-Ponty, 1994).

Through our subjective research focus, we will describe some observed examples and characteristic situations from kindergarten that can be understood as aesthetic encounters or experiences. We will also exemplify this through observations where the possibility to facilitate an aesthetic encounter is present.

An aesthetic encounter is an encounter where the artistic form affects you as a human being, that is, an encounter that creates traces within you which you will carry with you as a body memory to new encounters. An aesthetic encounter cannot be measured in other ways than giving a widened understanding of yourself in relation to your surroundings.

Parents' expectations towards kindergarten

In the research project Searching for Qualities, we have wanted to investigate the parents' views concerning themes related to art, culture and creativity. A survey was developed where we asked 1,988 parents with children under 3 years of age attending kindergarten about their opinions on what it is important to focus on when working with children under the age of 3. Of these, 1,183 parents answered.[1]

> Q29: What is, in your opinion, important to work with in the kindergarten when it comes to children under the age of 3?

In Table 12.1 we have chosen to focus on some of the themes that have often been debated when it comes to learning outcomes and, for many parents, also can be the reason why their child attends the kindergarten. From the table we can read that parents of children attending kindergarten most of all are occupied with the idea that their children get quality care from the kindergarten staff. The care aspect is strong in Norwegian kindergartens and is also an important part of the Nordic kindergarten model. As this is a table that says something about parents' expectations towards the kindergarten for their small ones, it might not be a big surprise that 97% say that good care is very important. In addition we see that it is important for parents that their children socialize and that the children

Table 12.1 Opinions about working with children aged under 3

	Very important (%)	*Important (%)*	*Not important (%)*
Children receive care and safety from adults	97	2	0
Children learn to socialize	91	8	1
Children are allowed to play with other children	88	11	1
Children have great freedom of movement	75	23	1
Emphasis is on learning the language	71	27	1
Children experience nature	70	28	2
Staff have pedagogical education	64	33	3
What the children learn is preparation for school	35	39	26
Children take part in various cultural activities	33	56	10
A certain percentage of employees are men	29	50	20
Children get experience with digital tools	12	42	46

n = 1,183
Source: *Searching for Qualities*, Gulpinar and Hernes (2014)

have the opportunity to play with other children. These values are strong in the Norwegian kindergarten tradition.

Ninety percent look upon socializing as a very important part of daily life in kindergarten, and as much of the process of socializing happens through a good play environment, it is not unexpected that the rate when it comes to the importance of play is 88% very important and 11% important. These answers say something about the parents' appraisal of play as a central activity when it comes to content in kindergarten. It suggests that there is coherence between the parents' views and the research in the field (Dencik et al., 1988; Strandell, 1994, 1999; Dencik, 1994, 2002; Gulbrandsen, 2000; Harris, 1995, 1998; Sommer, 1996; Corsaro, 1997; Frønes, 1999)..

Parents' opinions of the importance of play in kindergarten can be based on several factors. It might be their own memories of playing and the importance of play in their lives, or the kindergarten staff have informed them that it is through play that children approach their surroundings and through their bodies and actions understand the world and that children by being together and in good play environments socialize and develop language (Os, 2016). It is through good peer relations that learning occurs. In what we call the Norwegian and the 'Nordic model', play is central and is the core of activities in kindergarten. Both the Kindergarten Act and the Framework Plan underpin the importance of facilitating play in a socializing environment and also where children's own voices are heard and children's own culture is manifested.

Time spent on art and culture in kindergarten

In Tables 12.2 and 12.3 we are going to look into parents' and kindergarten teachers' opinions on time spent with aesthetic subjects in kindergarten.

Table 12.2 Degree of satisfaction with dance, drama, music and art in kindergarten

To great extent (%)	*To some extent (%)*	*Very little extent (%)*	*No extent (%)*
54	30	7	9

n = 1,183
Source: *Searching for Qualities*, Gulpinar and Hernes (2014)

Table 12.3 Satisfaction of time in the kindergarten with dance, drama, music and art

To great extent (%)	*To some extent (%)*	*Neither satisfied or dissatisfied (%)*	*Pretty dissatisfied (%)*
22	46	19	12

n = 398
Source: *Searching for Qualities*, Gulpinar and Hernes (2014)

Parents

Q16: To which degree are you satisfied with time spent with dance, drama, music and art in kindergarten?

Kindergarten teachers

Q5 (var.: 36): To which degree are you satisfied/dissatisfied with time spent with dance, drama, music and art in kindergarten?

These tables show among other things that 84% of the parents are very satisfied or satisfied with time spent on aesthetic subjects, whereas 16% are very little or not satisfied with time spent on aesthetic subjects. Most likely this means that according to their opinions, time spent on these subjects is too little.

When we asked kindergarten teachers almost the same question, 68% answered that they are very satisfied or satisfied with the time spent with aesthetic subjects, whereas 12% are pretty dissatisfied. We might assume based on their opinions that too little time is spent on this subject.

If we compare the parents' answers and the kindergarten teachers' answers, we see that 54% of the parents are very satisfied with the time spent on aesthetic subjects, whereas 22% of the kindergarten teachers are very satisfied with this. It might be that the kindergarten staff are clever to document the work done and highlight aesthetic activities. In this way the parents get the impression that the kindergarten is working more with this theme than they actually do, as only 22% of the kindergarten teachers are very satisfied with time spent with aesthetic subjects.

Justification for aesthetic subjects

The Framework Plan refers clearly to the importance of themes like children's formation and learning. One facilitates children's self-esteem, the art of being in a group and being able to cooperate in good environments for children. At the same time it refers to how important language is for the child to be able to express him- or herself in interaction with other children and adults.

In Tables 12.4 and 12.5 we have chosen to ask the kindergarten teachers how important aesthetic subjects are for learning, formation, self-esteem, cooperation and language.

Q17 (var.: 105, 106, 108, 111, 113): How important do you think aesthetic activities are concerning children's development?

From this table we can read that kindergarten teachers see aesthetic subjects as central to all of the five themes presented: learning, formation, self-esteem, corporation and language. Between 80 and 90% of kindergarten teachers say that these themes are important – and that they can be developed and strengthened through aesthetic subjects. Aesthetic activities constitute the content in

Table 12.4 Importance of aesthetic activities

	Learning (%)	*Formation* (%)	*Self-esteem* (%)	*Cooperation* (%)	*Language* (%)
Very important	49	39	52	47	53
Important	43	43	37	42	37
Slightly important	8	17	10	9	9
Not important	1	1	1	1	1
Do not know	0	0	1	0	0

n = 398
Source: *Searching for Qualities*, Gulpinar and Hernes (2014)

Table 12.5 Pedagogical work with art, culture and creativity in the kindergarten

Working much with (%)	*Working some with* (%)	*Working little with* (%)	*Do not know* (%)
41	46	7	7

n = 1,185
Source: *Searching for Qualities*, Gulpinar and Hernes (2014)

kindergarten. We have to do something together with others to develop abilities to corporate, and we must meet with new experiences to learn. If we are we going to talk together and develop the conversation, we must have something to talk about, to interact about and to elaborate, develop, explore and create. It is through the content in kindergarten that one meets with learning, formation, self-esteem, corporation and language.

Time and emphases of aesthetic subjects

We have also asked how often kindergarten teachers work with aesthetic subjects. We choose to see this question in relation to what parents mean about the emphases of art and culture. These are not precisely the same values, but we think they show tendencies we find interesting in our research. Parents might have an understanding that one is working more with aesthetics than actually is the case. Or one may have the idea that working with art and culture is important in kindergarten and therefore should be emphasized.

Parents

Q31: To which degree do you think that art, culture and creativity are emphasized in the pedagogical work in the kindergarten group your children are attending (the last 3 months) (Table 12.6)?

Table 12.6 Working with aesthetics in the kindergarten

	Fine art (%)	*Dance (%)*	*Drama (%)*	*Music (%)*
Daily	13	21	10	56
Weekly	72	52	44	36
More seldom	15	26	43	7
Never	*	1	3	1

$n = 398$
Source: *Searching for Qualities*, Gulpinar and Hernes (2014)

Kindergarten teachers

Q12: How often do you work with aesthetics in the kindergarten?

Only every 10th children's group meets with fine art and drama activities every day and every fifth children's group meets with dance. Music is the subject kindergarten teachers are working most with, and the group meets with this media on a daily bases in almost 60% of the kindergartens reporting.

We shall look into how the kindergarten teachers' opinions of how often one is working with the aesthetic subjects is confirmed by another question in the same survey.

Where do aesthetic subjects emerge in kindergarten?

Through Table 12.7, showing four chosen activities, we want to highlight what the kindergarten teachers are answering when aesthetic subjects emerge in the

Table 12.7 Aesthetic activities

	Singing (%)	*Dance (%)*	*Painting (%)*	*Dramatic play (%)*
Dedicated room	16	18	25	17
Wardrobe	67	27	2	21
During meals	51	0	0	4
Changing diapers	76	2	0	6
Circle time	96	62	4	53
Outdoor	73	45	27	49
By the table	61	1	92	12
Free play	76	75	13	70
Reading corner	38	2	0	7
Other places	27	28	10	21

$n = 398$
Source: *Searching for Qualities*, Gulpinar and Hernes (2014)

kindergarten. We claim that these answers give an indication of not only where aesthetic subjects emerge in formal settings but also where the kindergarten staff observe children in free activities without the staff necessarily being involved.

> Q13 (var.: 77, 80, 81, 72): In which rooms or situations are children involved in the following aesthetic activities?

Singing

As we can read from the table, singing seems to emerge in all situations, in all rooms in the kindergarten, and seem to be an ongoing activity throughout the day. This is not unexpected as this is the 'instrument' that is a part of you; both in the staff's communication with this age group and in children's own free activities, this is a very suitable media. Through focus conversations[2] with the staff, quite a few recognize these results. Singing is used both as an artistic form and as a 'tool' to soothe children, get a child to sleep, sing nursery rhymes and so on.

Dedicated rooms are not much used when it comes to singing. It might be that all kindergartens do not have a dedicated room for special activities. Singing is happening in circle time, and it happens in free play, both in formal situation as well as in situations where children have the initiative and where children's own culture emerges. Seventy-six percent of kindergarten teachers report that singing is happening in free play. This is the period where children play alone or together with other children and gives an indication that singing is a form children often use to express themselves in play situations.

Dancing

The reports on dance in kindergartens are maybe the most important finding in this survey. Seventy-five percent of kindergarten teachers report that dance happens during free play, and 45% report it also happens during outdoor play, where we know that children to a great extent play without involvement of adults. That indicates that dance is within the child and is to a great extent a self-initiated aesthetic expression that emerges in three-quarters to half of the observations reported by kindergarten teachers. Sixty-two percent of them also report that dance is part of the content in circle time. In other words, dance happens both in formal situations as well as in non-formal situations where the child has great freedom of choice as to which content he or she will spend the time.

This finding might have an effect on the education of kindergarten teachers in Norway as this is now not a subject. Dance as a subject might become a part of the education of kindergarten teachers who are going to work with the youngest children. This survey shows that dance is one of the aesthetic media children express themselves through in addition to dramatic play.

What we also see from the table is that the wardrobe is a very central place in the kindergarten. Both dancing and singing are activities that happen there. The wardrobe is an important room for many different activities most often initiated by the children. In conversations with staff working in the field, this view is supported. The wardrobe is created with a clear purpose and not necessarily for a certain activity, but it has an important function throughout the day in kindergarten.

Painting

Painting seems to a great degree to happen at the table in kindergarten. More than 90% of the informants report this. The table is and has always been a meeting point in kindergarten. In addition to being disciplined, it can also help a group to focus on activities being performed at the table. This is the traditional way to work with painting in kindergarten. Half of the kindergarten teachers report that they also work with painting outdoors. If we see this from the perspective on children's motoric abilities, they have easier access to paper or the object they are going to paint when it is laying on the ground or is placed on the wall. The children get greater control over the instruments and a better overview of where to paint.

The answers from the survey show that dedicated rooms are used to a greater extent for painting activities. It is easier to facilitate painting in dedicated rooms where materials and instruments are easily at hand, and in newer and bigger kindergartens often dedicated rooms are available. This is a place where you don't have to be too careful, and it is easier to take care of the creative process. Through our observations in kindergartens we found that painting is happening mostly on paper and more seldom on three-dimensional material. These observations seem to be verified by this survey.

Dramatic play

Dramatic play manifests in Norwegian kindergarten through this survey and supports the idea that children use dramatic play throughout the day all over the kindergarten. We also see that play emerges mostly in activities initiated by the children themselves and where children usually play with other children: 70% in free play and 49% in outdoor play – half to three-quarters of the informants report that dramatic play is reserved for the non-formal situations where children choose their own content for play. Dramatic play also happens in more formal situations like circle time, but we cannot tell from this survey how dramatic play proceeds in a formal situation. The wardrobe is also important here as a place that is actively used for dramatic play.

Premises for aesthetic processes in kindergarten

Aesthetic processes are happening in almost every room in kindergarten and in many different situations. This indicates that both adults and children are creative in relation to the use of rooms and situations. It seems like rooms and situations are permeated by aesthetic activities related to everyday situations in kindergarten.

The tables we have seen so far do not indicate that one is working much with aesthetic subjects in kindergarten. We have referred to much research that has commented that there is a decreasing focus on aesthetic subjects in kindergarten. When we opened up for comments in our survey, we asked: which factors are vital for you to work with aesthetic subjects in kindergarten? The kindergarten teachers answered that the most important things were to have enough time, to have enough competence and to have enough knowledge about aesthetic processes in kindergarten and that the staff had the ability to engage in aesthetic activities. We have documented earlier that it seems like some of the kindergarten teachers report that they seem to have enough time, and at the same time some report that they do not have enough time. These answers are not definite and might indicate that not all the kindergartens are good enough when it comes to structuring of time. This can also mean that they work in kindergartens where the logistics and timing of the day are dependent on other children's groups in the same kindergarten – meaning that they have the time but that they are not in a situation where they can decide to use the time as they wish.

Preliminary conclusion

Through the tables we have reports from the parents' expectations of kindergarten. The kindergarten teachers report how important they think aesthetic subjects are and how often they are used in kindergarten. They also report on where aesthetic subjects emerge. All the answers are based on the parents' and kindergarten teachers' understanding of what an aesthetic meeting is.

Our findings give an indication that working with art and culture is central in kindergarten – both children's own cultures as well as the importance of seeing aesthetic subjects in a pedagogical context where formation, self esteem, corporation, learning and language are central. This is highlighted in both the Kindergarten Act and in the Framework Plan. It is all about the individual child and his or her affiliation and possibility to contribute in group relations as the kindergarten is a group-oriented institution with the purpose to create a qualitative good environment for children.

We also find that the parents express that aesthetic activities are focused on in kindergarten, but most kindergarten teachers do not report this. This might have to do with how we define aesthetic activities, what we understand about art, culture and creativity and what it means that the kindergarten is supposed to be a cultural arena (Jæger & Torgersen, 2016).

Everyday life in kindergarten and possibilities for aesthetic activities

In relation to the surveys distributed to parents and kindergarten teachers, the researchers have had the opportunity to have focused conversations with both pedagogues involved in educating kindergarten teachers as well as staff from kindergartens. We have also made observations through different methods how children act in everyday life. Through this work we have observed many examples of children and adults. We have chosen to present some of these observations as examples for where and how we can experience situations that are or could become an aesthetic encounter.

Examples of aesthetic encounters based on play and exploration

We will through three small examples, observed in a kindergarten with children under the age of 3 in the course of 30 minutes, try to highlight how children through play and exploration make both bodily and aesthetic experiences in kindergarten. Children experience and learn from these experiences.

1 The child is standing in the small playroom looking out through the glass door. He has a play animal in his hand and starts to hit the glass with the animal. The animal creates a sharp sound; the child closes his eyes as a reaction to the sharp sound. He continues to hit the glass with the animal as he closes his eyes.

Can be read as an encounter with sound and rhythm.

2 The child climbs onto a broad window shelf. There is a square basket standing on the shelf. When the child stands straight, the window is exactly high enough. When the child climbs the basket, he bangs his head on the ceiling of the window shelf. He steps down again, straightens up, climbs the basket again and bangs his head on the ceiling of the window shelf.

Can be read as a bodily experience and exploring of space.

3 The child (aged 1 year and 7 months) is standing barefoot on a carpet and turning around till he loses control and falls to the floor. He stands again and starts turning around, falls to the floor again, smiles, stands up again and tries to turn around for the third time, falls to the floor, stands up and walks away.

Can be read as an experience with body and space.

The adults' possibilities

Observations from the kindergarten[3] of children's activities show that when children communicate through play, they use all possible ways of communicating with body and sounds. A variety of expressions gives possibilities to create nuances in the communication. Not only children but adults too should use variety in communication when involved in children's play. Voice, body, movement, props – everything might be treated and acted through. Through different dynamics this will create genuine and varied ways of communication (Laban, 1948/1975; Stern, 2010).

Play is an aesthetic practice if you as an adult want to focus on this. To have an attitude towards the play, an aesthetic attitude (Stolnitz, 1969) is vital for the aesthetic values of praxis. Aesthetics is about praxis, about practice. We through repetition, through imitation and fiction, act; we perform an aesthetic practice. It is important that in this praxis, the performers are taking part as equal participants; the staff and the children have the same approach to play, it is equally seriously to both, that it is equally real for both and the frames of fiction will be respected (Greve & Kristensen, 2015).

The Framework Plan (2006, s 27/28) states: "Play shall play a prominent role in life at kindergartens. Play has intrinsic value and is an important part of child culture. Play is an universal human phenomenon, which children are skilled at and enjoy. It is a fundamental lifestyle and way of learning through which children can express themselves . . . . Children learn and develop a complex set of skills through play".

This is this backdrop that shall be the guiding line for our pedagogical work. It is the pedagogue who shall be the play artist, the artist who can play, the player who can act and the actor who knows his or her pedagogical responsibility (Gulpinar & Hernes, 2016).

What we understand as participation in play is to be the adult who is present and can act together with children, know the rules of play, and can help and support a child to develop play competence as an equal participant in the playgroup.

The adult can take the lead and can be led in building play. It may be the room that has to be changed, or it can be agreements that have to be negotiated to get play moving. It can be common experiences, it can be suggestions on themes, and it can be adding objects for inspiration as well as a move to make the play more dynamic.

It is about constructing and inventing a point of departure for play. It is about starting associative actions and verbal sayings targeting what might occur and build for further actions, without letting associations becoming descriptive or demonstrative but open, conceptualized associations. In this work one has to introduce ideas and be a good listener to other ideas and actions (Bae, 2009).

As adults we shall be able to read the group and the dynamics of the group, where it is in its process, and be able to handle themes, establishing a place and situation. When play is at its best, or when one for other reasons withdraws, it is important to look at play from time to time to observe the progression and that all in the group have equal parts though with different roles.

Conclusion

According to Dewey (1934/2008), learning through bodily experiences is described. We learn by experiencing and living our lives. Maurice Merleau-Ponty

(1994) claims that we register the world through our senses. It is through the body that consciousness is created; the body is subject to the personality. Merleau-Ponty looks upon the body as experiencing, and searching for meaning; the body is both subject and object at the same time. Merleau-Ponty's' term 'circularity' describes the relation between the lived, subjective body and the physical, objective body. The body is our access to the world, and by altered bodily experiences our perception of the world will also change.

The cultural and artistic experiences we facilitate in kindergarten can become a competence or a capital that is useful for different parts of our society, according to Pierre Bourdieu (1995), who claims that the social world is constructed through actions that not always are conscious, reflected or justified (Bourdieu, 1995). Human beings develop, according to Bourdieu, a practical sense that is connected to our upbringing, where norms, values and behaviour patterns are imprinted as 'dispositions' in the individual. It is these dispositions Bourdieu calls 'habitus'. The term habitus implies two concurrent, interacting processes through internalizing – the individual acquires knowledge and culture – and externalizing – where the individual transforms this knowledge to practical actions.

Roland Barthes's (2001) aesthetic discourse is a discourse where the body sensation has its own form of recognition and where the individual experience is in the body. He calls these 'bodily recollections'. Daniel Stern (2010) is highlighting the term dynamic forms of vitality as a life form of its own. The lived life we carry with us as a part of our being. This vitality marks our being in our meetings with daily life as well as with art. The forms of vitality are a part of our recollections that are in the body and give life to our stories; they are a part of our earlier experiences. Our emotions are in our bodies, memories of earlier experiences, everything we have experienced in our lived lives but as well of expectations, preconceptions and biased opinions.

If we transform this for the art scene, writes Erica Fischer-Lichte (2008), where through a performance tradition looks upon the body as a shaping and controllable material, where you consequently recognize both 'being a body' and 'having a body', a coexistence of the phenomenal and the semiotic body. This says something about the body's presence in daily life and in artistic encounters. In play and working with aesthetic subjects, this describes the importance of the pedagogue's consciousness of his or her body memories and how one in kindergarten both plans and meets with children's bodies in their meeting with artistic, aesthetic activities.

If we accept that our lived lives affect our being in our encounters in daily life as well as in art, we will understand the importance of realizing that all staff in kindergarten also are mediators of culture. This is expected from the parents and as well from the government through, in this context, the Framework Plan and the Kindergarten Act. The question is if the framework for kindergarten facilitates the kindergarten teacher in a way so that it is possible to comply with the expectations and claims, not only in the role of a mediator of culture but also in all the other expectations of kindergarten to highlight learning, formation, self-esteem, corporation and language.

Notes

1 The target group was parents with children under the age of 3 attending kindergarten. TNS-Gallups's panel was used, and the survey was sent in June 2014. There was a response rate of 59.5%.
2 Focus conversation has been done in relation to observations in several kindergartens in Norway.
3 The researchers have done 30-minute observations in kindergartens in Norway.

References

Bae, B. (2009). Samspill mellom barn og voksne ved måltidet. *Nordisk barnehageforskning, 2*(1), 3–15. Retrieved from www.nordiskbarnehageforskning.no

Barthes, R. (2001). *Det lyse rommet. Tanker om fotografi.* Oslo: Pax.

Bourdieu, P. (1995). *Distinksjonen.* Oslo: Pax Forlag.

Bourdieu, P. (1996). *Symbolsk makt.* Oslo: Pax forlag.

Corsaro, W. A. (1997). *The Sociology of Childhood.* Thousand Oaks, CA: Pine Forge Press.

Dencik, L. (1994). *Børns tilegnelse af livskvalifikationer for den postmoderne tilværelse.* Ungepædagoger, nr. 7.

Dencik, L. (2002). *Socialisering.* Roskilde: Roskilde Universitetscenter.

Dencik, L., Bäckström, C., & Larsson, E. (1988). *Barnens två världar.* Uppsala: Almqvist & Wiksell.

Dewey, J. (1934/2008). *Art as Experience.* London: Penguin Books Ltd.

Fischer-Lichte, E. (2008). *The Transformative Power of Performance.* London: Routledge.

Framework Plan for the Content and Tasks of Kindergartens. (2006). *Ministry of Education and Research.* Retrieved from www.udir.no/globalassets/filer/barnehage/rammeplan/framework_plan_for_the_content_and_tasks_of_kindergartens_2011_rammeplan_engelsk.pdf

Frønes, I. (1999). Kammeraterne og moderniteten. In L. Dencik & P. S. Jørgensen (Eds.), *Børn og familie i det postmoderne samfund.* København: Hans Reitzels forlag.

Greve, A., & Kristensen, K. O. (2015). Lek i det muliges rom. In A. Greve, L. Pedersen, & H. G. Sviggum (Eds.), *Faglighet i barnehagen.* Bergen: Fagbokforlaget.

Gulbrandsen, L. M. (2000). Samspill mellom barn som kjønnskapte og kjønnskapende prosesser. Et analytisk perspektiv. In H. Haavind (Ed.), *Kjønn og fortolkende metode.* Oslo: Gyldendal Akademisk.

Gulpinar, T., & Hernes, L. (2016). Estetisk læring i barnehagen. In T. Gulpinar, L. Hernes, & N. Winger (Ed.), *Blikk fra Barnehagen.* Bergen: Fagbokforlaget.

Harris, J. R. (1995). Where is the child's environment? A group socialization theory of development. *Psychological Review, 102*, 458–489.

Harris, J. R. (1998). *The Nurture Assumption.* London: Bloomsbury.

Hernes, L. (2013). Barn, kunst og demokrati. In A. Greve, S. Morreaunet, & N. Winger (Eds.), *Ytringer (om likeverd, demokrati og relasjonsbygging i barnehagen).* Bergen: Fagbokforlaget.

Hernes, L. (2014). Kunstneren og den kunstneriske prosessen. In E. Angelo & S. Kalsnes (Eds.), *Kunstner eller lærer. Profesjonsdilemmaer i musikk-og kunstpedagogisk utdanning.* Oslo: Cappelen Damm.

Hernes, L., Horn, G., & Reistad, H. (1993). *Lek, dans og teater.* Vollen: Tell forlag.

Jæger, H., Hopperstad, M. H., & Torgersen, J. K. (2016). Barnekultur: kultur for, av og med barn. In H. Jæger & J. K. Torgersen (Eds.), *Barnekultur.* Oslo: Cappelen Damm Akademiske.

Jæger, H. & Torgersen, J.K. (2016). *Barnekultur.* Oslo: Cappelen Damm Akademisk.

Juncker, B. (2006). *Om processen. Det æstetiskes betydning i børns kultur.* København: Tidene skifter.

Laban, R. (1948/1975). *Modern Educational Dance.* London: Macdonald & Evans.

Matthews, J. (1984). *Early Child Development and Care. Children's Drawing: Are Young Children Really Scribbling?* London, UK: Science Publisher Inc. and OPA Ltd.

Merleau-Ponty, M. (1994). *Kroppens fenomenologi.* Oslo: Pax forlag.

NOKUT. (2010). *Evaluering av førskolelærerutdanning i Norge.* Del 1 Hovedrapport.

Østrem, S., Bjar, H., Føsker, H. D., Hogsnes, H. D., Jansen, T. T., Nordtømme, S., & Tholin, K. R. (2009). *Alle teller mer. En evaluering av hvordan Rammeplan for barnehagens innhold og oppgaver blir innført, brukt og erfart.* Tønsberg: Høgskolen i Vestfold.

Sommer, D. (1996). *Barndomspsykologi – udvikling i en forandret verden.* København: Hans Reitzels Forlag.

Stern, D. N. (2010). *Forms of Vitality. Exploring Dynamic Experience in Psychology, the Arts, Psychotherapy, and Development.* Oxford: Oxford University Press.

Stolnitz, J. (1969). The aesthetic attitude. In J. Hosper (Ed.), *Introductory Readings in Aesthetics.* London: Collier Macmillan Publishers.

Strandell, H. (1994). *Sociale möteplater för barn. Aktivitetsprofiler och förhandlingskulturer på daghem.* Helsinki: Gaudeamus.

Index

Note: Page numbers with *italics* indicate figures and tables.

acts of compassion 39, 41, 42, 43, 45–7, 48, 49
Ådnanes, M. 87
aesthetic activities in Norwegian kindergartens 11, 157–70, *163*, *164*; adults' possibilities 168–9; art and culture 157–9, *161*, 161–2, *163*; dancing 165–6; dramatic play 166; everyday life 167–8; justification 162–3; opinions about working with children under age 3 *160*; painting 166; parents' expectations 159–61; play and exploration 168; premises for processes 166–7; singing 165; time and emphases 163–4; two surveys 159; types of subjects 164–5
aggression 80, 81–3, 86, 88, 89, 91
Alasuutari, M. 144, 148
Amato, P. R. 80, 87
anxiety 83–4, 88, 152
Åsén, G. 56

Bäckström, L. 10, 158
Baig, T. 127
Ball, S. J. 96
Beach, D. 127
Beegle, G. 144
Bernelius, V. 108
Bialostok, S. 41
blended family 34
Blomqvist, C. 100
Blue-Banning, M. 144
Bodolica, V. 126, 137, 138
Borrine, M. L. 87
Bourdieu, P. 170
bourgeois family 33–4, 67
Braun, A. 96
Brewster, C. 127
Bronfenbrenner, U. 53
Brown, N. Y. 87
Buchanan, C. M. 89
Buckle, J. L. 128
BUP *see* child and youth psychiatric care

Castells, M. 29
Cerdin, J.-L. 127, 138
CHAT *see* cultural-historical activity theory
Cherlin, A. J. 88
child abuse 11, 94–6, 97–8, 103, 104
child and youth psychiatric care (BUP) 100
Children's House 42–3, 44–5, 46, 47, 48–9
children under age 3 *160*
City Preschool 52, 60
communities and blended family 34
compassion, acts of 39, 41, 42, 43, 45–7, 48, 49
compassion, rules of 43, 44, 45
compassion in early childhood educational settings 39–49; analysis 43; constituents of compassion 39–41; cultural-historical activity theory 41–2; ethical considerations 43; kindergarten 40, 41, 42–3, 44–7, 48, 49; study design 42–3
conduct of life 15–16, 23
conflict 13, 17, 18, 20, 21, 24; children and parents 22–3, 30, 99, 152; concept 86–7; Nordic model *65*,

69–70; between parents 10, 32, 80–1, 83, 84, 85, 86, 87, 88, 89–91; parents and teachers 10, 19, 60; state's interest and children 64
'Constituting Cultures of Compassion in Early Childhood Education (CoCuCo)' 42
constituting cultures of compassion in early childhood educational settings 39–49; analysis 43; constituents of compassion 39–41; cultural-historical activity theory 41–2; ethical considerations 43; kindergarten 44–7; study design 42–3
continuously changing conditions and mutuality 17–19
Corsaro, W. A. 158
CRC *see* UN Convention on the Rights of the Child
cultural-historical activity theory (CHAT) 41–2, 47, 49
Cummins, J. 111
curriculum 2, 3, 6, 42, 46, 53, 110, 111, 153; Children's House 43, 44–5, 47–8; Finnish 144; national 94, 103, 145–6; preschool 51, 54–6, 57, 59, 60, 70–1, 72, 74, 145–6, 154

Dağdelen, M. K. 127
Dahlgren, G. 56
Dahlström, E. 28
dancing 165–6
democratization 53, 68–9
Dencik, L. 158
depressive feelings 84–5, 88
Dewey, J. 169
Diné, M. A. 127
divorce, families and children 3, 10, 29, 30–1, 31, 32, 66, 79–91, 130; aggressive feelings 80, 81–3, 86, 88, 89, 91; anxiety 83–4, 88; conflict concept 86–7; conflicts between parents 83, 84, 86, 87, 88, 89, 90; depressive feelings 84–5, 88; not being heard 86, 89; shame and guilt 85–6, 88, 102
domestic abuse and child neglect 11, 97–100, 104
Dornbusch, S. M. 89
dramatic play *164*, 165, 166
Dreier, O. 16
Dwyer, C. 128
early childhood education and care (ECEC) 63–4, *64*, 65, *65*, 66, 67, 68, 69, 70, 71, 73, 143, 144
early childhood education, gender relations and equality in Sweden 63–75; challenges 72–3; changes in Nordic model and areas of conflict 69–70; equality for different kinds of families 69; family as a good enough socialization environment 72; feminist issue 68; gender patterns and stereotypes in preschool 74–5; gender perspective 67; gender squeeze 69; global world 73–4; historical perspectives 63–6; individualization, defamilization, democratization and radical changes in family life 68–9; international actors 66–7; preschool enrollment 70–2; shared responsibility and social investment 66; state feminism 65–6
ECEC *see* early childhood education and care
economic, social and cultural status (ESCS) and mathematics performance of immigrant students in the Finnish metropolitan area in PISA 2012 11, 108–22; data 113–14; method 115; results 115–21; students with immigrant background in Finland 109–12; students with immigrant backgrounds in PISA 2012 and ESCS 112–13
Einarsdottir, J. 11
Ekeland, T. J. 87
Emery, R. 83, 84, 85, 87
Engeström, Y. 41–2, 49
Epstein, J. L. 111
equality 2, *5*, 29, 30, 40, 53, 63, 122, 144, 147; education and equity in Finland 11; gender 10, *65*, 68, 69–70, 72, 73, 75; kindergarten 6; kinds of families 69; language 110; national curriculum 71; Nordic model 73; preschool 68, 72; situated inequality 24
ESCS *see* economic, social and cultural status
external context 96, 97, 98, 100, 103
Eydal, G. B. 71

family conduct of life and parental self-understanding 13–24; analytical challenges 15–17; continuously

changing conditions and mutuality 17–19; discussion across analytical themes 23–4; family research 14–15; self-understanding as a collective affair 21–3; when conducting everyday life become overwhelming 20–1
Family Counselling Service 91
family life 28–35; cohesion and departure 31–2; family today 29–31; history of family 28–9; lifelong family lives 31–2; lifespan and generative aspects 32–3
family research 13, 14–15, 16, 28, 29, 34, 35, 87, 104
family systems 2, 34
feminism 39, 68; state 65–6
Finnish Education Evaluation Centre 110
Fischer-Lichte, E. 170
Fleer, M. 39
Fotaki, M. 40, 48
Frankland, H. C. 144
Fröbel, F. W. A. 63
Frønes, I. 158
Furstenberg, F. F. 88

Gay, G. 111
gender: equality 10, *65*, 68, 69–70, 72, 73, 75; patterns and stereotypes in preschool 74–5; perspective 67; squeeze 69
generational family 33, 34
Gertsen, M. C. 129
Ginsberg, M. R. 136
Given, H. 41
Goetz, L. 40
Golombok, S. 32
guilt 85–6, 88, 102
Gulbrandsen, L. M. 158
Gulpinar, T. 11

Haavind, H. 17
Hallet, E. 51–2
Hammer, M. 39
Handal, P. J. 87
Harju-Luukkainen, H. 11, 112, 116, 121
Harris, A. 53
Harris, J. R. 158
Hernes, H. 65
Hernes, L. 11
Hetherington, M. E. 32
Hilton, A. 11
Hochschild, A. 31
Hogweed school 96, 100, 101, 103, 104
Højholt, C. 10
honour violence 97, 100–3, 104, 105
Hoskins, K. 96
Hughes, P. 144, 150, 151, 154
Hujala, E. 53
Humanities Secretariat for Women and Research 65
Husum, T. L. 87

immigrant families in Denmark 126–40; case studies 130–4; children's influence 139; cultural differences and perceptions of 'outsiderness' 137–8; data analysis 129–30; data collection 129; factors in support of integration 138–9; influence of family 136; integration challenges 137–8; language learning and intercultural understanding 138–9; method 128–9; reasons to leave Denmark 136; reasons to move or remain in Denmark 135; results 134–5; social and political challenges 136–7
immigrant students in the Finnish metropolitan area in PISA 2012 and economic, social and cultural status in mathematics performance 11, 108–22; data 113–14; method 115; results 115–21; students with immigrant background in Finland 109–12; students with immigrant backgrounds in PISA 2012 and ESCS 112–13
indispensability theory 28
internal structure of family 14

Jensberg, H. 87
Jensen, H. S. 90
Johansson, T. 11, 74
Jonsdottir, A. H. 11
Juhl, P. 10

Keith, B. 87
kindergarten 3–6, *4*, 11, 64, 66, 67; adults' possibilities 168–9; aesthetic activities 157–70, *163*, *164*; art and culture 157–9, 161–2, *163*; compassion as part of everyday life 39, 40, 41, 42–3, 44–7, 48, 49; cost and access *9*; dancing 165–6; dramatic play 166; everyday life 167–8;

Fröbel-inspired 63; justification for aesthetic subjects 162–3; language 131, 132, 137; painting 166; parents' expectations 159–61; play and exploration 168; premises for aesthetic processes 166–7; singing 165; time and emphases of aesthetic subjects 163–4; two surveys 159
Kindergarten Act 157, 159, 161, 167, 170
Kousholt, D. 10
Kriging method 109, 115, 120, 122
Kristjánsson, B. 29, 33, 71

Lamb, M. E. 80
Larsson, E. 158
leadership, pedagogical *see* pedagogical leadership and families in Swedish preschool
"Learners with an Immigrant Background within the Finnish Education System" (Finnish Education Evaluation Centre) 110
Leekeenan, D. 41
life becomes overwhelming 20–1
lifespan 28; generative aspects 32–3
linked family 34
Lipponen, L. 10
Lunneblad, J. 11, 127

Maccoby, E. E. 30, 89
Machung, A. 31
MacNaughton, G. 144, 150, 151, 154
Maguire, M. 96
Manni, L. 53
material context 96, 97, 100, 102, 104
mathematics performance and economic, social and cultural status of immigrant students in the Finnish metropolitan area in PISA 2012 11, 108–22, *117–20*, *121*
Meeto, A. 103
Merleau-Ponty, M. 169–70
Mirza, H. S. 103
Morgan, D. 15
Moxnes, K. 32
Murdock, G. P. 34
mutuality 16, 17–19, 23
Myklebust, V. 87
Myrdal, A. 63

National Agency parent survey 53
National Guidelines on Early Childhood and Care in Finland 43
Nelson, L. L. 144
network family 34
Nissinen, K. 11
Nordic comparison 3–6
Nordic model 1, 2–3, 6, 161; conflict *65*, 69–70; equality 73
Nordic policy around childhood 3, *4–5*, 6
Nordic policy for parents 6, *7*
Nordic population 3, 32, 66, 79; children 64, *64*; language 74
Nordic welfare support for children 3, 6, *8–9*
Norwegian Children Act 80, 89
Norwegian Framework Plan for the Content and Tasks of Kindergarten 158
Norwegian Kindergarten Act 157, 159, 161, 167, 170
Norwegian Research Council for Science 65, 157
not being heard 86, 89
nuclear family 14, 28, 31, 33, 34, 35, 79, 101
Nussbaum, M. C. 41

Oberhuemer, P. 144
Odenbring, Y. 11
OECD *see* Organisation for Economic Co-operation and Development
Olin, A. 53, 60
Olwig, K. F. 127, 137
Organisation for Economic Co-operation and Development (OECD) 66, 112, 115, 116
Ottosen, M. H. 90
overwhelming life 20–1

painting *164*, 166
parental engagement in Icelandic preschools 143–54; challenges 143–4; collaboration 149–50; education of staff 149; national curriculum guidelines 145–6; parents' satisfaction 146–7; participants and method 146; professionalism and participation 147–8; the study 146–52; time 151; transition to primary school 151–2
Parental Leave, Childcare and Gender Equality in the Nordic Countries (Gislason) 69

parents' expectations 159–61, 167
parents' rights 10, 80, 88
Park, C. 41
Parsons, T. 14
patriarchy 10, 14, 28, 29, 67, 79
pedagogical leadership and families in Swedish preschool 10, 51–60; context and leadership 54–5; head of preschool 56; policy documents regulating leadership and cooperation between home and preschool 55; preschool teacher 10, 51, 52, 54, 55, 57–9, 60
Perryman, J. 96
Pietka-Nykaza, E. 127
Pile, G. M. D. 87
PISA 2012 and economic, social and cultural status in mathematics performance 11, 108–22; data 113–14; method 115; results 115–21; students with immigrant background in Finland 109–12; students with immigrant backgrounds in PISA 2012 and ESCS 112–13
play and exploration 168
policy around childhood 3, *4–5*, 6
policy for parents 6, *7*
population 3, 32, 66, 79; children 64, *64*; language 74
Pramling Samuelsson, I. 10, 75
preschools: curriculum 51, 54–6, 57, 59, 60, 70–1, 72, 74, 145–6, 154; enrollment 70–2; equality 68, 72; gender patterns and stereotypes 74–5; *see also* parental engagement in Icelandic preschools; pedagogical leadership and families in Swedish preschool
preschool teachers 72; curriculum 145, 146; feminist issue 68; lack of qualified 74, 149; parent participation 147, 148, 154; pedagogical leadership 10, 51, 52, 54, 55, 57–9, 60
professional culture 96–7, 98, 100, 101, 103–4
Pryor, J. 32

rainbow family 34
Rantalaiho, M. 87
Rød, P. A. 19
Rodd, J. 53
Rodgers, B. 32
Rönnerman, K. 53, 60
Rostgaard, T. 71
rules of compassion 43, 44, 45

Schmidt, G. 127, 137
Schneider, N. F. 14
schools, child abuse and family support 94–105; child abuse and school 11, 94–6, 97–8, 103, 104; domestic abuse and child neglect 11, 97–100, 104; honour violence 97, 100–3, 104, 105; method, sample and methodology 96–7; results 97–100
Scrivens, C. 57
Searching for Qualities 157, 159
Searight, H. R. 87
Searle, J. 41
self-understanding 13, 16, 17, 19, 24; collective affair 21–3
shame 85–6, 88, 102; *see also* guilt
shared care 15
Sheridan, S. 74, 75
Sime, D. 127
singing *164*, 165
Siraj-Blatchford, I. 51–2, 53
situated context 96
social investment 66, 68, 69
Social Services Act 94, 99
Søderberg, A.-M. 129
Sommer, D. 158
Souto-Manning, M. 144
Spånberger, W. 99
Spillane, J. P. 53
Spraggon, M. 126, 137, 138
Stage, M. H. S. 90
star family 34
state feminism 65–6
Sternberg, K. J. 80
structural-functionalistic approach to family 14
Summers, J. A. 144
Swedish Education Act 51, 54, 55
Swedish preschool *see* pedagogical leadership and families in Swedish preschool
Swedish Trade Union Confederation 68
Swick, K. J. 144

Tallberg-Broman, I. 10
Thompson, R. A. 80
Thornberg, R. 41
Tulip school 96, 98, 99, 100, 101, 102, 104

UN Convention on the Rights of the Child (CRC) 33, 34, 89–90, 104

Van de Vliert, E. 87
Vesely, C. K. 136
Vettenranta, J. 11, 116, 121

Water Lily school 96, 97, 98, 99, 104
welfare support for children 3, 6, *8–9*
White, L. A. 66
Williams, P. 10, 75
withering away theory 28

www.ingramcontent.com/pod-product-compliance
Ingram Content Group UK Ltd.
Pitfield, Milton Keynes, MK11 3LW, UK
UKHW011015180926
475701UK00004B/749
* 9 7 8 0 3 6 7 2 7 1 9 5 4 *